Like a Swallow

Looking Back at a Polish Childhood

Nina L. Camic

LITTLE CREEK PRESS®
AND BOOK DESIGN

MINERAL POINT, WISCONSIN

Little Creek Press®
A Division of Kristin Mitchell Design, Inc.
5341 Sunny Ridge Road
Mineral Point, Wisconsin 53565

Book Design and Project Coordination:
Little Creek Press and Book Design

First Printing
June 2022

Printed in the United States of America

For more information or to order books,
www.littlecreekpress.com

Library of Congress Control Number: 2022908887

ISBN-13: 978-1-955656-21-4

Cover image: Shutterstock. Item ID: 1312353473
Benedictine monastery at sunrise in Tyniec near Krakow Poland.

For Caroline, Susannah,
and their little ones:
Alma, Lena, Sammy,
Sepi, and Serena

Preface

My memories of my childhood never receded into some fuzzy spaces in the back of my head as I had thought they would. Details of events, of the people who filtered in and out of my younger years, are as vivid now as they were sixty years ago. Everything I describe here is as real in my mind as the chair I sit in or the glass of tea I hold in my hand. I have not changed names, and I have not embellished for the sake of the flow of the narrative. Even conversations related here are approximations of ones I had or have had recalled to me by those who spoke the words. The characters that stumbled into this book did not ask to be included, but I hope they understand that they were central to my recollections of events that were taking place around me. In so many ways, these people wrote my story for me.

A word about the book's title: I have a simple image of a swallow tattooed on my back. One day I just walked into a tattoo parlor in Krakow and asked for it. Perhaps I was thinking of the swallows that came each year to nest in the corner of my grandparents' village house in Poland. Or maybe I was recalling the first time I sang what I thought was an American song to my Polish high school classmates. "Donna, Donna." Do you know the lyrics? They're about a swallow mocking a cow bound for slaughter. *Why don't you have wings to fly with, like the swallow so proud and free?*

Or maybe I just like swallows.

Chapter 1

1.

I heard the words first from a friend at school: "My mom said she'd rather be dead than red." There was no malice in the girl's voice. Her grin suggested that she didn't necessarily side with her mother on this. You don't typically prefer death when you're ten.

We were outside in the cramped courtyard, a make-do playground for the United Nations International School (UNIS) in New York. The other girls, intensely focused on winding string around their hands to form a cat's cradle, seemed not to have heard the girl's comment. For one small second, I wondered if Marie—a girl with drooping knee socks, stringy blond hair, and apparently a communist-hating mother—remembered that I was Polish. But, of course, despite my fluency in English, she knew. Everyone in my class knew. Didn't they all look my way and giggle whenever we sang "I'm the Man from Krakow," clearly labeled as a "Polish folk song," in music class? I was from Poland, and Poland was red.

We were Polish, but we were living in New York. My father had landed a plum job. After years of paying his dues as a lower-ranked foreign service staff member at the Foreign Ministry in Warsaw, he was appointed Polish ambassador to the United Nations. (When I asked later how that happened, he shrugged his shoulders, shaking off any insinuation that it was a political repayment for some act of loyalty on his part and said, "I worked hard on learning the English language. Really hard.") We had sailed to America with trunks and suitcases when I was just seven, not as immigrants fleeing Poland or communism, but as the family of a young and suddenly successful Polish diplomat.

We lived six years in the United States, from 1960 to 1966. I thought it was a great adventure, but I knew that Poland—a country I loved—was home. Still, it didn't take long for me to discover that my affections toward my homeland were neither understood nor celebrated in America. In 1958, at the height of the Cold War, Bertrand Russell, the British philosopher, wrote that the latter was preferable between the two evils—nuclear annihilation and communism. Better red than dead. But in the United States, in 1963, I heard the inversion of that sentiment.

It's a straight shot from fear and hatred to regulation and exclusion. At the beginning of our stay in New York, I knew nothing about the Cold War, about McCarthyism's impact on the lives of those who allegedly endorsed a communist agenda. But within a few years, I began to suspect that perhaps most Americans wanted to do everything in their power to keep the likes of us—Polish nationals with allegiance to their country—away from their communities. One evening, just weeks before the start of our school winter break, my dad sat in the living room of our Manhattan apartment studying the road maps we had picked up at AAA, marking a route south for what had become an annual winter road trip to Florida. I looked over his shoulder. His markings seemed jagged and irregular. He had scratched out portions of coastal Florida. He ran his pencil along the road west of it.

"Why don't you want to go by the Atlantic Ocean, *Tatek*?" I asked, addressing him as always by the Polish pet name for Dad. I had always felt a thrill when the road brought us closer to the ocean. Our vinyl car seats, too sticky and warm, seemed to relax their grip when I rolled down the window to let the sea breezes work their magic on the hot

Nina Lewandowska Camic

and cigarette smoke-filled air inside the black Chevy Impala. Why wouldn't he want to squeeze as much coastal time into the trip as possible?

"There is a new American law that permits counties and states to designate communist-free zones," he answered. "People from communist countries aren't allowed to set foot in them. We have to be sure not to drive through those areas."

"Are they only in Florida?" I'm starting to feel uneasy about traveling to the sunshine state.

"Not at all. Remember Lake George in upstate New York?"

I do remember. We had gone there for spring break, and I had loved it for the escape it offered from the loud chaos of Manhattan.

"We can't go back," he said matter-of-factly. "It's off limits now. Every state has areas where we aren't allowed to travel. Well, actually, one state has refused to set these limits. Georgia. We can go anywhere we want in Georgia."

"Let's just go to Georgia."

My dad smiled his tight-lipped grin. "There are plenty of places for us to see, even in Florida."

"But who's to know? If you don't stop overnight, it's not as if they can tell we're from a communist country, right?"

"We obey American laws so long as we're here, Nina."

He returned to his maps, and I retreated to the room I shared with my older sister, Eliza. I felt chastised by his words, and I wanted to defend myself, but I knew not to ever challenge Tatek—the man of a small frame but great stature, certainly in my mother's eyes and in the eyes of the diplomatic world. He wasn't home much, and I didn't really know him all that well, but I knew enough to stay quiet when Tatek talked.

My sister was a better audience.

"I wonder why we don't have to obey parking signs in the city." I said this as if the question just came to me at that very second.

"What do you mean?"

"Well, the car Tatek drives has DPL on the license plate. He's a diplomat. That means he can park anywhere, and he won't get a parking ticket!"

"So? It's not a big deal. He never drives in the city anyway."

She was right. My parents liked to walk, and for evening functions, they used the chauffeur from the Polish delegation. Still, those three letters "DPL" appeared to give him permission to break rules. And I'd seen him break that rule at least once when he had taken us for a Sunday outing to the Guggenheim Museum, and there was no legitimate parking nearby.

"Do you know that there are new rules about where we can't go? Tatek says that's a rule we have to obey." I zeroed in on the topic that was really on my mind, but Eliza had returned to her reading and had lost interest in my seemingly random questions.

The new restrictions on our comings and goings didn't really surprise me. Although I had no memory of hearing the word "communism" back in Poland, I often heard it after arriving in New York, whether on the playground, in the classroom, or on television.

"What did you do when the lights went out?" My teacher at UNIS asked the class after the night of New York City's complete blackout resulting from a Con Ed power failure.

"My mom had us all get into the bathtub." It's Marie again. The girl often spoke up without bothering to raise her hand. "She said it was a communist invasion. That the Russians were coming!" One girl let out a giggle, but I sensed it was because of Marie's habit of speaking out of turn, not because she had once again revealed her family's distrust of communists.

When did I first grasp the fact that I came from a country with a political system that was despised by the west? Certainly not before I left Poland. I was born in 1953, and my earliest years were split between the remote village house where my maternal grandmother and grandfather—*babcia* and *dziadek* in Polish—lived and the small Warsaw apartment on Nowowiejska Street where my parents lived. These were pre-television years, and my mom and dad—*mamusia* and *tatek*—never talked about politics at home. If I came across the word "communist" at all, it would have been in passing. The first of May certainly triggered talk of pride in the working people of my country. This was the day we celebrated, with bombastic clamor, workers' rights. Flag-waving school children joined the military parade that made its

Nina Lewandowska Camic

way up Marszalkowska Street, all the way to the Palace of Culture. But I was far too young to think much about the pomposity and the display of power intended for that day. Much more interesting to my young eyes was the Palace of Culture, where the dignitaries stood to salute those marching before them. At thirty-two stories, the Palace of Culture was the tallest building in Warsaw and all of Poland. It very much resembled a similarly designed building in Moscow. The Warsaw structure was Stalin's gift to my country after the war. Jokes about the building flow freely in Warsaw. You know that it offers the best views of Warsaw! It's the only place from which you can view the city without having to see the palace itself. Stalin asked the people if they wanted the palace or a subway system. The people chose the subway system, so he built them a palace! And so on.

"Who is Stalin?" I asked Mamusia one day as I caught a glimpse of the imposing palace on one of our strolls through the city.

"He was the leader of the Soviet Union," she said. "He died just a month before you were born. It was a shock! I cried when I heard the news."

"Was he a good leader?"

She seemed flustered. "At the time, it wasn't always easy to tell."

Had my father participated in the conversation, his answer would have been very different.

During the time we lived in New York, Eliza and I were somewhat protected from the worst of the hatred targeting communists. Our orbits, after all, were small and tightly controlled. The very first day we stepped off the magnificent *Queen Elizabeth* vessel that brought us to the piers of west Manhattan, we were whisked away by car to Flushing, Long Island, where much of the Polish delegation's staff resided.

I had fared well during the ocean crossing, but the first car ride in America was something else altogether. In Poland, few people had cars, and although I know I must have surely ridden in one, I have no memory of it. Now, on my first day in America, riding in the stop-and-go traffic of the Long Island Expressway, my stomach heaved.

"Mamo!" I wailed and then threw up on the back seat.

When we finally climbed out of the hot, stuffy car, I found no relief in being outside. I had never experienced air that was so still and humid.

We were in a neighborhood of two- and three-story brick buildings, each with a handful of apartment units. Short strips of lawn abutted the sidewalk, and yew bushes grew in cropped formations alongside the buildings. Nothing felt familiar, although the language spoken among the residents was Polish.

"Are we going to live here?" I asked.

"No, our apartment is in the city." My mother waved her hand, indicating another place, somewhere beyond all this. "But it's not ready. I have to unpack our trunks when they arrive and finish furnishing the place. Tatek has important work to do."

Oh, now that's a phrase I recognized! Back home, the absence of Tatek was always explained in this way. Important work—that's my tatek! Many years would pass before I began to suspect that my mother said it with just a tiny hint of sarcasm. In their early years together, it wasn't clear who contributed more to the family larder: my tatek, the government employee; my mamusia, the radio announcer and English language instructor; or maybe even my grandparents, who lugged meats and produce from the village to replenish stockpiles that could not easily be replenished with goods you'd find in Warsaw stores.

"You'll stay here with people from the Polish delegation for now," she said. "Babcia (her mother and my grandmother) is coming soon, and she'll look after you once she arrives." If my mother was searching for the familiar to offer reassurance, she succeeded, at least a little bit. Babcia had been my de facto parent for the first three years of my life. She was a soft-spoken woman, gentle toward her grandchildren, and always willing to let me hide my head in her ample bosom. I reached now for my book of Polish folk songs, a gift from Dziadek (my grandfather) back home. He knew I liked to sing. That became clear when we visited him this spring in Kamionka, the village near where he was born. It had been cold. Patches of snow made it seem that winter wasn't ready to fade just yet. We posed for a photo with Dziadek. Two girls in heavy blue wool coats and a man who knows how to build most anything. Late at night, I sat next to him in a smoky room right by the kitchen of the small house. He was engaged in a lively conversation with his friends. Men with wool caps, some with unshaven faces, many with thick mustaches and missing teeth. I could

Nina Lewandowska Camic

hardly see through the haze of tobacco smoke. I leaned on Dziadek's lap and tried to catch fragments of conversation. Impossible! These men clipped their words in ways that I could not follow. I buried my face in Dziadek's wool jacket.

"Sing for us," Dziadek prodded me. At first I declined, but he coaxed me with his kind eyes, good eyes, eyes that tear up at the sound of familiar Polish melodies.

I began to sing. *"Pyk pyk, pyk z fajeczki, duz duz duz duz golombeczki ..."*

Pipes and pigeons, a bench in a garden. Simple words about quiet moments.

"More. Go on, sing us another!" The room grew quiet.

I continued with a gutsy song of a country lad urging his horses on. *"Hej, wjo, hetta stary, mlody jary ..."* My little girl voice must have sounded funny to these men who prod their horses daily behind the long, wooden wagons. Dziadek looked down at me, and his old face melted into a broad grin. I have not failed him. He pulled me up on his lap, and I lost myself in his broad arms, worker's arms, arms that can saw timber and heave a pitchfork.

———

Now, in this strange new American world, I picked out my favorite song and practiced singing the notes just right.

"Ej przelecial ptaszek ... nie placz ty dziewczyno ... abo ci to swiat maly ..."

A bird has flown over a forest, don't cry, the world is a small place.

It didn't feel very small to me at all.

But like the pet cat or puppy that you bring home in a cage, keeping it there until it gets familiar with its new home, day after day, my sister and I were left in the Flushing community of Poles. Communists among communists, looking after their own. And within a few days, Babcia arrived. She boiled a chicken for a traditional *rosol* (chicken soup) and baked a *szarlotka* (apple cake). This should have put me in a good frame of mind, yet as I sat at the Formica table casually positioned by the kitchen window and looked out at the strips of dull green grass along the edge of the sidewalk, it didn't feel right at all. After a night where I woke up screaming from a nightmare and another where I sleepwalked my way to the door, it was decided that Babcia, my sister, and I would finally move into our Manhattan apartment.

The United Nations International School was another buffer zone for kids from countries with shady—even hostile—governments. We were a mixture of international and American. Half the school was like a geography quiz, testing your knowledge of the nations of the world. Rumania, India, New Zealand, Poland. Our teacher routinely distributed her favorite songbook, *Voices From Around the World*, in music class. We sang about Russian birch trees, Per Spelman from Denmark, and the Zulu Warrior from South Africa.

We sang about what binds us, not about what divides us.
We'll treat each one like a brother
By protecting one another
We'll be all for one and one for all!
And:
I have a little friend
Whose name ends with a ski
And yet my little friend
Looks just like you and me.
Last night I asked my father
Why a name like this should be
And this is what my father said
As I sat on his knee.
A ski or witz or off or cue when added to a name
Just teaches you the family of land from which he came
A name like Thomas Jefferson in some lands o'er the sea
Would not be Thomas Jefferson but Thomas Jefferski!

When we came to Thomas Jefferski, all eyes turned to me. But I kept my eyes focused on the floor, too embarrassed to say that I had been given a ridiculous name since coming to New York. Here, I was Nina Lewandowski, copying my father's last name, who was indeed

Nina Lewandowska Camic

Mr. Lewandowski. But anyone in Poland would tell you that you only end a name with "ski" for boys. A girl's name should end with "ska." At home, I was Lewandowska. By my fourth year in UNIS, I would grow bold and insist on a change back to Nina Lewandowska.

2.

When we first moved into our New York apartment, we were a family of five: Mamusia, Tatek, Babcia, Eliza, and I. But this was just a temporary state of affairs. My mother needed help, and Babcia was only filling in until a permanent live-in housekeeper arrived from Poland. Who to hire? Just about any Pole would find the idea of work in New York to be wildly alluring. There was the benefit of travel abroad—something that almost no one in Poland could afford—but perhaps more importantly, it would put dollars in the pocket of some Pole who had no other way of accessing western currencies.

My grandfather pushed hard for hiring someone from a village in the southeast of Poland. Dziadek grew up in that region, and when all the essential components of daily life would disappoint him— work, wife, community, politics—he returned again and again to the villages of his childhood where cousins and more distant relatives still resided. It was no surprise that he wanted to help some local family by arranging work in New York. Dziadek believed that if you show someone the path to a better life, if you help the person along just a wee bit, then their success will be yours, and their prosperity will be everyone's rich reward.

We called her Pani Nela. Even to my seven-year-old eyes, she seemed young. She came with a sturdy build but a delicate glossy smooth face that was always a bit shiny. Pani Nela projected an image of freshness and coquettish innocence. She shared a room with my grandmother, and between the two of them, I rarely heard more than a murmur. Babcia always spoke in a hushed voice, as if anything she said would be an intrusion. And you got the feeling that Pani Nela saved her words for the men in her life. As for written words—well, forget those. Pani Nela was illiterate. And she did not know how to cook. Babcia put on her apron each morning and set out to teach her, step by step, but Pani Nela resisted. My mother quickly became exasperated.

"Give her time," Babcia would say. "Give her time."

Pani Nela spoke no English, and when she left the apartment and stepped out onto the streets of a city that had to have shocked her senses, she always had one destination in mind—a Catholic church with a Polish congregation. There, she found people familiar with her ways, people who, like her, prayed for a better life than the one they knew back home. But on many Sundays, she skipped church too, preferring to rest in bed, turning the pages of countless magazines.

Our apartment on East 46th Street was at least three times the size of our Warsaw home on Ulica Nowowiejska. The layout was slightly unconventional and not altogether friendly toward family life. In reality, our apartment wasn't really one unit at all. It consisted of three small apartments at the end of the ninth-floor corridor, closed off and converted into one residence. My parents inhabited the first "apartment," an L-shaped studio immediately to our left as we came in. It must have had a kitchenette at one point. My mother used the alcove now as her sewing corner. Eliza and I, along with Pani Nela lived in the two rooms of the second unit to the left, while the third, positioned across the hallway to the right, had been turned into a living-dining room combination.

Our kitchen was a curious U-shaped room, created out of two separate kitchens, with a wall knocked down at the midpoint. The Polish government rented the apartment and furnished it with standard 1950s modern pieces that I recognized from what I was seeing now on television. My mother had a decorating budget to add needed furniture, but the budget must have been small because the apartment looked much the same on the day we moved out as it did when we first saw it in the summer of 1960.

I should have liked our room. It was much larger than the space Eliza and I shared in Warsaw. But it had a northern exposure, and I saw it as dreary and dark. When I think about the room on Ulica Nowowiejska, I have an image of sunshine coming in through the window, and I see a reproduction of a Monet painting with bright red poppy fields on the wall. The room in New York surely had a picture on our bedroom wall, but I do not remember what it was. And the window came too close to the back of the building on the next street. Effectively, our bedroom looked out onto the rooms of the YMCA on East 47th.

"Do you see him? He's staring at us," I said, peering into a dimly lit room at the YMCA.

"Close the blinds," Eliza told me, but neither of us touched the Venetian shades. I moved closer to the window, pretending to look elsewhere, but out of the corner of my eye, I studied the man in the room across from ours. He looked despondent. Shoulders hunched. Very still. I shook off any worries about him and walked over to the rooms across the hall. I sat down on the living room couch and looked at an oil painting of fishing boats.

"Are we rich now?" I asked my mother, who was flipping the pages of the newspaper. I had never thought of our Polish life as harsh, but our life now seemed far removed from what I had known in Warsaw.

"No, we are not! We will be spending a lot of money sending you to a good school. I could buy a fur coat with the money we'll spend on school!"

"But we live in this big apartment! And Tatek has a chauffeur!"

"The Polish government pays for these things. None of this is ours. Your father gets a salary, and it's not very large. Not even a small fraction of what an American lower-ranked diplomat earns. It's only large by Polish standards."

I heard a version of this story during our entire stay in New York. Yes, we were very privileged now, but cash was tight. We were living a borrowed life, where money remained elusive. One afternoon, when I was old enough to ride the city bus alone, I asked my mother for an extra quarter for the fare to Long Island to visit my friend there. My mother burst out crying.

"You just asked me for some money an hour ago! I just don't have it right now!"

Our requests for anything that costs money nearly always upset my mother, so we learned quickly not to ask. Still, I was surprised that she should worry about a quarter. We were living in Manhattan. Our refrigerator had food in it. We had new clothes, and though they were mostly sewn by her, they felt more colorful than anything we had worn in Poland. The hues were brighter, and we no longer wore brown lace-up shoes, even in the winter. And yet we always seemed to be at the cusp of a financial crisis. One wrong move, one excessive purchase, and we would sink. Forget about those coveted PF Flyers advertised on television—sneakers that would make me jump higher and run faster! We made do with Korvette's bargain bins.

If my parents spent money on a consumer good, it was always with an eye toward its usefulness when we would be returning to Poland one day. Underwear was purchased in bulk, in various sizes. My mother collected scores of American paperbacks. My father collected classical music albums. For daily stuff now, my mother improvised. She purchased a sewing machine and made her own evening dresses for the numerous receptions she attended. She was familiar with every bargain basement in the city. And toys were never on anyone's shopping list. Johnny, my Polish doll, with a faded imprint of shorts and a shirt on his pink rubber body, was as important to me now as he had been in Warsaw.

"Are you going out to a party tonight?" It was a rhetorical question on my part. From the first month in New York, my parents were almost always out for the evening. On this evening, I had come into their room tentatively, trying to stay out of their way. I liked being there. My father had just come home, and he was changing into an evening suit. My mother was working on her clouds oh high, puffy hair died inky black, spraying herself with cologne and adding strands of Polish pearls to her newly stitched evening dress. The television was in their room, and I could watch it in small amounts. But right now, I flung myself on their bed, riveted by the transformations taking place before me.

"We are having dinner with the representative from Ghana. And before that, a reception at the Russian Delegation," my mother answered.

"Do you ever have dinner with American diplomats?"

"Sometimes. Not too often." She paused a little, almost not liking her response, then continued to tease and spray her hair.

"How about the French?" I knew about France now. We passed through Paris to get to New York.

"No, not very often. We see a lot of people from the other Eastern European countries."

"Like who?"

"No one you know." And she went off to the bathroom to work on her makeup. Everywhere she walked, she left behind a scent of hairspray and perfume.

Their social life seemed to be a carefully scripted affair, often consisting of two or even three events on any one evening. And when a Polish dignitary came to New York, like the foreign minister, Adam Rapacki, or even the general secretary of the Polish United Workers Party, Wladyslaw Gomulka, I hardly saw my parents. They disappeared into the chaos of diplomatic functions: receptions, teas, lunches for my mother, and formal evening dinners.

"Do you like going out? I wish I could go to so many parties!"

My mother shook her head. "You wouldn't like it if you had to do it every day."

I considered this. I wasn't sure I believed her. "I think I'd like it anyway!"

For all her words, my mother did not appear to be unhappy. She stood tall and proud, quite content to be dressing up in her hand-sewn brocade dresses. I could tell that she was pleased with the impression she created. She was a surprise on the diplomatic stage—from the Eastern Bloc, but savvy in the ways of the West.

The fact is, my mother was no newcomer to New York. Her parents had attempted to settle in America when she was young, so she lived in this very city most of her childhood years. Not surprisingly, she was completely fluent in English and very familiar with the city.

And my father? As he tied his black neckpiece deftly to form a bow, I noticed a twitch of a smile as well. My mother made the grand entrance, and then he worked the crowd with carefully crafted tales. Better at telling stories than listening to them, he now had countless opportunities to perform. Yes, this life appeared to suit both of them just fine.

"What do you talk about during the parties?"

"The women talk to each other, and the men have separate conversations. We talk about our children and home life. The men?

Oh, politics, I should imagine." She smiled to herself as she thought back to a recent dinner at the Polish delegation headquarters on 66th Street. One of the guests had been the Swedish ambassador—a woman. Should she join the men in the room where cigar smoke hung in the air and cognac glasses were filled and refilled? No, she chose to sit with the wives and join in their conversation.

"Are these women your friends now?"

"I like some of them, and they like us. We cut a good picture! People can't believe I'm Polish!" My mother spoke with a laugh in her voice. It's as if being completely Polish put you in a disadvantaged category.

Once my parents stepped out of the apartment for the evening, a stillness settled over all the rooms. With Babcia back in Poland now, Pani Nela took on babysitting responsibilities. But her reclusiveness meant that Eliza and I were, in effect, left to our own devices. Realizing that Pani Nela was not capable of providing help in the kitchen and not very interested in providing child care, by springtime of our first year in New York, my mother told Pani Nela that she should plan on returning home. Her services were no longer needed. Pani Nela listened in silence as my mother explained that she would be booking a passage for her on a ship that would sail to Poland in June. If Pani Nela was disappointed, she did not show it. Message conveyed, my mother breathed a sigh of relief and began to look into other live-in help. But one Sunday, shortly after this exchange, when Pani Nela left to attend Polish church services with a congregation in lower Manhattan, my mother noticed that she was especially well dressed for the event.

"Do you have somewhere to go after the services?" she asked.

Pani Nela shrugged her shoulders and slammed the door behind her.

Evening came and Pani Nela had not returned.

"Where is she? Maybe she got lost? She doesn't speak much English," I said.

My mother shook her head. "Maybe she is visiting friends in the Polish community."

Pani Nela never returned. An organization of Polish Americans had offered her both means and a method to escape from our home and

Poland in general. We never saw her again, though we did read about her in the Polish-American newspaper, where she was portrayed as a victim of communist oppression and, more specifically, a victim of too much work, too little pay, at the hands of her communist employers—my parents.

"They did not let me practice my religion! They're communists! I was not allowed to believe in God!" she was quoted as saying. The article emphasized the repressiveness of the Polish regime and its hold over the minds and activities of the common people.

"Did we keep her from going to church?" I asked.

"Of course not!" My mother was outraged. "She wanted to stay in America. She was told to say that. It's propaganda, that's all!"

3.

When Pani Nela left, my parents hired another woman from Poland, Pani Pola, who had experience working in diplomats' homes living abroad. She was a quiet, older person who had a twinge of affection for us but was far too shy to display it, especially when my parents were present. Pani Pola stayed with us for only a year. She missed her family and asked to return home. By then, my mother decided that we could make do with a local babysitter and that she could hire local part-time help to assist with the formal dinners and receptions in our home. And still later, when I turned eleven and my sister was twelve, we were allowed to stay home alone.

When the apartment became too quiet for my liking, I went to my parents' bedroom and flipped on the TV. And very quickly, I got hooked on many of the programs. My parents surely felt ambivalent about my love of television. Very early, they established rules about how much I could watch. "One hour per day is plenty," my mother told me. But when they were gone, I got a break. "Okay, you can watch something when you're eating supper."

I went to great lengths to fix an elaborate meal for myself. I boiled hot dogs or ears of corn, put them on a tray, and carried them to my parents' bedroom. There I curled up in my father's big leather chair and enjoyed a very, very long supper to the sound of commercial jingles, punctuating the sitcoms and adventure series that I had grown to love.

One evening, my parents returned from a reception to find me still glued to the TV, watching *The Man from U.N.C.L.E.* It was an immensely popular spy thriller, unusual in that it portrayed an American and a Russian working on one side to defeat the encroachment of evil from what appeared to be a transnational power. The show was much discussed and reviewed by my friends in school. Girls bantered as to one star's virtues and good looks over the other. I admitted to liking David McCallum.

"No, Robert Vaughn is more manly!"

"McCallum has great eyes!"

"Vaughn is sexy!"

The episodes were fast-paced and entertaining. In my mind, they were not unlike the James Bond movies my parents loved and occasionally took us to when a new one appeared in movie theaters.

As he hung up his evening jacket and unraveled his tie, my father paused to watch the show with me.

"What is this?" He sounded irritated. I wondered if his performance of stories and schmoozing had not gone well for him that night.

"It's *The Man from U.N.C.L.E.*"

"It's nonsense! Propaganda! You shouldn't be watching this."

"Tatek! Everyone else is watching it!"

"I said no." The TV was turned off.

If my father appeared bothered by the politicized depictions of good and evil on television, he surely could not have thought that this was our only exposure to propaganda. Protected as we were, I assume he knew that we heard anti-communist messages from any number of sources. Was he now feeling obligated to take an authoritative parental stand just because he happened to be there, witnessing a political message on television not to his liking?

———

"Look, Tatek!" It was the weekend, and I had been flipping ahead in my social studies book, counting how many pages were left in my homework assignment. I was not a fan of homework. "There is a paragraph about the Soviet Union: 'In communist Soviet Union, if you disobey the government, you are sent, along with your family, on a slow-moving train to Siberia.'" I giggled at this sentence since my parents had taught me to be skeptical about anything I learned about Eastern European and so-called communist countries as described in American writings.

"It's propaganda," my father said. "Let me see that book." I handed it over, feeling suddenly foolish. I hadn't wanted him to make a fuss.

"It's only a small paragraph," I answered in defense of the book.

"You should not be using that text in your school. I will look into this further."

For me, any description in the press, textbooks, or reading matter of life under communism was suspect. From early on, I learned that there were agendas at play. Americans were hell-bent on depicting communists as evil. Since I could not reconcile the bits and pieces of such reporting with my own memories of life back in Poland, I tended to treat the whole as propaganda. At the same time, even in my childhood years, it became obvious that Eastern Bloc countries portrayed images of economic success and progress in excess of what was real. And so, for me, all messaging was either incomplete or sometimes even patently false. Where was the truth then? It lay in what you witnessed and what was spoken in your closest circles of association. But what was also obvious to me then was that most Americans, regardless of how well-off or well-read they were, accepted the depictions of a harshly politicized everyday life in Eastern European countries to the very last detail, which I knew to be wrong. In contrast, no Pole that crossed my path believed the stories of their own country's successes nor descriptions of western imperialism as portrayed in our press or on the radio. Perhaps one reason for this was that it is far easier to deceive an audience about what goes on in a faraway place that they are never likely to visit than it is to deceive your own people about how good their lives are compared to those of relatives who send you dollars and consumer goods from abroad.

Following my exchange with my father about the slow-moving trains to Siberia, I expected any day now for the principal to come into class and conduct a grand sweep of our offensive textbooks. But he did not come, and we continued with the book. My father did not mention it again, and I began to doubt that he even remembered the incident the next day.

4.

Winter in New York. Who would think that a city could be so bright and colorful in December? In the winter months, Warsaw grew dark early and stayed dark late. But it wasn't the stalled dusk that made evenings brighter here. It was the presence of street lamps, office lights, headlights, neon lights, flashing lights—lights that came on even before the sun hid behind the tall buildings. If you weren't impressed with their luminescence, you would surely be impressed with their color and pizzazz! I could spend a good many minutes just watching the open sign do its rhythmic dance by the pizza joint. One letter at a time, blinking slowly, then rapidly, and then fully on. We're OPEN, and isn't that grand? An announcement of who is boss. A defiant attitude toward darkness. In New York, light triumphs, even in winter.

But if New York was dazzling, my images of Warsaw remained strongly positive, perhaps aided by a protective defensiveness I learned to adopt when talking about my home country.

"Is it true that they have men with guns in schools, standing outside the classrooms so that the kids don't escape?" a classmate asks.

"No."

"Do they make you learn things? Do they brainwash you?"

"No." Do they? "No."

Sometimes, though, I hesitated. I wasn't sure what it meant to be brainwashed. Did it mean to force you to like your country? I liked my country. I liked America too. Was I being brainwashed by the people in power here?

When I was ten years old, a classmate raised his hand during our homeroom discussion of everything and nothing.

"Mrs. Inez, why don't people like communists?"

"How would you like it if someone took away all your money?"

Mrs. Inez was my fifth-grade teacher, and she had an edge to her. She was tall, wiry, and sharp in her tone. I shouldn't have given much thought to her blunt outburst, but I couldn't help minding it. Was this why she didn't like me? Because I came from a communist country? I had noticed that she always seemed to look past me, but up to now, I had dismissed it as a manner that she had toward most of the kids in her homeroom. I had the feeling that she just didn't like being around children. But I took her words now to heart because I knew she was merely saying what others around me were thinking. But did communists take away your money? By now, I knew something about communism. I had asked at home for a definition, and I was told that under an ideal communist system, decisions were made for the good of the many and wealth was distributed for the benefit of all. It struck me as a plausible way to proceed. We did not have much money back in Poland. But neither did our friends and neighbors. And weren't we merely sharing what little we had? If the government took our money, where is it? Who has it?

From the moment I first stepped into a grocery store in New York, I understood that Poland was not a prosperous country. At the same time, it was obvious that New Yorkers were not uniformly well off. But where do you find the roots of poverty in either country? My inclination was to fall back on history rather than hold government systems responsible. I merely thought of Poland as postwar poor. Our starting point had been prewar economic stagnation, followed by wartime destruction. My father had been a young boy before the war broke out. He had no good words to say about life in Poland just before Hitler invaded the country. Poland, according to him, was an economic mess. "Corrupt, semi-fascist government," he told me. Failing institutions. And then came the war and with it the tremendous loss of life, the calamitous destruction of towns and cities. Warsaw had to be completely rebuilt, raised from the rubble. Is Poland now catching up or falling behind? Were the very poor in America better off than the poor in Poland? Or was it more important to look at the vast majority? The vast majority of Americans would not want anything to do with Poland. The vast majority of Poles would not mind at least visiting America.

Eventually, I shrugged off Mrs. Inez's comment. I was used to people not knowing anything about Poland. Even at a place like UNIS, we buried our cultures. We lived in what we shared. School and New York. My best friends were from Ceylon, Romania, and Lebanon. I knew nothing about these places. One friend had strict parents. Was it because she was Ceylonese? I didn't know. We learned to be polite. Respectful. Accept what you see and move forward. It was a workable approach to childhood. Differences were confusing, and we didn't have the language to sort it all out yet. Cultural blindness was a synch compared to confronting why so many Americans hated communists.

And over time, I got used to being the odd communist in any roomful of people. I was, in fact, a little bit proud of being so different from the rest. Americans were afraid of communists. I thought these fears were irrational, especially as they pertained to Poland. Hatred of capitalism, fear of communism—slogans exaggerated to bolster a political purpose.

But very early in our New York stay, something happened that rattled all of us, and suddenly the juxtaposition of the East and the West was no longer just a textbook discussion of which system of governance was fairer. It was October 1962. The minute my father returned from work, he turned the television on, and it stayed on all evening. Tatek sat in the leather chair facing the set—a coveted spot that I usually appropriated when I was in their bedroom. He was smoking, and although I had gotten used to the scent of burning tobacco, I noticed that he was lighting one cigarette after another this time. A crumpled Chesterfield packet lay to the side. My mother was watching the television, too, from her usual perch at the head of their bed, leaning against the wall, a piece of fabric and a needle in hand, sewing as she usually did, methodically, evenly.

The news broadcasts described the rising tension as Khrushchev, the leader of the Soviet Union, deployed missiles to Cuba. As the potential for armed conflict between the two superpowers grew, I understood that the responses from the two leaders, Kennedy and Khrushchev, were immensely important.

"Is there going to be a war?" I asked, with a small quiver in my voice. The aftermath of war had been with me my entire childhood. Suddenly, I was panicking. Was it real, this talk of firing missiles?

I was nine years old. I knew about nuclear weapons. I knew what would happen when superpowers dropped nuclear bombs.

"Tatek, would the Soviet Union use nuclear weapons against the United States?"

"Be quiet. Let's listen."

"But would they? And would Americans start a war against the Soviet Union?"

"Everyone is trying to avoid this," my father said, but I could tell he was distracted.

"If there were a nuclear war, we would all die." I said this, hoping that someone would deny the inevitability of such an outcome. "What president would want that? Kennedy has children. He wouldn't want his children hurt, right?"

I took it to the level of family. I had this in common with the presidents. I was part of a family. They were too. Americans had families. Russians had families. Poles had families. Surely this must matter to them.My father's face revealed just a shadow of a smile. He leaned back in the leather chair and pushed the few strands of straight hair from his forehead. My mother continued to sew, rhythmically, quietly.

"Yes," he answered, "President Kennedy has a family."

5.

We returned to Poland several times in the six years that we lived in New York. But not the summer after our first year abroad. Eliza and I were rapidly becoming fluent in English, and my mother decided that camp would be good for us. It would solidify our English language and keep us out of trouble. In part, she was following the course taken by the previous Polish ambassador's wife. Mrs. Michalowska had sent her boys to camp. And to UNIS. And so my mother signed us up for two months at her predecessor's choice, Camp Robinson Crusoe in Massachusetts. Left-leaning East Coast families favored the camp, predominantly New Yorkers who hadn't the antipathy toward socialism or communism that other Americans seemed to have. I was put in a cabin with the youngest age group. I was to spend the summer living in Cabin 1A, a white house with bunk beds at two levels with other girls my age.

"Will we see you at all?" I asked my mother. Having spent every summer of my childhood away from my parents, I didn't regard the announcement that this year there would be camp as strange. In Poland, we were always sent to the familiar village house where Babcia and Dziadek lived. My mother would visit nearly every Saturday. Camp would be something altogether different.

"Your father and I will be vacationing on Cape Cod, at a beach cottage, for a couple of weeks."

"Can't we go?"

"You have a whole summer to fill! We'll be in the city much of the time you're at camp. We'll come for a visit halfway through."

The only thing that camp had in common with a summer spent cavorting in the village where my grandparents lived was that both were away from the hot, sticky chaos of summer in the city. Everything else was entirely new for me, including activities I'd not considered before, such as archery, nature hikes, and swimming. And it was all planned and carefully structured, in stark contrast to our lackadaisical habits and play routines during our summers in the village in Poland.

At camp, during the obligatory naptime after lunch, we were encouraged to write letters home. I had special stationery and a sheet of flower stamps that I could lick onto the writing paper as a decoration. All these items were on the packing list the camp had sent us before our arrival. As I lay on my bunk bed, I tried to think of something to put down on the sheet before me.

Dear Mamusia and Tatek, I'm learning to play the guitar here. Can I have a guitar when I come home? love, Nina

My sister didn't like camp. She pleaded, with no success, to return home midway through. I didn't know this initially, as we were in separate cabins and our paths rarely crossed. For me, camp was fun. I was dismayed that I was one of the few who could not swim. The counselor patiently started me off with the dead man's float in the shallow water. I thought I was good at outdoor sports, but I was stunned at how difficult it was to pretend to be dead in the water. The lake where we did our daily swim routines was clean and clear. The water was so refreshing, especially in the heat of July, and yet each time I tried to do what seemed to come so naturally to the others, I sank. It took the whole summer to get me to swim even a very short distance.

The other plunge into the exotic and unusual for me came at mealtimes. The food at camp was like nothing I had ever seen before. I had never eaten a baloney sandwich. Hot dogs with beans on the side? Bizarre. Sweet fruit juice, called "bug juice" for no reason that I could understand, was nothing like Babcia's gently diluted stewed fruit compote. We were measured and weighed at the infirmary early into the summer, and the camp nurse told me bluntly that I was too thin.

"Can you eat more?"

"I'll try," I said without much enthusiasm.

"We'd also like you to come up here once a day for an extra milkshake. Anything you like: chocolate, strawberry, vanilla."

And so, for a month, I forced down milk mixed with ice cream, something that, too, was unusual for me. My cabin mates were envious, but I was happy when I was relieved of the trips for the extra dish of calories at the end of the month.

Despite these small thorns, I liked my days at Robinson Crusoe. I made friends with several girls in my cabin. I was especially drawn to Cindy Hellerstein, a pixie-haired girl with a generous disposition. She was a New Yorker from the upper west side of Manhattan. I didn't understand then that camp was camp, and you could live just blocks from each other back home and never see them again. At camp, Cindy was my hero. She knew what's what. She swam, played archery, and sang all the songs. And somewhere along the line, her parents taught her to be a good kid, even toward communist friends at camp.

I marked off the six years we spent in New York by where we went for vacation during the summers. After Camp Robinson Crusoe the first year, we returned to Poland the following summer. The third summer put us on a road trip across America. The summer after that was Poland again, followed by Russian camp. The last summer, it was YMCA Camp and Poland. And then Poland for good.

I took the prospect of my first summer return to Poland in stride. I had been in New York for two years, enough to move my center of attention away from our Warsaw apartment on Ulica Nowowiejska, away from my Polish classmates, from the inkwells and uniforms, away from the local bakery where we bought fresh doughnuts with a dab of plum jam in them, and the ice cream shop where children lined up for vanilla and cocoa scoops served between thin wafers. I preferred, instead, to think about the hand-clapping games we played on slabs of concrete during recess at UNIS and to look forward to pizza that Tatek picked up for us nearly every Saturday night, bringing it home just in time for *Gilligan's Island* that we liked to watch in my parents' bedroom. At least in some small ways, I had become Americanized.

Perhaps sensing our growing attachment to our new school friends, my mother made a point of reconnecting us with the classmates we had left behind in Warsaw. When we had been in New York just short of a year, she told me to write a postcard to all the children in my Polish class. I balked.

"What should I write?" I was only eight years old with no great thoughts worthy of scribbling to kids who were virtually strangers.

"Tell them about New York," my mother prompted.

Dear girls and boys—I began. I looked at the photo on the card my mother put in front of me. It was a picture of a New York skyline.

There are many tall buildings in New York. I miss you and send greetings to all of you. Your friend, Nina.

Phew! What a chore. I was glad to be done with it. I didn't give the recipients of the card a second thought.

We journeyed back to Poland in 1962 in much the same way we had arrived just two years before. We sailed across the Atlantic on the great *Queen Elizabeth*, and from the port in Cherbourg, we took the train to Paris and then to Warsaw.

After a two-year absence, Warsaw seemed sweetly familiar, even as I felt a detachment from my childhood years there. We had to stay in a hotel, as my mother explained that our apartment was not available. I did not question why this would be the case. I liked the hotel just fine. The room that I shared with my sister was smaller than rooms I had seen in American motels, but the parquet floors were polished to a deep shine, and the two single beds were comfortable and freshly made up for us each day. We ate breakfast in the dining hall downstairs and the main midday meal at the milk bar just a block down Krucza Street.

Milk bars were ubiquitous and just about the only places where Poles would take a meal outside of home or workplace. They served simple Polish food, high on calories and low on sensory appeal. Many soups. Boiled potatoes with perhaps a *kotlet smazony*. Fried ground meat. Lots of *pierogi* and blintzes. All self-service. Eat and run. No lingering, no socializing. I preferred Babcia's pierogi and cheese blintzes, but there was a certain grandness to being in Warsaw as an almost guest rather than an old-time resident.

Shortly after our arrival, my mother told me that we would be treating all my classmates to ice cream at the local ice cream store.

"But they're not my classmates anymore! I don't know any of them!"

"You'll be returning to school here someday. You have to make an effort," she answered in a tone that shut down further discussion.

I greeted the large class of children with trepidation. I was wearing a simple skirt sewn by my mother and a T-shirt with bright stripes at the neckline. My former classmates were all in school uniform. I stood out and I knew it. I sensed that my mother knew it too, but she seemed happy to be nudging me toward the group as if reintroducing the child who had had a grand adventure back into the fold of those who had stayed behind. The children were already outside, clustered in a group, boys giving each other playful shoves, many girls with braided hair, all lining up in pairs now, as if used to walking in this orderly fashion through the city streets. A girl with large ribbons pleated through her braids came up to where I was standing next to my mamusia.

"I'm having a name day party tomorrow. Can you come?"

I had already forgotten that name days were causes for celebration for Polish people. In this way, I had stood out even before I left for America. I was that rare child who did not have a name day associated with her name. My mother chose names for her daughters that had no saint designation. She got some pushback from the authorities when she listed me as Nina on the birth certificate, but my mother was not easily deterred. She typed up a long letter of complaint, decrying the unwritten rule that only a Catholic saint's name may be used for a newborn. *It is appalling that even under communism, there should be a requirement to name a child after a saint!* she wrote. It was not the last letter that she would send off in her life, listing grievances and injustices that she felt had been committed. This time she prevailed, but as a result, I was the odd duck who could not bring treats to school on her nonexistent name day. I found myself grousing about this to Eliza, who also lacked a name day but seemed not to mind.

"Why don't you celebrate under Janina?" she suggested, seeking to find a compromise. "The nickname for that is Nina."

"That's cheating! I'm stuck with just an irrelevant birthday. No Polish person cares about birthdays!"

Now, at the suggestion of a name day party, I looked at my mamusia anxiously, hoping she would tell this girl that it was impossible, that I was too busy, that I was about to leave town, perhaps for a long, long time. Instead, my mother smiled a broad smile. "What a lovely idea, Malgosia! Yes, of course, she can go."

It was a done deal. I suppose I once knew this girl. Maybe we played in the schoolyard together. Maybe I was her seatmate in class. I had no recollection of any of it. At the party, I sat quietly at a long table with former classmates on both sides of it. The girls chatted excitedly to each other, and I smiled what I hoped was a convincing smile. The mother of Malgosia gave us coins to toss.

"Play heads or tails," she told us and then returned to the grown-up conversation at the other end of the room. I thought back to the one birthday party I had attended in New York. We had played many games, and there were presents for the guests, too. I walked away with a beautiful sparkly pencil case. I had never seen anything with so much glitter before.

Here, the heads or tails coin tossing quickly fizzled at the table. Groups of girls gathered by the window, and one of them pointed to the cactus plant growing on the sill.

"Look! It has bugs!" she said with a grimace.

Another girl reached into the pot, took out one of the small bugs, and placed it in another classmate's hair.

"Fela Fastman, Fela Fastman, you have bugs!" she chortled. Fela began to cry, and several adults came over to see what had happened. Someone whisked Fela to the bathroom to clean her up and wash her face. I sat quietly to the side, wishing so much that the party would end.

Back in the hotel room, my mother took out a pencil and a notecard. "Please write a thank you note," she said.

Dear Malgosia,

Thank you for inviting me to the party. I had a very nice time.

Nina

After our fourth year in New York, we again packed our bags for a return visit to Poland. I was eleven, and Poland felt far more remote than during the previous visit.

"Will we stay in the hotel again?"

"Yes, the same one. But you'll be there only for a few days. After that, I'll take you to the country to stay with Babcia and Dziadek for a month. You are lucky that you don't have to stay in the city during the summer. Very lucky."

I accepted this readily enough. I would not have known what to do with myself in Warsaw. In New York, I was now permitted to visit friends, walk to the store, the library, and the skating rink. I hadn't any idea where to go in Warsaw. To the ice cream shop again? To the bakery? To the milk bar? We could not shop for food. We hadn't a place to cook. There was no mention of visiting classmates, and after three days, I was happy to be back in the village of Gniazdowo, where my grandparents lived. There, Eliza and I picked up routines that were both familiar and comfortable. And we expanded on them. Now that we were older, we had the freedom to roam. To go to the river with other children who were spending summers in the village. To go to the next village and buy bread for Babcia. To go to the forest and pick mushrooms. Very lucky, I repeated to myself. Very lucky to be here, away from the city.

"But why only a month? Can't we spend the whole summer in Gniazdowo?"

"I have things to attend to back in New York, and your father and I thought it would be a good idea to return early and send you in August to Russian Camp." I noticed her reference to this as a joint decision.

I was genuinely puzzled. "Russian Camp? You mean like Robinson Crusoe?" I remembered liking camp activities. Would they be the same?

"It's a little different. The Russians run it for the children of the

Soviet diplomatic staff in New York. You'll be exposed to the Russian language. We're hoping you'll pick up some of it. You'll need it when we return to Poland for good." My mother was referring to the fact that every child in Poland began the compulsory study of the Russian language in fifth grade.

The camp was on Long Island, at a fenced compound near Oyster Bay. It seemed spacious for an estate, but it hadn't the feel of a forested, natural habitat. It's as if you were spending the summer at someone's grand mansion, one that perhaps needed some updating. There were grassy sports fields in the back and some wooded areas by the fencing, giving the place a sense of isolation. You couldn't see the outside world, nor could the outside world see you. The main red brick building had upstairs girls' quarters at one end and boys' quarters at the other. Downstairs, there was a large dining room.

We arrived in midsummer. It was obvious that most of the children had already had a month of camp. Upstairs, my sister and I were assigned places to sleep on the girls' side, but we were not close to each other. The white wrought iron beds were in a straight line, much as I imagined would be the case in a large hospital ward. Girls were effectively placed in ascending order of birth. I was near the younger end of the line. Eliza was closer to the middle. Once again, I was in a world of incomprehensible sounds and utterances.

The summer program at the camp was, at times, excessively structured and completely open-ended at other times. Girls roamed the fenced-in fields in groups and pairs during these free hours. Eliza and I held back. For me, the feeling of a slow passage of time was intense. I sensed that the counselors were keeping a motherly eye on us that was protective and ready to direct. But the Russian girls were oblivious to us, and we never crossed the invisible barrier that separated us from them.

A bugle call. We washed up and appeared for flag raising. But it was a Soviet flag, and there was a count off in Russian.

Boys and girls were lined up by size, and I was at the beginning of the line. "*Raz, dwa, tri....*" Alright, I got it. Counting wasn't hard, and I didn't have far to go. I was safe.

We marched to breakfast like little soldiers in step to the long tables in the dining hall. The food amounts were copious, and I was reminded vaguely of nursery school food back in Warsaw. Milk soups, warm cereals. I played with my food, willing myself to take a bite.

"Why aren't you eating? You can't get up until you're excused. Finish your food, and then we'll excuse you." This in broken English.

I tried. And I asked, in Russian, because it was expected that I pick up the Russian words spoken so effortlessly by those around me. "May I be excused?"

A shrug and a wave. *"Da, da ..."* *"Spasiba!* Thank you!" Gratefully I sauntered off until the next meal, when it all started again, and I sat tensely waiting for the words of reprieve. *"Da, da, haraszo.* Go now."

On good weather mornings, a bus took us to the beach. But the ocean was like a mirage—water you wish you could enter, even as you never got close enough to melt into its cool embrace. For most of the morning, we were kept away from the sea.

"Children! Stay out of the water! Come here for snack time now! No, you cannot go in the water after eating." The air was hot and sticky, and I thought back to my mother's words about being grateful to be out of the city. The city had air conditioning. The beach was horribly warm and muggy.

Toward the end of the morning, we would be given a few minutes to splash in the shallow waters just where the waves rolled gently onto the shore. After that, we'd come back to the hot sands, where I counted the minutes until it was time to travel back to the compound.

If the beach was unpleasant, the bus ride there and back was quite the opposite. The bus windows were open wide, and the minute we picked up speed, the breezes cooled our faces and hot, sticky bodies. The children sang Russian songs, and though I never fully picked up the lyrics, the melodies stayed with me for the rest of my life. *Russian folk music is very beautiful*, I thought. I closed my eyes and listened, and I wondered if it was odd for all these kids to be here, in New York. The despised Soviets. Though I knew being Polish, too, came with the baggage of being a communist, in my mind, Poles were one notch up the likability scale from the Russians. No wonder the compound was so isolated, so inaccessible to the public.

Lunch. "May I be excused?"

"Alright, alright."

"Spasiba!"

After the midday meal, we were told to strip down to our underpants and lie on top of our beds for a rest period. The older girls were allowed to talk quietly. At my end, we were to be silent. Well, that was fine by me. I couldn't say a word to the girl next to me. She and I occasionally exchanged smiles, nothing more.

At my sister's end of the room, there was another girl from Poland her age. Joanna was the daughter of another staff member from the Polish delegation. Over the course of the month, she and Eliza became great friends. If my mother had hoped we'd mix with Russian children, the presence of Joanna dashed that hope quickly enough.

I didn't exactly hate camp. I just found the days to be terribly long and punctuated by meals that I disliked. American camp food was also strange at first, but hot dogs and baloney were easier to get used to than, for example, the ubiquitous Russian eggplant caviar, a gloppy dish that swam on your plate if you let it sit there long enough. And it's not true that I left camp without learning a thing. I did walk away with new knowledge about girls' breasts. I had never seen so many naked teens in one room before, and here I had before me a full range of developing girls, stripped to their underpants, spread out on beds like young goddesses, some plump, some merely plump in discreet areas of the upper torso. I revised my image of adult breasts. And I began an impatient wait for mine to start doing what I had seen on the girls around me.

If I acquired language skills, they were not what my mother hoped for.

"Can I have Joanna sleep over?" Eliza asked when we were finally back in our New York apartment.

My mother was not enthusiastic about our associations with the rest of the Polish delegation children in New York. But Eliza persisted, and finally, my mother agreed.

On the weekend of the visit, I stayed for a while in the room, listening to the older girls talk. Joanna's cot was in our bedroom, and I leaned against it, resting comfortably with my feet up on Eliza's bed.

"Get your fucking feet off my bed!" Eliza told me.

"Oh, fine." I slipped them down to the floor. This was standard big sister little sister chatter, with the addition of a new vocabulary acquired over the summer. But my mother happened to hear the exchange. When Joanna left later that day, she came into our room and glared at Eliza.

"What did I hear you say when Joanna was here?"

"I don't know, what?"

"Did I hear you use a curse word?"

"Did you?"

"Yes, I did. That calls for punishment."

"But everyone talks like that."

"You are not everyone. I don't want Joanna here again. Do you understand?"

The lifelong misalignment between my mother and my sister had begun.

Chapter 2

1.

During our six years in New York, I let my Polish self take on some very un-Polish behaviors and beliefs. Even at my young age—we moved to New York when I was seven and left when I was thirteen—I knew that I could never again feel just Polish. What I didn't fully grasp then was that my parents had been drifting in a porous world of shifting identities and allegiances all their adult lives, with my mother veering closer to markers of her Americanisms and my father appearing, on the surface at least, more comfortable with his Polish identity. How is it that these two Poles were tossed between two countries at a time when so few moved effortlessly between America and Poland? For this, let me take you back to the years before our New York adventure.

Note: Nina moves from past tense to present tense for the remainder of the book.

Nina Lewandowska Camic

It is springtime in Warsaw. A striking woman, a thoroughly modern woman, makes her way to the hospital on Woloska Street. She is about to give birth. She is walking briskly and without a trace of anxiety. Of course, I don't know that since I'm focused on placing myself in a good position in her belly to make an unremarkable exit into the world.

Producing offspring. As if she was a launching pad for a life yet to be. I was her second child in less than two years. She clutches the handrail of the bus that she knows will take her right past the entrance to the hospital. Such a casual thing! Hoisting her body up the bus step, like countless others going to work or to run an errand. It's after the morning rush, and the bus is less crowded. People make room for her. She is clearly with child. At the hospital stop, she lifts herself out of the seat and steps down. The bus's doors close behind her, and the driver pulls away, looking not at her but over his left shoulder at the persistent and grinding progression of trucks—no nod to the pregnant woman or words of encouragement. By the time the bus belches a cloud of dark exhaust fumes and rejoins the city snarl, she is on the walk leading to the entrance of the brutalist concrete building with rows and rows of windows. It's set back from the street, and there are extra steps that she must take. She is determined. She walks steadily, resolutely, without a show of emotion.

"I'm here to give birth," she tells the hospital attendant, almost unnecessarily.

"I'm sorry, the nurse is on lunch hour. Can you wait?"

"No, I can't." Did the attendant detect that her voice cracked just a little?

The pregnant woman has short, jet black hair pushed securely behind the ears. Her lips are full and painted a deep red. Her dark eyes stay focused on the attendant. There is no trace of a smile on her face. The older woman behind the desk stirs the tea in a glass before her, delaying, delaying, but finally, she pushes her chair back and, with a sigh, gets up to call someone in from lunch.

We pass this spot five years later. I am now a young child, holding on tightly to the sleeve of my mamusia's voluminous wool coat. We are out on an errand that takes us to this very set of blocks in Warsaw. I'm concentrating on not letting go of her arm, on not being lost in the crowd of women and men, walking too briskly, with dangling netting bags ready to be filled with cabbage, apples, pickles, white cheese wrapped in newspapers, chunks of bread. Hurrying, always hurrying. Callous almost in their indifference to the plight of a small person struggling to keep up with her mamusia. I see before me the mammoth structure that houses the hospital. My mamusia tells me, "You were born there. I got off the bus and gave birth to you." My eyes grow wide. My mamusia is so smart! She knew where to go to have her baby! It does not strike me to wonder why she should have come here alone.

My world right now, at this moment of birth and for months to come, is completely centered on my mamusia, this very modern woman who, they say, looks just a touch foreign. Some will shake their heads and click their tongues and claim she is Americanized, and in later years, I wonder what exactly they mean by it. Is it that she attends to her clothes with unusual care? The longer skirts, so full and tightly held at the waist? Few Warsaw women hand over that much fabric for a skirt! Is it the neatly tucked-in blouse? The scarf, clasped to the side as if following a fashion directive? Maybe it's that she has such even, white teeth. Or maybe it's the skin tone. She looks dark. An olive complexion. She tells me many times, "Your sister has an olive complexion, just like me." My skin is not dark-toned. I come into this world looking very Slavic.

"You have such fine Slavic hair! You have your father's Slavic nose." I'm Polish alright.

Where did my mother pick up her style, her independent habits? That's easy. She left Poland with her family when she was just six. The immigrant. To Detroit, to New York, finally to D.C. And now, twenty-odd years later, she is back again in her country of birth, Warsaw, this time married to a Pole, a lower-ranked Polish diplomat who is away in New York during the birth of his second daughter.

The year is 1953.

2.

Such a sickly infant. I'm back in the hospital within two months. Pneumonia, diarrhea, sick, not thriving, and not digesting properly. Cows milk? Bleh! And what happens when maternity leave is up and a mother's infant is still very ill?

———

I'm released from the hospital. My mamusia gets on the train with her frail baby and waits for the locomotive to wheeze out the dark smoke that signals departure. Finally, there is a violent lurch. The wheels turn slowly, and the train moves forward. She leans back against the wooden slats of the bench in the wagon and closes her eyes. Her child is swaddled tightly, even though it is nearly summer. The train is crammed with people with baskets and packages wrapped tightly in paper, but they have made room for her. And now she pays them no heed. She is lost in her tiredness. Willing her newborn child to stay quiet.

The train is moving toward the north and east, slowly, with frequent stops, pulling its weight toward the border with the Soviet Union. But the mother disembarks just two hours into the ride in the provincial town of Lochow. An old man waits for her on the platform. His eyes squint from behind wire-framed glasses until they find her. He hurries to help her down the awkward steps of the train car. His hands are roughened by outdoor work, but they are steady and gentle as they reach for her arm and the yellow woven suitcase that she struggles with as the baby shifts inside the swaddled blanket. He carries the suitcase now and guides her to a long, wooden wagon, hitched behind a hefty, old-looking horse. She is not prone to tears, but she is crying now. It was not supposed to be like this. A birth happens, and there is joy in the family. Everyone smiles and tickles the baby under the chin. Why else endure the hardship of motherhood if not for these moments of deep pride? Her tears wet her face and drip down to the baby's blanket. The child is quiet. The mother weeps.

That old man is my grandpa Dziadek. He looks worried, but it could be an illusion or an exaggeration. Dziadek's face, creviced with age, displays emotion easily and without apology. A light chuckle becomes a radiant expression of mirth. A frown sags so deeply, folding in the eyes, forehead, mouth, drawing and redrawing lines of sorrow so that you imagine a pain so profound that you almost have to look away.

Babcia is back at the village house, looking after Eliza, the firstborn. Babcia's face is harder to read. Sometimes it softens with silent mirth, and then you can tell she is content. But every once in a while, if I stare long enough, I'll catch the almost invisible tears that occasionally spill over to her cheeks. Though not today. She has spent this day doing laundry in the tin tub outside, and she is checking the clothesline that's suspended between the three tall pines in the front yard when the horse-drawn wagon pulls up to the house. She smiles broadly at the sight of the woman—her daughter—and the baby.

———

The village house is small, and Dziadek and Babcia inhabit just half of the building. A fence runs right up to the middle, on both sides of the structure. It's a compact half of a house, with just two rooms and a kitchen. It wasn't easy to find even this much space and so close to a train station, giving my grandparents a direct link with Warsaw. Over the years, Dziadek will add rooms. First a verandah, where we will eat meals in warm weather months. Eventually, they will purchase the other half of the house, and Dziadek will add the second floor, where my parents will stay on summer visits.

He is the housebuilder, and she is the homemaker. She is the one boiling soup on the stove as my mother arrives with her swaddled infant. Babcia, too, is keeping a vigilant eye on my sister, sleeping now in a large stroller in the shade of the great pines. How did they find themselves in this deeply rural landscape of Poland? Dziadek and Babcia are failed immigrants who returned to Poland because America did not exactly deliver on a promise.

It takes me a lifetime to pull together pieces of my grandparents' lives. At first, the pieces handed to me didn't fit. If Dziadek had first

Nina Lewandowska Camic

traveled to the United States in 1907, he must have been twenty-two. Why did he go? Was he seeking adventure? Yes, that, but I am told that he also wanted to escape an "invitation" back home to serve in the Austrian Army. (For over a hundred years, Poland had been partitioned between Austria, the Kingdom of Prussia, and the Russian Empire, effectively disappearing off of the map of Europe. His home in the southeast corner of Poland was under Austrian rule.) Then came the matter of marriage. I learned that his first wife was a Polish-American woman. They met in Detroit, and they had a child. He worked hard to secure a job in the automobile industry, and he was successful for a while. But he was a man of high ideals, and from early on, he was drawn to political organizations that united men and women with a socialist vision of society. He joined the Polish Socialist group in Detroit. Being on the side of the "reds" did you no favors in those years. Within thirteen years of coming to America, he was thrown in jail with hundreds of others on trumped-up charges of attempting to overthrow the government.

It took weeks to get Dziadek out of prison. Only after his employer, the Motor Products Corporation, stepped up to vouch for his character was he released. But support for Dziadek was short-lived. Just months after returning to work, Dziadek was fired. He was a liability to the company. And his former employer wasn't the only one scared of having Dziadek on board. No one seemed willing to hire the young man with radical viewpoints. Unable to find work, Dziadek returned to the newly re-emerging Poland, freed after the Great War from her oppressive rulers. Again, he traveled alone. His wife and now two little children stayed in Detroit, refusing to go back to Poland.

My mother later told me: "His wife, she didn't want to 'build the new Poland.' She wanted a husband with a decent job. She tells him, 'You find work first, then maybe we'll go back to be with you.'"

Poland is emerging from a devastating war. Dziadek returns to the southeast and eventually finds an abandoned farm near Lwow. And this is confusing to my young mind as well. According to my geography books, Lwow is now in Ukraine. But in 1921, it was in Poland, though with a hefty number of Ukrainians living in the region. My dziadek takes up farming, and his wife and their two children travel back to be with him. But when she becomes pregnant again, she panics. "No more children!" She attempts an abortion and bleeds to death. Dziadek comes home, horrified. How could this be? He hadn't even known she was pregnant!

And this is where the story has a happy detour. Dziadek, needing help with the two children, looks for a second wife. My babcia, then a young woman from a nearby village, fits the bill. She has experience with children. She dropped out of elementary school early to care for her sisters and brothers when her mother died. This proposal comes at a good time for her. In 1923, when she is just twenty-two, they are married.

Dziadek and Babcia. In a farmhouse near Mazow. And within a year, my mamusia is born. Well, not a mamusia yet—Helena Maria for now. And soon after, a brother, Jan—my uncle Johnny. Dziadek the farmer, Babcia the farmer's wife, the mother of two, the stepmother of two more.

I see that Dziadek, like me, has that gene of restlessness. He hears stories from his engineer friends in Detroit. They're moving ahead with their careers while he's tending crops in southeast Poland. Maybe he should give America another try? He has American citizenship. Surely he'll find good work there. Off he goes, leaving Babcia with the four children.

When I'm old enough to count on my fingers, I tick off his trips to America. In 1928, here comes trip number two! This time, he finds work at the Hupp Company as a draftsman for a car manufacturer. And so Babcia travels with all those children to America. This is the first big trip for her and her two younger ones, and they cannot understand that they are leaving their familiar village home. But Babcia understands. She hates the upheaval, the strangeness of the new country. She is lonely without her extended family. And she is pregnant again, so she has an abortion. She falls ill. So back they go, Babcia and the children, to Poland once more a year later.

But a man needs his wife! Dziadek sends for her, and in 1931, she returns with the children. Now they are all together in Detroit. And this time, there is an air of hope. Dziadek has made improvements to their home so that it is comfortable. Babcia's sister travels from Poland to keep her company. I am told that life was good for them for a brief period. But not for long. In 1932, Dziadek loses his job. Welcome to the Great Depression and the land of the unemployed.

It would take more than ten fingers of both hands to count the number of ways in which this jarring ending to a promising career in auto manufacturing affects the lives of Babcia and Dziadek. Unemployed, Dziadek devotes himself to the organization of Polish-American workers. He is the head of the Polish section of the International Workers Order, but he has little money to pay the bills. The family moves from a spacious house in Detroit to a tenement flat on the lower east side of Manhattan. Babcia gets work cleaning offices and museums and processing breads and doughnuts for commercial bakeries at night. Dziadek fights injustice while Babcia fights an infestation of rats and cockroaches in her home. Dziadek frets about the powerlessness of unemployed Polish immigrants, and Babcia frets about having enough food for her family of six. In these prewar years in America, he forms alliances with labor groups. She has four abortions.

During World War II, Dziadek's political activism grows. I learn this part of their story fairly early in my life. My mother tells it, and my father affirms it. This is a period where American distrust of anyone with sympathies toward communism is on the rise. Once more, my dziadek is in trouble. Moreover, as he works at organizing Polish labor in America, his health begins to fail. He and Babcia abandon any hope of making a life for themselves in the big cities and move to Cross Village, a hamlet on the northern shores of Lake Michigan, where they run the Polonia Rest Home for vacationing Polish workers.

But Dziadek's long affiliation with the labor movement stays on record, placed in secret files for further consideration. The label "communist sympathizer" resurfaces, and friends warn him that his socialist politics are regarded as unpatriotic. Disheartened, five years after moving to Cross Village, he decides to return to his country of birth. So in 1951, Babcia and Dziadek travel to Poland, and here's the surprising part. They come not too long after their daughter, my mamusia, moved back to Warsaw to marry a young Polish diplomat.

My dziadek, the returning Americanized communist sympathizer, and my babcia at his side say a tearful goodbye to her stepdaughter and her beloved youngest son, Johnny. (Her other stepchild went off to war and never returned.) Wojciech and Stefania by name—Babcia and Dziadek to me—my two protectors, guardians, and caregivers are now in their small village house in Poland, by the River Liwiec, far from paved roads, electricity, plumbing, or phone lines.

3.

"I'm leaving my child with you," my mamusia tells Babcia a few days after arriving in the village with her sickly infant.

"Please leave her with us."

Babcia knows about young children and knows village life from the bottom up. She grows robust vegetables to feed the family. She is skilled at putting an ax through a chicken's neck to make chicken and dumpling soup for lunch. And she knows how to work yeast miracles in the kitchen. She makes them all: breads, bundt cakes, cookies, fruit bars. In her spare time, she scrubs everything within reach.

"Don't go into the sleeping rooms during the day! You're bringing in dirt! Stay outside or out on the verandah!"

She places the quilt in a white cover, and it smells as fresh as the wind that passes through the tall birch trees on a spring day.

Though she lived in America for more than twenty years, Babcia never learned English well enough to be completely fluent. During her time in the United States, she struggled with being understood. It was slow going. Off she would march to the store, pointing to the needed detergent on the shelf, the pound of butter, the gallon of milk. Then in the evening, she would be among her own again, at the Polish Workers' Club, where Polish immigrants sang songs and staged plays in their native language. When papers needed to be signed at home, her Americanized children explained the words on the pages before her. All her life, she spoke English haltingly and with a heavy accent. But oh, did she know how to sing! Polish, English, it did not matter. I am told that she had a voice that melted hearts!

So why is it that I remember her as being so quiet?

Nina Lewandowska Camic

"Good night, good night. I'll see you in the morning." She sings this to me at night, but it is in a hushed tone, barely whispered. A few notes to demonstrate that she has a voice, whispering, humming. A quiet hiccup of a laugh, no more. Her great big bosom shakes, her eyes crease at the sides in gentle laughter, but if your back is turned, you may not even notice she is laughing.

Years later, my mother scoffs.

"Quiet? Oh, she gave me a mouthful of opinions! I would tell her, 'Ma, enough already.'"

And now, I am the ailing infant, left here in the village house, along with my sister, Eliza, born eighteen months earlier. At the end of the week, my mamusia walks to the train station and takes the next train back to Warsaw, where she will resume her work. If you had a radio, you could listen to her English-speaking voice on the program broadcasting carefully scripted news about Poland, coming from Poland, news intended to be heard by the world beyond our borders.

She returns to Babcia and Dziadek's village the following Saturday.

My mother often recalls that first trip back to see me. "I thought you'd be dead when I next went there. So sick. You had been so sick."

I appear to have turned the corner.

"Sour milk! Babcia fed you sour milk, and you turned the corner! I came back next Saturday, and Babcia held you out for me to see. 'There, Halinka, you see? She's fine. Your baby is fine!'"

I never heard anyone call my mother by that nickname, except for Babcia. To the world, she was Helen.

4.

And my dad was Bohdan or Dan, or Daaahn as I heard it said by Mamusia. "Daaahn, please, not in front of the children!"

———

She met him in Washington D.C. in the years after World War II. She is an English-speaking secretary at the Polish Embassy in the nation's capital. She was born in Poland, but that's just a distant memory. Most of her schooling was in America, and she sees herself as a fully assimilated American girl speaking faultless English. But, unlike so many at the time, she was not afraid of communists. Dziadek taught her to look beyond her own small orbit, to pay attention to politics and the fate of others, especially those living in the newly emerging Polish People's Republic under the leadership of a communist government.

Dziadek had helped her land her first good job, working as a secretary for the Science Section of the Soviet-American Friendship Society. She liked the work. She met important men of science— doctors from Princeton, astronomers from Harvard—all interested in forging scientific ties with their Russian counterparts. But as relations between the Soviet Union and the United States chilled, the society's work came to a halt. She was grateful when a former secretary of the society brought her on board to the newly forming Polish Embassy in Washington, D.C., and this is where she meets my father, Tatek.

He is a government employee from Poland in D.C. on assignment. He's a bright young man, beginning his climb up the wobbly diplomat's ladder. A perfect love story? Well, not really so perfect. She likes to think that she can run with a classy crowd. Never having a shot at a college degree herself, she nonetheless has boyfriends who are academics and scientists. And my father merely finished a Polish post-high school course of study in the foreign service.

Who is this man anyway? Who are his parents? They are the Lewandowski grandparents, and we call them Dziadek and Babcia Lewandowski. It's a mouthful! Their real names are Zygmunt and Stefania. I have two grandmothers with the same first name, but that is all they share. Babcia Haracz never finished grade school. Babcia Lewandowska works for a news agency. And unlike my maternal Babcia, this one lives in Warsaw. And she has little time or interest in being a nanny to her grandchildren.

"I've already raised mine!" she protests when Mamusia asks her to look after me when she has to return to work.

"Just for a few months! I can't take her to my parents now! There aren't any doctors in the village, and Nina is so sick!"

But she does have to take me to the village. Babcia Lewandowska raised her two sons.

What kind of a boy was he, this tatek of mine? Did he cause trouble at home? Was he a bad student? A rascal?

No. He was not the difficult one in that household. Ask anyone, and they'll tell you the difficult one was his father, Dziadek Lewandowski. He was a school teacher and a man of letters. A man of harsh words to his wife and quite likely to his son.

But never mind all that. Tatek's childhood can properly be summarized by fairly calm, routine prewar years, living with his family in Warsaw and then, suddenly, the war years. In 1939, when he was just thirteen years old, the Germans bombed Poland. From then on, life was metered differently. There were the war years, and then there was life after.

How does a young boy cope with war? Initially, there is fear, but Babcia Lewandowska calms her sons. "We lived through the first war. We'll live through this one!" But my tatek wasn't convinced. He tells me many decades later that he knew then that this war would be different.

The immediate impact on the Lewandowski family is severe. They are ousted from their apartment near the city center and moved to a German-occupied compound on the other side of the Vistula River. His schooling, too, is suddenly in chaos. He was admitted to the most prestigious public high school in Warsaw, Stefan Batory, and now, his classes are interrupted at the time of war.

And he joins *Szare Szeregi*, "the Gray Ranks." Young boys were effective messengers and spies. Germans would shoot men, but they did not know to go after boys. My tatek is doing small sabotage like slashing tires of German military vehicles, and he is good at it. He is asked to join the intelligence network, which provided information to the Polish government in exile in London.

"We watched the bridges across the river, we noted the German vehicles crossing it, and we could tell that these units were heading east. Hitler will attack the Soviet Union!"

Churchill didn't believe it. Stalin, cozying up to Hitler, didn't believe it. But my father and his team of three teenage boys could see the writing on the wall.

Was my tatek really a spy? In fact, he was recruited into the school of officers of sabotage and intelligence, but then he got sick.

Years later, I tell him, "Such rotten luck to get sick during the war!"

He shakes his head and tells me, "Terrific luck! I was in the hospital for two months, and I was too weak to be active." Forever after, his lung is collapsed, and he walks with a lean toward the right side.

"Don't worry," the doctor tells him as he releases him from the hospital. "Mark my words. You'll live to be thirty-five." My tatek lives until the age of eighty-six.

In the remaining years of the war, he is relegated to desk work and odd jobs that come along, including being a camp counselor at a Catholic camp just outside Warsaw. And if you don't believe in luck, how do you explain that he, his brother, and his father—none of them Catholics—are all at camp, outside the city, when the Warsaw Uprising, the greatest resistance movement of the entire war begins.

"What a crime that was! The leadership of the Home Army should be put before the Nuremberg Tribunals for allowing it to go forth!" he tells me many, many decades later. "Heroism? Where's the heroism when 200,000 civilians were killed? They could not win! The whole city was destroyed! Some of the best people perished!"

I think about this. "But Tatus, maybe they were expecting help and reinforcements?"

"The Polish units of the Soviet Army tried to cross the river, but they were shot down by the Germans!" His face is getting red, and his hand shakes. His agitation is so great that I am afraid his heart will give out.

The Warsaw Uprising began on August 1, 1944. By January 1945, Warsaw, soon to be my Warsaw, was almost entirely gone, leveled to rubble.

Tatus, of course, was not in Warsaw then, but he was close enough. The Germans picked him up along with his brother and sent them to a transfer camp. They were to be deported to Germany to do forced labor there. But the two teenage boys escaped! Into the woods they went, and there they hid for several months, picking anything they could find to eat and scratching lice from their scalps and tired, dirt-crusted bodies.

Nina Lewandowska Camic

Fifteen years later, my father is the acting president of the Security Council at the United Nations. In the evening, he attends a dinner, and he is placed next to the visiting Queen of Denmark. "Just a few years ago, I am licking lice out of my hair, and here I am, eating dinner alongside the Queen of Denmark! Anything can happen," he tells me. "Anything can happen in life!"

Both Mamusia's and Tatek's parents were sympathetic toward communism. The Lewandowkis did not join the Polish Communist Party before the war. They knew not to get in trouble. Stalin, to the east, was no friend to communist organizations, and neither was the Polish government at the time. I listen to my father's recollections, and I try to make sense of this. Is he saying Stalin was no friend to communists?

My tatek tells me, "My family, we were progressives. But we knew about Stalin and the *czystki* (cleansing) he conducted. A communist visiting from the Soviet Union put it this way: 'Under Stalin, today you're a minister, tomorrow you're shit. And then, after the war, when Stalin went after the Jewish doctors, the whole world knew that he was nothing more than a Hitlerite fascist.'"

Toward the end of my tatek's life, I ask him, "You knew about Stalin, and yet you joined the communists in Poland after the war?"

Again I see the exasperation, the raging frustration within him.

"I was asked to join, and I did. Before the war, Poland was under a semi-fascist, repressive leadership. After the war, so many of us joined with so much hope! And look what the postwar government accomplished. They rebuilt this country! And everyone had access to education, health care, and jobs in a country that was in ruins! I am proud of that period! I have no apologies to make for it!"

I know that after the war, my tatek first went to medical school, but when an opening presented itself in a training program for diplomats, he applied and was accepted. Because he spoke good schoolboy English, in 1945, he was sent to San Francisco to assist with the opening of the Polish Consulate there. The California consulate idea was scrapped, and he was sent to Pittsburgh, then to Chicago and finally to Washington D.C., where he met the Polish American secretary, my mamusia.

5.

A romance ensued in the nation's capital. My tatek had timing on his side. She is with him, but then she is with someone else she prefers. That other man, John Tate, is a well-heeled Princetonian who is about to be appointed professor of mathematics at Harvard. She has aspirations, and she likes his world. But when he takes her home to meet the family, they recoil. A left-leaning Polish woman with ties to the Soviet Scientists? That's just not right! John, her lover, her man of letters, makes plans to go to Harvard without her. Her heart is broken, but my tatek is there to catch her. She waves off dismissively the classy crowd. She is living in a D.C. apartment with Bohdan, the Polish diplomat three years her junior.

He is infatuated! True, he is quick to fall in love. Yes, always in love! But this stately woman appears to be responsive to his romantic overtures. She is without inhibition. And not only is she ready for new love, but she is also ready to move away from America. A family friend who is in the loop has been warning her: "They are building a file on you. Your past is fodder for them. The American-Soviet Science Society is saying it was a cover for spy activity. They are setting you up. You will be the next scapegoat." And she knows this is no idle rumor. On March 10, 1948, an article appears in the *Washington News* with a large photo of my mamusia under the heading: "Suspicious Characters? Who's Who Among Dr. Condon's Acquaintances." Dr. Condon was denounced just the previous week in a report by a House subcommittee on un-American Activities for forging relations with the Soviet Union.

My tatek tells her, "Leave Washington. Come back to Warsaw with me." Hope lay in the city that was being raised from the rubble.

In early September 1948, they are heading back to Poland together, a mere three years after the war. He wants first to see if she—so Americanized and thoroughly modern—can stomach a city completely demolished by Hitler's forces. But she doesn't like this kind of uncertainty. She wants a commitment, so they marry within two months of their arrival in Warsaw—on her lunch break from work.

These are the postwar years. There is but one war for those growing up now in postwar Poland. We are the children of survivors.

Nina Lewandowska Camic

But I am only half that. My mother, after all, lived in America during the war. She wrote letters to American soldiers on the frontlines, rationed food at home, and saved metal bits. She was in the thick of the war effort but not in the thick of the war. On the other hand, my father was never far from the center of fighting. His story belongs in a volume of war stories. That he is one of the living, that he is himself a father now is a story of sheer luck.

Years later, when tempers flare, and Mamusia comes crying to Babcia and Dziadek about Bogdan this and Bogdan that, they remind her: "You have to understand. He lived through the war."

The war is over now, yet it hangs over the city like a heavy, waterlogged net, leaking stories of untold suffering from every block. Each step I take as a child is along a piece of a damaged landscape. I am born eight years after it all ended. I never heard the rifle fire, the explosion of bombs, yet I am learning to live in the echo of these noises. I know, too, that I am the next generation. I am the one with life. The dreams of those whose lives were so abruptly cut short are now my obligation.

Except at this time, in the village house of my grandparents, I am still struggling to keep milk down. Even as my parents attend political meetings in Warsaw with their colleagues or comrades, I am looking the cow in the eye and defying her strong white stuff.

"See?" Babcia smiles. "Your Ninoczka, she is doing well." To Babcia, I am Ninoczka. To my high school boyfriend I am Ninka. To my mamusia and tatek I am simply Nina.

Chapter 3

1.

In the decade after the Second World War, Warsaw transformed itself. Though the historic districts were painstakingly reconstructed to mimic the boulevards and houses that stood there before the war, the residential streets took on a new and different appearance. Postwar architecture became a mishmash of housing projects, many of them modeled in the image of Soviet developments. At the city's peripheries, indifferent rows of apartment buildings sprouted quickly and without attention to design or detail. The shortage of apartment units was acute, and for many decades, the demand for housing far exceeded the supply.

To any Warsaw resident, the city after the war became a confusing amalgam of the familiar and the new. There were the familiar Old Town squares (though newly rebuilt), stately parks, old churches, and the occasional old bakery or café that had managed to retain shades of a prewar life in the process of reconstruction. But, too, the city sprouted new residential neighborhoods, new public schools, new state-run stores that struggled to satisfy basic levels of consumer demand. New flags suspended from lamp posts: the Polish red and white without the prewar crowned eagle and next to it a red flag symbolizing international solidarity with the proletariat. There were new libraries and bookstores but no new churches. Old farmers' markets flourished, but new restaurants did not. Were you to dine in one of only a handful, typically appended to a hotel, you'd be told that most of the items on the menu were only suggestive. "*Nie ma*" (we don't have any) became the common phrase uttered by waiters and clerks standing indifferently behind the store counter. No one ate in restaurants anyway. Your midday meal was served at work or school, and your evening supper would be at home or the subsidized milk bars.

If Warsaw appeared to be digging through rubble and moving toward a new urban landscape rapidly, the Polish village remained stagnant and unchanged. Most farming in Poland stayed under private ownership. Families divided land among offspring. The cultivated fields were like narrow, colorful ribbons, barely economically viable. Tractors were not available, so workhorses pulled plows, and when not working the fields, they were used to pull wooden wagons for transport. You could hop-skip from village to village and never see a car or truck. Children pastured cattle in the open meadows, and old women made cheese and gathered wildflowers to sell on city streets. They rode the trains with full baskets and buckets in the morning, and if the day was good, they returned to the village with empty containers at night.

I am a child of the city, but my first three years of life are in the village or hamlet, with some twenty houses, half of which back up to the forest and half, like ours, to the meadow and river. It is a strange old settlement, surrounded by farmland even as none of its residents are farmers. Several raise chickens and keep bees, but otherwise, the people work in provincial towns or, like my grandparents, are retired, living off a small pension, growing foods for the table, huddled together like old hens and cocks with nowhere else to go. The village name, Gniazdowo, is roughly translated as "the nesting place." How apt! A cluster of brick, stucco, and timbered homes, here in northeastern Poland's deeply rural flat landscape.

About a mile up the road amidst tall Scots pines, there is an old, crumbling orphanage for wayward boys. If an emergency strikes and you know the director, you can ask to use the orphanage phone. Gniazdowo itself has no electricity, and a paved road is several miles away. The nearest train station is an hour's walk unless you want to get wet and plunge across the river. That'll save you ten minutes. To get to the provincial town of Lochow, where you'll find a doctor, administrative bureaus, and a handful of stores, you need to have or hire a horse and wagon. If you have sturdy legs for the sandy dirt road and then nerves of steel once you reach the narrow and often congested piece of asphalt cutting through Lochow, you can pedal your way there on a bike. Otherwise, your contact with the outside world is by mail, delivered and picked up daily by a not always sober mailman, pushing his very old bicycle along a sandy path.

Dziadek plants fruit trees in the yard, and Babcia grows vegetables and berries. A mixed thicket of pines, birches, and poplars lines the fence to the east. The birches are old and very tall, and I can always hear their leaves moving with the gusts of wind that pass through our small homestead. If you leave by the back gate, you'll find the pond with tadpoles and frogs leaping into its murky waters. Sometimes big fat frogs wander into our yard, dragging their wrinkled bodies with each crawl forward.

The village house grows. Dziadek improves rooms and adds the verandah and attic. But many years pass before water is pumped inside. I move from diaper to potty to outhouse. No matter. We have the cleanest outhouse in the village. In all of Poland, maybe. Babcia insists on it. Dziadek spreads white calcium over the day's waste, and the smell isn't too bad. And our garden is thriving!

The new verandah is made of mellow, knotty pine boards. Windows on two sides bring in the morning sun. A bit of America makes its way to the village house when Dziadek builds window screens to keep out flies, yellow jackets, and mosquitoes. In my years growing up in Poland, I never saw screens in any other home. The verandah and our tiny bedroom are the only rooms where you could throw open the windows and not think about bugs. In our village house and every other Polish home, sticky rolls of paper are suspended from the ceiling. Once they fill with flies, you toss the roll and hang a new one.

Below the verandah, there is a cellar. In the early summer, it is nearly empty. It's too soon to line the shelves with apples. The fruit syrups are not yet made, and the potatoes that grow in the fields just beyond our hamlet are not nearly ready for digging. Babcia stores everything that's perishable in the dirt cellar, but by the end of spring, the shelves are crying for a harvest.

The best foods though are upstairs, on the verandah table—apple *szarlotka*, a crumbly cake topped with cooked apples, and poppyseed cake—all baked in the coal-burning kitchen oven, then placed on a wooden board and covered with a cotton dishcloth. And jugs of pine syrup, made from May pine buds. Dziadek plants pine trees to keep the sandy pastures by the river from eroding. To his dismay, Babcia picks the new buds in May to make syrup. The environmentalist and the homemaker are at odds with each other over pine buds. It's probably about more than just pine buds, but all that is outside my field of vision. Babcia and Dziadek are my world now. I am too young to know much else.

I live in the village with my grandparents and my sister for the first three years of my life. My mamusia comes nearly every Saturday and leaves the next day. No goodbyes, no tears. She thinks it's best to exit quietly when no one is looking. Here one minute, gone the next. She is a disappearing mamusia.

And my father? The man whose Slavic features are so evident in my own face. He's not a country man. He lives and stays in the city, where men smoke cigarettes late into the night and talk. "Your tatus is a gifted speaker!" my mother tells me repeatedly. Yes, and he knows it, too. Someday, he will be respected for his long expositions and commentaries. Now, he is merely practicing on his friends. He is either in Warsaw or traveling abroad on work assignments from his place of employment, the Ministry of Foreign Affairs. I know nothing of the city. I'm a village child. My orbit extends from the riverbanks, across the vast flat fields of wheat and potatoes, to the pine forest that separates us from the next village. It's a world of pastel colors. Cornflower blue and hollyhock pink. An expanse of meadow grasses and acacia blooms.

My mamusia takes me on Sunday to the riverbank, and we pick flowers. We look for forget-me-nots and buttercups. I hold her hand

and look up at her. She is tall, even by adult standards, but especially to me, and I can hardly catch her face. But I know her dark eyes well. "Gypsy eyes," I say when I am slightly older. I'm parroting what I've picked up from a grown-up conversation. She denies it at first with a laugh, then later with a frown. "We have no gypsy blood. We are from the southeast corner of Poland."

Now I know that. Dziadek's family was a good, law-abiding farming family from Ruda, near the southern provincial town of Rzeszow. Not like the gypsies that I sometimes hear Babcia talk about. When I am older and take to roaming the pastures and riverbanks on my own, she warns me. "Watch out for the gypsies! They steal children! Run from them. Stay away."

And I do run from the groups of dark-skinned nomads that pass through neighboring villages now and then, burning their fires into the night, disappearing the next week, stealthily, to trick us into thinking they were never there. They leave stories behind. Farmers complain of stolen chickens but no stolen children. Not this time. We run when we see them building fires in the woods. We are safe. Even so, when I look at Mamusia's dark eyes, I see gypsy eyes.

2.

"You lived in the village with your grandparents, but when you were three, you wanted to come back to Warsaw." My mother is certain that I pushed for the move back to the city.

Maybe I merely wanted to follow my disappearing mamusia. How could I possibly know what it means to live in Warsaw? What's a city to a young child who has never used a faucet and cannot remember what a lightbulb is for? We traveled to the city once a year for doctors' visits. Maybe some small memory of Warsaw sticks in my head, haunting me every Saturday when Mamusia would arrive, laden with foods and hand-sewn clothes for her girls and bulky packages of supplies for pantry shelves, all from the city.

The horse pulls the wagon to the train station. My sister and my mamusia are with me. We say goodbye to Dziadek and Babcia, who will be staying behind in the village house. I'll spend summers with you! Every summer of my childhood! You'll see. I'll be back! But now I'm heading for the city to be with Mamusia and Tatek. I'll get to know my tatek now, won't I?

"Do you want to go to the park with Tatek on Sunday?"

"What will I do in a park?"

Mamusia laughs at that. "Feed the squirrels!"

"We never fed the squirrels in the village."

She doesn't have a ready answer, but she nonetheless stuffs a few hazelnuts into our pockets. "Go now! I have a meal to prepare."

My mother enrolls me in a nursery school she says is good. It's for children whose parents work at the Ministry of Foreign Affairs. That's my tatek! You see? He is indispensable, after all. His place of work will determine where I will spend my childhood days.

Children in Poland live in the bubble of their parents' jobs. Nursery schools and vacation homes, several hospitals, and many of Warsaw's apartment buildings are not open to the general public. They serve families within specific occupations. Ministry workers may stay in designated guest houses in the mountains and by the sea. Journalists can vacation in hotels dedicated to those who belong to the Association of Polish Journalists. Rumor has it that apartment complexes, preschools, and vacation homes for coal miners are the best in the entire country. Is it true? Do these perks of affiliation create a hierarchy so that we grow to envy the benefits that are bestowed on some but not others? It surely is the case that creating homes, resorts, and nursery schools for workers in your circle of employment limits, for the most part, your contacts with those outside your workplace. But your children will play with children of your colleagues and children of workers at all levels of employment. There is also a benefit to those whose work is more isolated and remote. Writers meet other writers in guest houses limited to their trade. And farmers can meet other farmers and those with only an academic interest in agriculture in places like Dom Chlopa (Peasant's House) in Warsaw.

The notion that Warsaw should have a hotel specifically targeting the agrarian population was born years before the Second World War. Still, it wasn't until 1956, when the government allocated funds and hired architects, that the construction of the Dom Chlopa began. The 565-room hotel was created to give the rural population, still referred to as the peasants of Poland, access to the city. It was designed on the outside to mimic the undulating wheat fields of the Polish landscape, and it occupied a prized location in the center of Warsaw. Dom Chlopa opened in 1961. From the beginning, it boasted nearly one hundred percent occupancy rates. In addition to guest rooms, the hotel provided a library, meeting rooms, and social services targeting the rural population. A staff of doctors, lawyers, and agricultural experts were on hand to give advice. Here young village people could conduct meetings of the Association of Rural Youth (Zwiazek Mlodziezy Wiejskiej), an organization not unlike the urban-based Association of Socialist Youth (Zwiazek Mlodziezy Socjalistycznej). In the evenings, agricultural workers and urban residents might attend poetry readings on Polish rural life or folk music and dance performances in the large coffee shop. But if Dom Chlopa was also to bring rural life to the hearts and minds of Warsaw residents, it surely failed to trickle down to my family. In all the years I lived in Poland, I don't think I, my parents, or anyone I knew ever stepped through the doorway of Dom Chlopa.

3.

When I moved back to Warsaw, my father's position within the Ministry of Foreign Affairs was unremarkable. Nonetheless, nearly every perk and benefit seemed to materialize as a result of his employment there. The apartment on Nowowjeska Street, so very small, but so coveted, was allocated to my family by the Ministry. The nursery school and the vacation homes, too, were Ministry operations. I also learned that when my sister was born, my mamusia went to a very good hospital. She told me as much later. "See?" she says, unfolding a piece of paper. "I kept the hospital stay certification!"

I look at the sheet before me. Yes, she was there. "Helena Lewandowska, wife of Bogdan Lewandowski, employee of MBP." Wait. Isn't that the Ministry of Public Security? But wasn't he a staff member of MSZ, the Ministry of Foreign Affairs? Which Ministry did Tatek work

Nina Lewandowska Camic

for in the end? It could be that any person specializing in western relations at the Foreign Ministry was, too, an employee of the MBP.

Much later, I asked my mother if he ever spoke about the nature of his connection to MBP. There would be some irony in this. The MBP was the intelligence unit that tracked anti-communist activity in Poland during the Stalinist era, between the years 1945 and 1954, in addition to tracking those linked to the Polish Home Army (*Armia Krajowa*, or AK), which aligned itself with the anti-communist government operating out of London during the war. Once the Soviet Union successfully established a communist government in Poland, AK was deemed a threat to future governance. Many AK fighters were arrested and sent to Soviet labor camps. Some of its leaders were reportedly executed. Others simply disappeared without a trace. In his youth, my father had done work for the Polish Home Army's espionage unit. Was he now protecting himself from his past? His affiliation with the Polish Home Army was his most closely guarded secret, and for the rest of his life, he tracked which of the young men who knew him at the time of the war were still living and could potentially betray him before the communists in power. But his connection to MBP was news to me.

My mother shakes her head. "We never talked about it. He would be embarrassed, especially before all his friends in the west, to admit even an insignificant link to MBP."

I take my first city walk with my mamusia. We go to *Plac Konstytucji* (Constitution Square), the vast square just around the corner, lined on two sides by freshly built, five stories high, solid, Soviet-style apartment buildings. I like the stroll to the Plac. Vaulted arcades at the ground level allow me to get up close to the store windows and stare inside, even in bad weather. I especially like the corner store called the "22nd of July." It's a chocolate shop named after the date of the beginning of the new socialist state in Poland. My mamusia once brought a box of 22nd of July chocolates home for us. I had never tasted anything so sweet and good! My favorite was the piece wrapped in glittery red foil. The box had only one such chocolate, and I was allowed to have it. I kept the little piece of paper for a long time, repeatedly running my thumb over it to smooth out the creases.

On this first walk to the Plac, I look up at a store off to the side and tell my mamusia, "There is an *apteka*," (a pharmacy). My mamusia looks at me curiously, as if I am a package whose contents she does not really know. I am three years old, but I have spent nearly all my days away from her.

"When did you learn to read? Who taught you?" She asks.

"I don't know. Dziadek showed me words on a piece of paper." His face now comes back to me—that face with so many creases, showing years of laughter and worry. I remember not so long ago sitting on my bed in the village house crying. I had been scolded at the table. He knocks gently on the door and comes into the bedroom.

"Why are you crying so hard? There now, blow your nose. Come, come. It can't be that bad!"

"It wasn't my fault!" I retort. "It's so unfair!"

"Well now, yes, I can see how some things are just so unfair. But listen, I'll tell you a little story." He sits next to me on the bed and spins a tale of little girls tending geese, of ducks and ponies and butterflies. I lean against him, and my shaking shoulders go limp against his large frame.

"But the word says *apteka*, doesn't it?"

"Yes, it does." My mamusia smiles now. She has learned something about me that makes her proud. Of all the discoveries that she slowly makes about her daughter, this one she wants to store in her memory and repeat for years to come.

We walk back to the two-room apartment four flights up. One of the rooms and the small kitchen face the courtyard. The second room I share with my sister faces the street, Ulica Nowowiejska. It's a noisy street. The tram stop is just outside our window. The tram pulls up with a warning ring and pulls away with an even louder, double shrill. I know it's good to have warning shrills. I am told that people in the city are hit by tram cars all the time. The tram cars are the gypsies of the city. They steal children and hide them under their wheels.

And they are crowded. My mother and I ride a tram home from an

Nina Lewandowska Camic

errand across town. "This is our stop," she tells me. "This is where we get off." But I lose her hand, and she is already off the tram. I hear the shrill, warning whistle. The tramcar is about to pull away, but I am still squashed between people, big people. I let out a loud cry as the car lurches. Someone inside pushes me out the door. I tumble out onto the cobbled street, crying uncontrollably.

My mamusia picks me up and stands me on the sidewalk. She looks at me with anxious eyes. My coat is muddy, and my face is dirty from tears and snot. What if I did not make it out the door in time? Where would I get off? How would I go home? I imagine myself riding the tram for a long time, squashed between people who do not see me, wondering if my mamusia had made her way back alright and was now fixing supper, setting the table for only three. I cry even harder at the images that race through my head. Mamusia looks at my red and smudged face and wipes my nose with her handkerchief.

"Does anything hurt? No? Well now, good." She takes my hand, and we walk home.

Our apartment has a bathroom—no more potties at night and dark outhouses by day. There is a toilet in a separate tiny room, and it has a chain that you pull to flush. I sit on the toilet comfortably for a long, long time. I study my toes in the bright light of an overhead light bulb. I see that my big toe curls up! Am I deformed? What's wrong with me? When did that happen? Did living in a city make my toes curl up?

In a separate part of the bathroom, there is a big tub too big for me to climb in by myself. A hand shower allows grownups to run the water over their bodies, but my little body doesn't need a hand shower. I can wash myself in a tub just half full of warm water.

But to get that water to the proper temperature, you have to light the gas heater suspended on the wall at the foot of the tub.

"Watch those flames now! They cannot go out! If they go out, gas will escape, and we may all die of gas poisoning. That's what happened to Irka's brother. You know Irka. She is in your nursery school. Her brother was in the tub, soaking, and he did not notice that the flame had gone out. He was found dead by his little sister right there in the bathtub."

I stare at the flames all the time now. What makes them go out? A draft? A splash of water? I don't know. I know it can happen anytime, most likely when you are not thinking about it, so I try to think about it every minute I am in the bathtub.

Nursery school is an all-day affair. My mamusia works from early in the morning until late afternoon and then many evenings too, reading those English texts on the radio and giving English lessons to classes of adults. It tires her, but she is proud of her work. Her knowledge of the English language is brilliant! Enviable! At the radio, her coworkers are intimidated by her. "That American! She can push us out of our jobs!" But she has no intention of doing that. On the other hand, she doesn't always like the text she is told to read. In fact, one day, it infuriates her. All that nonsense about how the Soviet Army brought about the surrender of Japan! There is no mention of American soldiers, those same ones who received her letters of encouragement and support! She marches to the radio director's office.

"Excuse me, Mr. Billig, but this is not correct. People who listen to this will know it's not correct. There is no mention of American heroism at all!"

Mr. Billig puts down his folder of papers and listens to her politely, then shakes his head. "Don't change a thing. It's not your job to write the text. You are to read the English translation. That is your job."

Mamusia is indignant. At home, she recounts the episode to Tatek. But if she thought he would be sympathetic, she was wrong. He pushes his chair back and paces the small space between the table and the kitchen window.

"Don't ever, ever do that again!" He is shouting. She rarely hears him raise his voice, but he is definitely shouting now. "Politics—that's my domain! You have yours. You make decisions in the home. Leave politics to me. You do not understand this country!"

She wants to say something, but she checks herself. She knows politics. Dziadek taught her to feel compassion for the working poor and stand on the side of political parties that represented their interests. Still, she stays silent. Tatek is very young, but she thinks him to be brilliant. He knows things she does not know. She knows English. She would continue sticking to the English text.

They mix in a world of English and Polish. Free of childcare

Nina Lewandowska Camic

obligations, they make time for friends. So many friends! She knows people from the world of English-speaking radio. My mamusia isn't the only one who returned to Poland after the war. The radio and the English language school draw from a handful of Polish Americans and Canadians who have now returned to Poland. One was asked to leave America because of his political associations. Another wanted to leave, sensing that his left-leaning beliefs would gain him no favors in Canada. Yet another came because her husband was Polish.

As a staff member of the North American Section of the Foreign Ministry, my tatus is surrounded by Poles, but these people, too, are familiar with the ways of the west. And so my parents join the stream of young couples, moving from one house to the next, sipping tea, sipping vodka, smoking, talking. These couples who live in Poland have insight into the world beyond. And, my tatus is there, always the one with a long story up his sleeve. "You have the gift of gab," she'd say to him after, with a touch of pride and maybe just a little exasperation. She says it in English. He likes to improve his language skills, and she, too, prefers it this way.

Eliza and I do not know any English words, but my mamusia teaches us a song.

"It's in English. Sing it with me!

Have you ever seen a lassie go this way and that way?" She shows me how to kick my leg up in this direction, then that direction. I like it, especially the leg kick!

"Teach me another!"

"My Bonnie lies over the ocean. My Bonnie lies over the sea." She translates the words. *Such a sad little song,* I think to myself. Is Bonnie a little girl separated from her mother?

"Bring back, bring back, oh bring back my Bonnie to me! To me!" I look at my mamusia's face, so pretty and different from my own! I am filled with happiness that I live now on Ulica Nowowiejska and that she is there to tuck us in each evening promptly at seven so that she can go off to work again as Tatek settles in for an evening at home, smoking cigarettes and talking to his visiting friends while we sleep.

"Bring back my Bonnie to me!" No, I don't like that one! "Another song!"

"London Bridge is falling down, falling down ..."

Why are English songs so tragic? But Mamusia shows how she and Eliza can catch me as I dance around their falling bridge and in their arms. I am safe again.

Knowledge of the English language is such a prize! Both Mamusia and Tatuś speak it, though he doesn't sound like an American when articulating the words. He sounds like a Pole, speaking English. But few Polish people would hear this. When my parents stand in line to go to the movies and deliberately speak English between themselves, the people around them think they are foreigners and push them to the front of the line. No language brings with it as much capital as English. For the rest of her years in Poland, my mother speaks English whenever she can, loudly, deliberately.

4.

I have a cubby at nursery school, where I keep my coat and shoes. The first year it has a picture of a little red mushroom with white spots on it. Everyone knows that this is a poisonous mushroom. Never eat a red mushroom with white spots on it! You'll die instantly.

"Did you read the story in last night's paper about the whole family who died because they picked poisonous mushrooms?" Mamusia says this emphatically so that we all can hear and take note. It's not that she distrusts the mushrooms Babcia pan fries on the kitchen stove. It is a warning of a more general nature to remind us that nothing in this world is really safe.

I have often picked mushrooms in the forest by Dziadek and Babcia's house. After a day of rain, we go out with baskets, and we walk among the tall pines and push away spent needles and shriveled plant leaves at their base in our search for the orange clumps. We call them *kurki* or chanterelles in English. I know to pick only the *kurki*. Sometimes we find the brown caps, *prawdziwki* or *maslaki*, but I always check with Dziadek before putting those in my basket. Babcia cooks our mushrooms in butter until they are intense with flavor. But we avoid all other mushrooms. Only stupid children touch red mushrooms with

Nina Lewandowska Camic

white spots on them! But then, why is my cubby decorated with this red-capped bit of poison? I want a different picture.

The next year, I am given a cubby with a drawing of a little African boy over it. He comes to my cubby from a story of jungles in faraway places. He wears bright red shorts and is smiling at me. I keep him over my cubby for the rest of my time in nursery school.

My nursery school teacher, a woman with soft brown hair and a gentle smile, is my hero, my beloved person whose hand feels safe and strong when it holds my own. And I do not mind when she helps me dress in exotic robes so that I am made to look like a little Japanese girl for picture day at the nursery school. That paper flower in my hair hurts so much, tightly twisted into my fine, golden brown Slavic strands, but I'm alright with that. My teacher put it there.

"There now. You are a proper Japanese little girl."

"What is that?"

"A girl with different eyes than yours. See, like this! And she has a fan, held just so and a dress just like yours."

But on picture day the following year, I am curiously dressed. What kind of outfit is this? I am wearing my cotton jumper. We all wear cotton jumpers every day, but why the plaid flannel pants? That's just me being distracted.

"When you come into nursery school, remember to take the flannel pants off and comb your hair for picture day!" My hair looks fine. My forgotten warm winter pants stay on.

At the winter party, the children at my nursery school wear paper hats made by my mamusia and me. The little boys are to be coal miners, and the little girls are to be little girls wearing tall, spiked hats with stars and specks on them. My job at home is to glue the stars and specks onto the crepe paper. We make the hats and take them to school, and all the children dutifully wear the hats that my mamusia made, except me. I can't find my paper hat. I am too enthralled that my teacher and Mamusia are in the same room, my school room, filled with children and mothers or fathers from the Ministry of Foreign Affairs.

I like nursery school just fine. But I am fearful of the food we are served and its smells. No one has fed me milk soup before. Warm, milky broth, with rice or noodles swimming in it. On the days that we have milk soup, I smell it in the corridors even before I get to the room where we eat. Waxed floors and milky soup. Strong odors, not repelling, not enticing, but a warning. Institutional smells that remind you of an institutional indifference to your likes and dislikes, quirks or inclinations. Milk soup for breakfast today. Eat!

5.

Our apartment on Nowowiejska Street, like most apartment buildings in Warsaw, has a courtyard where children play. "Go play outside. I'll call you when it's time for supper." Every Polish mother uses these words to push her kids out the door after school. She has so many chores: taking out packages of food from her grocery net, waxing the floorboards, and washing the white collars for the school uniform. She doesn't want the kids underfoot.

But my sister and I are never sent down to the courtyard. It could be that we're too young, and our kitchen window doesn't offer a good view of the playground. My mamusia might be fearful about not being able to keep an eye on us outside. All you can see from the kitchen is the apartment across the way, where a frightening, evil, old woman who stares at the wall lives.

"Look, Eliza. The old woman is there, staring again! She takes countless medicines and gives herself shots with big hypodermic needles."

Mamusia shakes her head. "Where do you get such crazy ideas?"

I don't mind not going outside to play. I dislike going up and down the four flights of stairs (the European third floor). At least they don't smell of urine like so many of the other stairwells in the city. But I worry that the city drunks will loiter in the hallway on the ground floor, near the mailboxes. Now that's a dark, scary place! If there is a light switch, I do not know where it is.

Our building has an elevator, and by age six, I am allowed to use it on my own to go down to the mailbox.

"Don't forget to close the doors inside, or it won't move." I know, I know! I press the button to call up the elevator. It comes, and I open the door, but a man is sitting in a heap on the floor, drooling and laughing at the same time. He holds out his hand, curling up his finger in a "come here" gesture.

"Come here, little girl. Come closer." I scream and slam the door shut. I run back to the apartment.

"What happened?"

"There was a man on the floor."

"Did he touch you?"

"No."

"Well, alright then."

My mother returns to her sewing. For her, there seem to be two worlds of problems—ones that are real and ones that are over and done with. She must feel the first to be a very large set because she rarely has patience for the second. One evening, she finds me in bed crying. She picks me up, sits down with me, and asks in a concerned voice, "What happened?"

"The song made me cry."

"That's it?" She exhales heavily, shakes her head in exasperation, and lightly pushes me off her lap.

The hours after nursery school are short and dark, especially in the fall and winter. City lamps offer little reassurance, dimly lit with a flickering pale amber light. The gloom seeps in, unexpectedly, in early November and stays until March. Warsaw becomes a place of shadows. The only relief can be found in our small but warmly lit apartment on Ulica Nowowiejska.

We play in our room. My sister's bed is against one wall, and mine is against the other, and underneath the beds, we each have a cardboard box holding all our toys. Perhaps my box has more than just one doll, but right now, I only remember ever playing with the one doll. He is made of rubber, and I name him Johnny because my mamusia tells me it is a good name. I do not really understand then that her brother, who remained in America after she returned to Poland, also has the name of Johnny. My uncle Johnny named his son Johnny too. My rubber doll is third in the line of Johnnies.

Eliza and I talk as we play with our dolls. Her Maggie is just a baby, but my Johnny is at least a schoolboy. His little rubber body is imprinted with short pants and solid-looking shoes, though over the years, the colors fade, and he becomes peachy pale all over. Eliza and I make our dolls do acrobatics. Occasionally, my sister reminds me that our dolls are misbehaving, so we spank them. This fills me with a sinking feeling of being a bad mamusia to my doll. In the quiet of the night, I whisper apologies to Johnny for spanking him, but I know it does not make any difference. I am the kind of mamusia who spanks her doll, even though my mamusia never laid a hand on me. The physical expression of emotion toward others is not in her nature, and I have never known her to sweep me up with joyous affection or slap my behind for misbehaving. My tatek is far more likely to squeeze his wife's hand or slap the bottom of his child, though not very often. He is off and away far too much to track his daughters' misdeeds and occasional successes.

When I think of my tatek's absence, I do so without much sadness or disappointment. As a child, I do not know him to be more than an occasional Sunday tatek, and often he is gone for months on end, so even Sundays with him are replaced by Sundays without him.

On the weekends when he is in Warsaw, we return again and again to Warsaw's magnificent park, Lazienki.

It seems that everyone in the city is out for a promenade in the park on a good weather Sunday. And, like us, everyone is dressed with care for the occasion. Or is it that they are dressed for church? Nearly all of Poland is Catholic now, but I know nothing about church attendance. In these early years of my life, I have never even been inside a church. If asked, I say I don't believe in God. To my knowledge, my parents do not believe in God either. They never mention a God, and I never ask.

I learn all about church during my childhood summers when I visit Dziadek and Babcia in the village. The people from neighboring villages all walk to the nearest church every Sunday. I watch them pass by our small, atheist house. First one way, then back again hours later in their Sunday best. I know for sure Dziadek does not believe in God. I know he thinks the church hasn't been paying enough attention to the needs of the men and women in the village. He is forever trying to organize the village men to work together toward a common goal that is not church related. His project now is to build a community hall—free from church oversight—for the people of the village.

But the people walk to church nonetheless, and the newly constructed community hall is vandalized after a particularly raucous night of hard drinking by the village men. Dziadek will eventually move from the village, leaving Babcia to tend to the house and garden while taking his activism south to the region where he was born. My roaming grandfather. My roaming father. The men in my life come and go. The women make sure the water for the tea is hot and that there is toilet paper in the closet.

I am amazed at the number of rolls of coarse toilet paper in my babcia's hall closet.

"Why do you have all those rolls of toilet paper, Babciu?"

She chuckles at my question. "Because tomorrow there may be none in the stores."

Tatek, my sister, and I put on our outdoor shoes and go out for our Sunday walk. We stroll up and down the wide alleys of the most beautiful park in the world. Tatek likes to take pictures of us feeding park animals. We buy pretzels and share them with the swans and the birds. This is the day when we wear our pretty Sunday dresses. Each year, my tatek travels to New York as part of the Polish delegation to the General Assembly of the United Nations. He is gone for two or three months, and when he comes back, he brings with him a dress for my sister and one for me—our Sunday best dresses for the godless two little girls of Ulica Nowowiejska.

The park is filled with parents, grandparents, lovers, and children. And my tatek with his two in tow are there, mingling with the rest. Never Mamusia. She is not one for Sunday outings. We are not a family of four; we are two families of three. I am with Mamusia and Eliza, or Tatek and Eliza.

I love the park! I even like the weekly piano concert in the park's rose garden, by the statue of Chopin. I am not restless. I know how to be still. The music is pretty, and scores of families surround us. War heroes, some of them. Survivors and their children.

We walk back home past one of the many memorials to the victims of the war. "In this spot, twenty brave citizens lost their lives to the

Nazis. December 1944." Or 1939. Or 1942. Candles flicker, and fresh flowers are tossed by the stone slab. "Here, fifteen women and children were brutally shot by the fascist army of Hitler." A brick wall remains pot-marked by bullet holes and dust that hasn't yet settled after the war. We are reminded that it must never fully settle. My country is and perhaps always will be in pain. Do not forget! We'll make sure that our children hear the stories told now, while the memories are so vivid and the pain is so raw.

It's afternoon now, and time to turn around and head home. Tatek has taken the photos. He is not a man who likes to linger. Not on Sunday walks. We head out of the park gates onto the wide sidewalk of Aleje Ujazdowskie. It's not far from home, but I know we won't be returning straight to our apartment. My tatek will want to visit the two spinsters living on the ground floor of a new housing project just a few short blocks from Lazienki Park. They're older than him, but they are all such good friends that I am told to call them *ciocia* (aunt). Ciocia Janka and Ciocia Wanda.

"Come, you can play with their dog while I rest a while," my father tells us.

Their dog is not interested in playing with Eliza or me, so we sit quietly while my father and the two ciocias smoke cigarettes and talk. Incomprehensible words and sentences. Politics, most likely. Like my father, but unlike my mother, the spinsters know the Warsaw of the prewar years. Surely they must be recalling it now? Or, are they looking ahead? Are they speaking the language of the new Poland? The People's Republic of Poland?

The room takes on the hazy blue color of three adults smoking cigarettes. Ciocia Janka likes to paint. Her easel is up, and I stare at a picture of an old man, half-finished. Each week, it has a few added brush strokes, but it remains on the easel as if it is a weekend project, an excuse to sit down, let your cigarette accumulate a stack of ashes while your glass of sweet tea grows lukewarm. Ciocia Janka has turned now to my father, and the words come pouring out, interrupted by unexpected bouts of laughter. On the rare occasion I am asked a question, whatever answer comes from me inevitably leads to that same hoarse laughter from both ciocias. My father smiles as well,

Nina Lewandowska Camic

though, as is his habit, he smiles a tight smile with closed lips. The sisters are never guests at our house, even though they live just around the corner. My tatek's world of chatty, laughing friends is his, never shared.

———

All the adults I know drink tea in a glass. Not me. Not yet. I need to be school-aged to be served tea in a glass. It's placed in a metal holder, so your fingers burn from clutching the hot handle rather than the glass.

My sister has started school, but I'm still too young for it. I am still attending the nursery school of the Ministry of Foreign Affairs. I am five, and she has just turned seven. In Poland, school begins when you turn seven. I fuss about this. Most likely, I cry. My sister tells me, "You cry at every little thing!" Do I?

In the middle of winter, just before I turn six, my mother stops sending me to nursery school. I am told that I may stay home and amuse myself. We have an older woman coming in to look after us while my mamusia is at work. Pani Malgosia, with the tight bun and the drooping shoulders and the warmest crinkle of a smile on her face. After Eliza has left the house, I spend all morning pretending that I, too, am going to school.

On some afternoons, Mamusia is home, and we walk together to pick up my sister after school. Eliza hates this, and I am certain she must hate me too. "Why are you walking me home? I can walk by myself!"

School is a ten-minute walk, but we have to cross the congested streets that run into Plac Zbawiciela. Saviour Square, the one with the church, ugly by so many accounts but familiar to me, towering with its narrow, dark spires over all of us, even the two little atheist girls from Ulica Nowowjejska.

On one such walk to school, Mamusia spots a line by the grocery store. Immediately we fall in place at the end of it. She asks those before her, "What shipment are we expecting?"

"Lemons."

I don't think I have ever even seen a lemon! They are worth the wait. My mamusia worries about the absence of vitamins in our meals. Sauerkraut, rich in vitamin C, is a winter staple, but there is little else to feed the vitamin starved blood cells of little girls. And serving tea with a lemon slice to guests would be a fine way to entertain!

She glances anxiously at her watch. I know that frown that sweeps over her face. It's a thinking frown. She is gauging the risks. Eliza will be leaving school shortly. Mamusia looks at me, her little almost-six-year-old. Lemons.

"Go," she tells me. "Cross the street only on the crosswalk, with other people. Stand by an adult and cross with her. Find Eliza at the school and bring her back here."

I am beaming. I am entrusted with the highest responsibility! I wonder if people notice this little girl walking alone? I am moving rapidly, milling with the crowd as it crosses the streets. I know where to turn, and I know which school is my sister's. I am almost an adult!

The school has a long flight of steps spilling out to the sidewalk. Students are pouring out, still in uniform, with leather backpacks filled with pens and notebooks. I find my sister, who looks at me with furrowed dark eyes. Gypsy eyes, like my mother's, I think.

"Where is Mamusia?" she asks.

"In line at the store. I have to take you there," I say with an air of importance.

Eliza saunters ahead, wanting no part of this.

"Why did you send her? Why can't I walk home alone?"

Mamusia is distracted. There may be no more lemons by the time it is her turn. They are expensive, and so she is hopeful. We wait with her. She buys a kilo for the tea served in glasses. All of it is squeezed and reused: juice, pulp, and rind.

The lemons are precious, but I am too young to understand that I live in a country with frequent food shortages. I go to the local food store and see old cans lining the shelves. I hardly know what they contain. Mamusia ignores all of them and heads for the counter with cheeses. She buys a chunk of Gouda and a kilo of white farmer's cheese. At the side, a large barrel stands open with fat pickles swimming in dilled brine. She reaches in and takes out several, placing them in a scrap of

Nina Lewandowska Camic

newspaper. She pays for these items, stuffs them in her net and heads out the door.

We rarely go to the meat store. When we pass a meat vendor, I look in and see only a few kielbasy hanging on racks against white tiled walls. The shelves are otherwise bare. I like these fatty sausages sliced on buttered bread, but they are expensive, and we rarely eat them. Sometimes my mamusia will bring home a piece of liver, her share of meat brought into town by someone with a direct link to a private supplier. I learn that stores are not the only place where people buy food.

Our kitchen, like most in Warsaw, is never without bread. We can get loaves of sourdough at the grocery store, but often we walk to the bakery, where Mamusia and I pick up warm Kaiser buns, yeasty crescents, and long loaves that are too tempting for a hungry, small child. *Przylepka* is the crusty end ripped off and eaten on the walk home.

Like so many other families, we have a connection to a village. My babcia comes to town by train once a week, as long as the snow doesn't prevent her from getting to the train station. She brings chickens, slaughtered and plucked by her, eggs, white cheeses, and butter. In the growing season, she brings garden vegetables and fruits and always puts her baked cookies and cakes into her baskets.

Mamusia protests. "Ma, you bring too much food. Who'll eat all this?"

Babcia answers in a matter-of-fact tone, "The girls will eat it," and she places the packages on the table. I listen to this exchange for many years, but I cannot tell if Babcia feels rebuffed or whether she senses the gratitude that surely my mamusia feels toward her now. I watch the kitchen shelf go from almost empty to overflowing as Mamusia puts the food away, and I think it looks better full. Mamusia doesn't say as much, but I know, even in my younger years, that grownups leave out a lot of words when they talk to each other. Every Pole knows that you have to listen for things left unsaid. Words aren't everything. And sometimes, they're nothing at all.

One evening, so very late that I have long been asleep, my mamusia turns the key to the apartment on Ulica Nowowiejska. My father is washing glasses in the kitchen sink. His friend gets up to leave when he hears my mother returning home. She sits down now at the kitchen table, tired from the evening at the radio station. She tells him small gossip details about her coworkers. He listens, but she senses his distraction. She is used to it. He never talks about his work, and she wonders if he really takes in all she tells him about her own.

Does Tatek feel anxious about his job? I do not know. He does travel a lot. There is the September trip to New York for the United Nations General Assembly, and there are other trips as well. He is busy when he is in Warsaw, but he has time for friends. Still, there are signs of stress. His health causes stomach pains. He has an aggravated gall bladder, and more than once, he has been prescribed a longer rest period at a sanatorium in the country. When summer vacation comes for my mamusia and tatek, he goes to the sanatorium, and she tries to get away for a brief vacation. She needs the rest! Not only are her English lessons and radio broadcasting days and evenings taxing, but she is sometimes asked to act as an interpreter when dignitaries come to Poland. She translates for Indira Gandhi, who arrives with her father, Prime Minister Nehru. She translates for Mrs. U Nu, who visits Poland with her husband, then the prime minister of Burma. She doesn't mind these additional jobs. She is proud of her language skills and likes to dress well for the visiting dignitaries. She has a string of pearls that she thinks contrast well with her black sweater.

But, she does mind giving up free time to attend political meetings at work. Meetings about agricultural production bore her, even though she knows that Tatek is attending meetings. He is, however, often at the front of the room, teaching fellow workers about the political process. She would rather be home resting. And so when summer comes, and we are sent to be with Dziadek and Babcia, he recuperates at his sanatorium, and she goes up north to a workers' guest house by the Baltic Sea. But she doesn't like the crowded room, the shared beds, the loud social banter late at night, so she returns south to Warsaw and eventually to Gniazdowo to rest on a swing chair carefully positioned in the yard of Dziadek and Babcia's house.

But if Tatek feels himself to be quietly responsible for maintaining a smooth sail for the family through the political upheavals that seem to forever plague Poland, does that mean that my mamusia has forever turned her back now to politics? Conversations with her father had left their mark on her. Dziadek's vision for lifting the underprivileged, hardworking members of society out of their distressed circumstances was real and full of hope. In his old age, my father said to me, "Dziadek was the one true communist among all of us. You have to admire him. He was the real deal."

My mother was raised on a steady diet of worker solidarity, equality, and shared responsibility for a better future. She knew this language well. And indeed, her interest in politics in Poland rebounds when in 1956, Stalin is publicly denounced. Boleslaw Bierut, the Polish prime minister who aligned himself with Stalin, dies mysteriously during a visit to Moscow. And a new, more open-to-the-west leadership comes to power in Poland. Wladyslaw Gomulka is now at the helm, and learned diplomat Adam Rapacki is appointed foreign minister. Both Mamusia and Tatus sense the seismic change in the political climate.

Optimistic about the direction the country is taking, my mamusia joins the Communist Party and even travels to Moscow with a friend, just to see life beyond the Polish eastern border for herself. She comes back shaken. If life in postwar Poland was tough, life in Moscow feels even tougher. Mamusia returns to her home thinking that surely Poland is on the better path. Look! You can now get foreign press here! The *International Herald Tribune* is on sale at the international bookstore in central Warsaw. French musicians perform at the Palace of Culture. If there is change in the air, most everyone agrees that it is a change for the better.

6.

My persistent voice of protest at staying home finally works, and at age six, I am enrolled in school. I'm a year too young, but my mother convinces the school authorities to take me in. She knows that I am bored at home. I am also very jealous of my sister's leather school pack. It closes with two metal buckles, and it's stiff as cardboard. I want one just like it!

I get a navy uniform, like all the others. It's a shiny fabric, and I'll snag it if I'm not careful. And here's the first important rule: every day, I must change the white collar that fastens at the neck of the uniform. We all have to do that. It's a show of cleanliness. If you don't wash your neck properly, you'll still come to school looking decent. The collar at least will be fresh.

And for the sleeve, I'm given a blue badge that says "Primary School Number 43." If I wear a coat, I need a badge there as well. No child can enter my school without that badge.

"Quickly, give me your coat! It's too cold to just wear the uniform. Let me sew on your badge. Hurry up!"

My sister and I walk to school together without speaking. We are a quiet pair. She must be thinking grown girl thoughts. She is, after all, eighteen months older than me. She has a serious, pretty face, lined with dark hair parted at the side and clipped back away from her lovely hazel eyes. Like Mamusia, her skin is less fair than mine. When we pose for my tatek's camera, even at her young age, she strikes a beautiful pose, with shoulders slightly drawn back, eyes smiling. Despite the frozen frame in these still pictures, you can tell that she moves with grace. I'm the imp whose hair never stays in place and who cannot affect a serene pose for any camera.

In school, I am in a class with forty other children. I am assigned a seat and a seatmate. We sit in three rows of school desks, and each desk has two students. We wear slippers in school. All children in all Polish schools wear slippers. Of course! The parquet floors are waxed and shiny. Outdoor shoes do not belong here. We leave them with our coats in the cloakroom by the entrance.

My first-grade teacher is very young. She has the same wavy brown hair that my nursery school teacher had, but this teacher does not look my way much. I think she would not notice if I stopped coming to school. But she knows how to keep order. She tells us to open our reading books, and she has us all pointing to the words under the picture: *Ala* and *As*. Ala is a girl, and As is her dog. Such easy words for me! But I hide my thoughts on this reading lesson. Easy is good! Above all else, I want to blend. Already I know that I am the young one here—too young to know how to make the teacher smile. I point my finger to *Ala* and *As* and say the words aloud, very slowly, like the others. Our teacher walks up and down the aisle, making sure our fingers point to the appropriate words on the page.

At home, I study the text Elementarz, an elementary textbook introducing each child in Poland to the written word. I glance at the pages toward the end, ones we won't get to for many months. I like what I read there. The poems make me feel warm and happy. I've translated one for you now:

All for All

A builder builds houses.
A tailor sews clothing.
But what could he sew
If he had no home?
And the builder, of course,
Could not get to work
Had the tailor not sewn
Pants and a cloak for him.
A baker needs shoes.
To the shoemaker he goes.
But without a baker,
The tailor would have no bread.
And so to each a common good
And to a common good for all
Everyone must work
My dear friend!

On another page, there is a picture of children waving different flags. I ask Tatek where the flags are from. He can give them names! Bulgaria, the Soviet Union, Poland, China, Czechoslovakia, Lebanon, Italy, and France. The text is so beautiful!

These are friends, from near and far, from many countries. We don't know each other yet. And we know little about each other. But when we get to know one another, we surely will have love to offer. We will study cooperatively. And we will work cooperatively. Let's all take hands and make a large circle. We will play together, happily, together.

And finally, on the very last page of the Elementarz, there is a tribute to my very favorite city in the world!

How large Warsaw is!
So many houses, so many people!
So much pride, so much joy
Awakened in our hearts for our capital.
So many streets, schools, gardens,
Squares, stores, traffic, noise,
Movie houses, theaters, cars,
Promenades, spaces too.
The old Vistula River is joyous
To see the capital grow so much,
It remembers when the city was small
And today it is so grown up!

I share in this pride. I love my city! I love the wide Marszalkowska Street, the Palace of Culture, the row of pastel houses in the Old Town, the parks! There cannot be a more beautiful city!

In class, we learn to write cursive letters. Unlike reading, this, to me, is a challenge. My teacher's letters appear neat and rounded on the blackboard. The big *A* flows into the *l* and small *a* perfectly. The words *Ala* and *As* look beautiful up there, where she writes them. But I find it hard to use the wooden pen with the replaceable steel tip. Dipping it in the common ink well is fine, but I press too hard on the page of my notebook, and the tip splits right down the middle. I get a splat of ink on the page, and my fingers are streaked in ink.

I try again, but I am impatient with my writing. The teacher moves quickly through the written alphabet. By springtime, we will be writing long sentences with curves and graceful letter transitions on the blackboard and my inadequate imitations in my notebook.

Each writing exercise is to be separated in our notebooks by colorful borders that we are to sketch ourselves. Mine are too complicated to be pretty. Swirls and swigs and dots and leaves. Walking ducks, bunches of flowers. At home, I rush through the assignment so that I can get to my complicated borders. But at school, the teacher frowns at them. "These are uneven," she tells me. She is, of course, correct. But I cannot resist building the design into something absurdly grand. Yes, childish doodles are true enough, but we are given free rein with them, and I'm pleased to fill this little space with color. Only I wish my complicated borders would be more even so that the teacher would smile at me.

In the fall, our class walks to the park. We pick fallen chestnuts and acorns and make toothpick animals out of them. My chestnuts fall off the toothpicks, but I like the project anyway. The chestnuts have the most beautiful brown sheen! Their skins are smooth so that if you rub your thumb across the belly of the nut, it feels like polished wood.

Autumn in Warsaw. I think I like this season best here. My city is not especially green in its center, but the parks are vast and beautiful, and the trees there have golden leaves now. Linden, chestnut—noisy leaves that rustle when the red squirrels jump from one pile to the next.

But winter is tough to love. The snow falls, and there are piles of muddy slush at every corner. Pedestrians create small paths through the mounds of snow and ice, but it is hard for me to get through without slipping, or at the very least, getting my brown lace-up shoes wet.

Mamusia takes us to the seamstress. We need new heavy coats with big buttons and matching hoods, with fake fur around the edge.

"Stand still! I want the coats to fit you well," she chides me as the seamstress takes measurements.

"And please," she tells the very tired-looking woman with pins in her mouth, "make the sleeves longer."

The coats are ready in time for the cold weather, but they are awkward, and I feel stiff and clumsy in mine. On goes the badge. Elementary School Number 43. It will stay there for many months.

One misty and particularly biting day in December, my mamusia takes us to the local outdoor market after school. Next to it, a small space has been flooded with water to create ice for skating. Mamusia sits me down on a concrete slab and screws a skate to each of my brown shoes. The skates are like little sleds with double rows of blades on each foot, making it nearly impossible for me to fall.

"Now stand up and move. You'll warm up if you do that."

I stand up on the ice, but nothing happens. Mamusia takes my hand. She is not skating, but she balances well on the ice.

"Glide forward," she tells me. "Glide, like this." She pushes one foot forward, then another. I try to keep up with her, but the ice is rippled, and the blades aren't sharp enough to sail over the rough spots. I am discouraged. I am not skating. I am a little girl stuck on two sets of blades in the middle of a dark patch of ice. The night lamps are turned on, even though it is only afternoon. I sit down on a snowbank to the side of the makeshift rink and feel the hot tears running down my face. Am I the only one who cannot draw beautiful, even borders that make the teacher smile, and who cannot glide on four blades across the ripples of ice?Mamusia shrugs off the first attempt at skating. "We'll try another time," she tells me. "Come on. Let's go home."

Just before St. Nicholas Day, which in Poland always falls on December 6, Eliza and I visit St. Nicholas himself at the Central Department Store on Aleje Jerozolimskie. He's a skinny man, and he wears black-rimmed glasses, and I am not quite sure why he is there and why we are sitting on his lap. But a photographer is standing by, and we are told to talk to St. Nicholas, and I do as I am told. I tell him his white beard is fake, and my mamusia reminds me to be polite next time. My cheeks burn with shame.

We have a Christmas tree. Everyone has a Christmas tree, and we are no different in this regard, even though my only associations with Jesus are exclamations made in frustration. *"Jezu kochany!"* My dear Jesus! I still have never set foot in a church. My babcia Lewandowska once came for a visit along with her sister, Ciocia Benia, and it was Ciocia Benia who suggested that Eliza and I should be baptized, but my mamusia would have none of it.

"Ridiculous!" she exploded. "I have no time for this nonsense." None of us ever saw Ciocia Benia again. Nonetheless, my sister and I make paper chains and tissue paper snowballs with a million colorful points for our Christmas tree. My mother has given us a book of instructions on making decorations. We have paper and glue, so we set out to do our Christmas work.

My sister's decorations are perfect. Each snowflake peak is positioned beautifully. Each chain link is cut to an identical width. I am impatient and can't make my fingers do the tricks that her fingers can do. My chains have fat strips of paper, and the glue doesn't always hold the links together. But I keep at it. The tree stands empty, except for the candles clipped to the sparse branches and a half dozen painted glass balls. Our ornaments will fill the branches with color.

Mamusia and Tatek play Christmas music on the small record player in their room. We listen to carols sung by the popular Polish folk group, Mazowsze. We know these singers and dancers well. We went to their show last spring. We watched the men lift the women and swirl them in the air as their petticoats flopped up and down and their beaded vests sparkled like cold fire from a firecracker. They sang about cuckoo birds and Laura falling in love with Filon and meadow flowers and peasant boys driving farm wagons with sturdy horses. And they sang about Warsaw.

"Jaka piekna jest Warszawa." How beautiful Warsaw is!

Yes, here it is again—a reverence for my city. And my city is indeed beautiful. Truthfully, I have never been to any other city on this planet, but I know from pictures that none can compare.

Plynie Wisla, the River Vistula flows through it, serenely, gracefully dividing my city in two. Yes, my city. Warsaw is mine, and I am her child. Warsaw, the city of parks and, of course, the towering Palace of Culture. As a young schoolgirl, the Palace of Culture is majestic, almost like a castle. On a warm fall day, my tatek, Babcia, and Dziadek Lewandowski take me to the top of the thirty-two-story building.

There is a balcony on the uppermost floor. It's a perfect place for a photo of your children, so Tatek takes his camera out of the leather case. The view is astonishing to a little girl who has never climbed higher than the fourth floor of her apartment building. The city blocks below look oddly irregular. The sloped roofs of apartment buildings cluster around the courtyards, and the tramcars move slowly. The streets appear distant, remote.

Dziadek Lewandowski, a bald-headed man with a pointed beard not unlike Lenin's, takes me by the hand and points to the square below us.

"No, I don't want to look. It's scary," I tell him with a shake of my head. I take a few steps back from the railing.

"Not at all. Here, you can't be scared. Let me show you." He lifts me nimbly over the banister and sways me over the city. "See? I'm holding tight! Nothing will happen! You are safe."

I feel anything but safe. I am dizzy and see nothing around me except swirling air, threatening to rip me away from his hold. After a minute, he lifts me back to the balcony, throwing a smug look at my tatek, who stands to the side, camera suspended. I refuse to go near the banister again. The Palace of Culture has lost a layer of grandness. It is a building from which children can be dangled and dropped to the pavement below.

7.

Eliza and I are mostly healthy now. Mamusia heats up milk and crushes garlic into it if my nose feels stuffy. "Drink this," she tells me. "It will clear up your head." But I cannot swallow it. The harsh bite of the garlic undoes the sweetness of the milk. Together, they produce a smell that makes my stomach heave inside. I know I am displeasing my mamusia, but I put the mostly full cup on the kitchen table and tell her that I am feeling fine. I do not need to be made well.

"Drink it," she tells me more sternly.

I do not like medicine, nor do I like doctors or nurses. I worry that if I become very sick, I will have to be taken away from my mamusia. Who would explain to the doctors what I need? Mamusia always speaks with conviction, as if she knows exactly what the next step should be. I want that voice to be there, next to me, speaking loudly and clearly on my behalf. I don't want to be cared for without her there. If I ignore a hurting stomach, no one will put me in a hospital. So when I break out in hives after eating tomatoes, I ignore the rash and eat more. I do not want to acknowledge frailty. I like to imagine myself as being tough and strong, even stronger than the boys in my class. Tougher than my best friend, Janek. Tougher than Eliza's school friend, Jerzyk. Not sickly, not delicate, not vulnerable at all.

On a wet autumn day, we walk to Mamusia's friend Irena's apartment just two blocks up Ulica Marszalkowska. Irena is the mother of Jerzyk. She is a robust woman, wide in girth, cheerful, with an engaging habit of teasing her son's friends, but never in a way that would make them cringe. Her husband is a doctor, and he has received a small supply of a special smallpox vaccination from his friend in Switzerland. The children of Irena's friends are lining up outside his study. Privileged children! Children who will not get a dreaded disease because of their special connection to a doctor with access to valuable medicine.

It is my turn, and I am shaking with fear.

"Hold still!" I am told. "Hold still, already!"

But I do not hold still. I am wiggling in this strange room where a man is threading a needle onto a syringe. I jerk away, and a portion of the vaccination spills. The doctor shakes his head. "She'll get some of it." "You see what you did! There is no more!"

Tears spill down my cheeks. My sister and all her friends will live. But I will not be spared, and it will be my fault. Eliza will get a room to herself. My Johnny will be hers now. She stands still. She will live.

In the winter of my first year in school, Mamusia decides it is time we are exposed to the English language. She gives a weekly lesson to Eliza and Jerzyk and me at our apartment. We sing songs about that bridge in London that falls down and about poor Bonnie lying over the ocean, and we learn to say, "My name is Nina. My name is George," the English word for Jerzyk. I am a restless student, and I fidget and look forward to the minute when Jerzyk's mother comes to take him home. He is a boy, and I think that boys are incompetent. He is two years older than me, and he cannot tie his shoelaces. Each time I kneel down on the floor and do it for him, our mothers laugh while Jerzyk blushes ferociously.

I do like another boy, though. I like Janek, also the son of Mamusia and Tatek's friends. We live in the city center, and our school is designated as our neighborhood school. It is only chance that places us in classrooms with children of family friends. Janek and I play during recess, and our parents make sure that he and I have a school Christmas photo taken together. Janek is in a cowboy costume with a plastic gun slung over his belt, and I am in my most treasured Mazowsze folk costume with a colorful flowered skirt sewn by Mamusia, a white petticoat, and lace apron, and a vest with beads and sequins that glitter like cold fireworks.

Janek tells his parents right then and there that when he grows up, he will marry me. I am pleased to hear him say this, even though our parents cannot stop laughing. I am sure they are laughing at the idea of me being married to anyone. I make ink blotches in my notebook, and I cannot glide across rippled ice, and my big toes curl upwards.

Over Christmas break, our family takes the overnight train south to the Polish High Tatra Mountains. It is not our first trip to the mountains. The Ministry of Foreign Affairs, like so many other workplaces, has a vacation house in the popular resort of Zakopane for its employees. We stay at this small guesthouse called Magnolia. We are quickly becoming regulars.

The Tatra Mountains are beautiful! My tatek loves these mountains more than life itself and has said as much. He speaks of boyhood hikes across the pristine valleys and up to the summits, and I know he wishes we would follow him to those summits now, but we are too little, and we prefer to ride in the horse-drawn sleighs that go up and down the snow-covered streets of Zakopane.

My sister's friend Jerzyk is in the mountains too, and our mothers take the three children skiing. We have wooden boards that fasten onto our brown lace-up shoes. I can wear my jacket now. The heavy blue wool coat is not good for winter sports. Jerzyk, Eliza, and I push our way across the valley, and we side-step up a small hill and plow down again and again. Jerzyk shows off by whizzing by fast, but I am not impressed. I know that someone had to tie Jerzyk's shoes before he could slip on the skis. I move effortlessly across the snow, happy that the skis, unlike the skates, make it easy for me to glide.

8.

It is spring, and I am about to turn seven. My mamusia plans a party for me, and I am bouncing with excitement when the day comes.

"I have some party games for your friends," she tells me.

"Like what?"

"Oh, Pin the Tail on the Donkey and Ring Around the Rosy." She uses English names, and I know she learned these games when she lived far away, in the country where people do not speak the Polish language. I am relieved that the pinning of a tail on a very rough drawing of a donkey is popular with my friends. We laugh with great hilarity as we pin the tails onto the wrong side of the animal.

We sit down to eat the fantastic hazelnut cake with nut frosting baked by Jerzyk's mother. It's her specialty. We have stewed fruit compote to drink, and I am delighted with sitting at the head of the table. Everyone sings for me. *"Sto lat, sto lat!"* A hundred years, a hundred years, may she live for us! Secretly, I do not believe that I will live to be an adult. If the gas heater doesn't poison me, the tram car will surely run me down. Or, more likely, I will become sick, and no medicine will be potent enough to cure me. I try hard not to imagine this set of cataclysmic events, and I succeed at least on the day of my birthday.

At the table, stretched out to its full length, we play the game of telephone.

"Whisper something in his ear, and then he will whisper what he heard in yours!" I laugh so hard at the twisted messages that come my way that I bite down hard on the glass with the fruit compote. It's not tempered glass, and shattered shreds of it fill my mouth. My mother panics and rushes me to the kitchen sink.

"Spit it out! Spit it out!" she shouts. I am so surprised at my mouth being full of glass that I offer no protest for once. Out goes the glass.

I am learning. I am learning that laughter often ends quickly. Shattered glass, a bruised elbow, a call to the homework table—events cutting short a moment of pleasure. "Put that away now." "Turn out the light." How old will I be when I no longer have to turn out the light?

I am becoming devilishly athletic. I have grown to love my bicycle more than I love Johnny. But my athleticism is jerky and bold, and it does not translate well onto the dance floor. My sister laughs at me when I try to imitate the dancers we saw in a Mazowsze performance. Perhaps in response to this, my mamusia enrolls us both in ballet class.

"Mamusia, do you think I can dance well?"

"We'll see," she tells me.

She sews us ballet dresses made of the same shiny fabric as our school uniforms, but these short little skirts are a lighter blue. We lace up our ballet slippers and make our way to the bars at the side of the school gym floor. First position, second position. I try hard to point my foot in the way the teacher tells me to. Someone is playing the piano, and the tune for the bar exercise will stay with me forever—slow, melancholy. Hands out, feet turned out, up and down, up and down.

I think I am managing the dance positions well enough, but my sister continues to laugh at my attempts. We practice at home, and I know I am doing the exercises just as the teacher showed us, and still she laughs.

"Look Mamo, Tatek. Come look at her!" They, too, smile at my antics.

I stop liking ballet classes and count the days until spring when I can ride my bike again on the dirt roads by Dziadek and Babcia's house.

In spring, the streets are full of women from the villages selling tiny bundles of flowers. Old women with kerchiefs covering their graying hair and wrinkled faces with gold caps on their front teeth crouch behind tin buckets and large washbasins. You can also pick up farm foods from them, but my mamusia prefers to buy them from the farmers in Babcia and Dziadek's village. Still, I coax her into buying the flowers. I am entranced with the sweet-smelling lilies of the valley, tiny violets, pink sweet peas, English daisies, and forget-me-nots. Small posies are held together by a rubber band or a thin sliver of silver foil. Riverbank flowers announce the end of winter's gloom.

9.

It is the spring of a new decade. We're standing in line again for ice cream, served between two wafer squares. Delicate flavors to choose from: raspberry, strawberry, cream, cocoa. I am near the end of my first year of school. Our class at Elementary School Number 43 is celebrating! Come to school in your best party dress! Pretend you're a

Nina Lewandowska Camic

fairy. Bring a magic wand!

My mamusia doesn't have time to sew me a fairy costume, but I have two good dresses from my father's last two trips to America. I have not grown much over the year, and both still fit me. I have been saving my favorite, the one with two layers of lace on the collar, for this occasion. I explain to Mamusia my dress choice. "It will be almost as good as a fairy costume."

I am completely taken aback by her response. She tells me that I will not be able to attend the party. It appears that we are moving. Tatek is going to be working in New York. He has been appointed ambassador to the United Nations. We will be leaving Warsaw for New York in the middle of June.

I understand none of this. New York? Where is that?

I am barely seven, and my orbit has been small. Summers with Babcia and Dziadek. Sometimes a week in the mountains. A week by the Baltic Sea one summer. A train journey to visit Dziadek's relatives in southeast Poland. And once, we boarded a plane and traveled outside Poland for a two-week vacation by the Black Sea in Bulgaria. I disliked the bumpy airplane ride tremendously and was sick both going there and coming back. I am not used to any form of locomotion except for trains and tramcars. I have rarely even been inside a car.

"How will we get there?"

"We'll be traveling by boat."

I most certainly have never been on a boat. The River Liwiec that runs through Babcia and Dziadek's village is too shallow for boats. I can sit down in most places on its sandy bottom and feel the water trickling between my toes. If I wade carefully, picking out the right spots and lifting my skirts, I can cross the river without getting my underpants wet.

The United Nations appointment came as a surprise to both my parents. My parents knew that Tatek was being considered for a high-ranking diplomatic post. He spoke English well now and was familiar with life in the West. Earlier in the year, rumor had it that he might be the next ambassador to Indonesia.

"Indonesia?" my mamusia had asked in shock. "With the children? Absolutely not!"

His name was withdrawn, and they heard nothing more of Indonesia. But New York? How did it come to pass that this young man, about to turn thirty-four in June, would represent Poland on the world stage of the United Nations?

"Luck!" my father tells me much later. "So many things came my way because of sheer luck!"

I do not realize how happy my mother is with the upcoming move.

"We will be taking a train to Paris."

Our small family from Ulica Nowowiejska will be in Paris? I don't know a thing about Paris.

"And from Paris, we will travel to Cherbourg."

I cannot take this in. What's Cherbourg?

"And from there, we will be sailing on a large ship to New York."

My mother, the daughter of a labor movement organizer, the woman who confidently moved back to what was thought of as Communist Poland, the mother who took the bus to give birth to her second daughter in the local hospital, is returning to the place where she had gone to elementary school and high school and just a little bit of college.

"Remember all your English words!" she tells me now.

I remember none of them.

"Practice!"

"My name is Nina. My name is Nina."

Chapter 4

1.

I have the taste of pizza in my mouth and the sound of the Beatles in my head.

There are places I remember all my life, though some have changed
Some forever not for better, some have gone, and some remain ...

It is July 1966. After a six-year term, my father's appointment as the head of the Polish Delegation to the United Nations comes to an end. We are leaving New York forever. But I am thirteen, and I don't think in those terms. I don't worry that I may never return. I'm not even focused on what lies ahead for next year back in a country where I haven't gone to school since grade one when I learned to write *Ala* and *As* in my notebook, between colorful borders carefully designed with my six-year-old hand. I think only about New York friends who will go on to eat lunches together and dance at parties together and go to the movies together—without me. Should I seek out my first love, Michael Charles, to say goodbye? Should I write to him?

Dear Michael,

I wanted to let you know that I liked you very much. If you want to write to me, this will be my summer address:

Nina Lewandowska, u Haraczow

Gniazdowo – Kaliska

Powiat Wegrow, Wojewodztwo Warszawskie

Poland

Your friend,

Nina

Uff! An address that only a Pole could understand. Eventually, Michael does write, copying the lettering dutifully, putting the appropriate airmail stamp on the envelope.

Dear Nina,

You were a good friend and I will always remember the fun we had in school. We will miss you.

Your friend,

Michael

I cry hard to the sound of the saddest of sad songs replayed without pause on the portable record player.

Our return trip to Poland is again by sea, on board the *Queen Elizabeth*. Six years ago, I was a quiet kid, happy to sit on the deck with a kerchief tied snugly under my chin to keep the wind away. Now I'm a teenager with a stack of *Seventeen* magazines at my bedside, wanting nothing more than to find the perfect remedy for skin blemishes. And I pay attention to boys. Take the Stokowski boys who are crossing the Atlantic with their father, Leopold Stokowski, the famous conductor. I'm told their mother is Gloria Vanderbilt, and though I don't know much about the lives of the rich and famous, I do know that the Vanderbilt family name is given to a street in midtown Manhattan just blocks from where I live—lived. My sister and I are introduced to the rather senior Mr. Stokowski and his sons, who are slightly older than us. I don't know what prompts the introductions. Maybe someone thinks that a Lewandowski should meet a Stokowski. However, when I ask my parents if Mr. Stokowski is Polish, they respond elusively "of Polish descent," as if that's not the entire story, but that's all I'm going to hear about it. It doesn't take me long to grasp that the Stokowski men mix in different circles than we do and that even a shared voyage on the *Queen Elizabeth* will not bridge the vast differences between us—not even for the short trip across the ocean. The boys are handsome, always immaculately groomed, and terribly indifferent to us.

Curiously, in my time in New York, I'd not had much experience with status hierarchies. We were poor compared to others on Manhattan's east side, but we surely lived very comfortably in a building with a uniformed doorman and air conditioning in each bedroom. The apartment wasn't really ours, but we still lived there. And we went to a private school, though one that attracted families from a range of economic backgrounds. Status was not apparent to me. But here, on the ship, evidence of social class is palpable, and I know that we are only pretending to be part of this rarefied world of travelers on luxury vessels. Communists, returning home. And maybe my mother feels it as well because there is a new cautionary note in her demeanor, as in, "Don't get too comfortable here. This isn't ours."

We dock in Cherbourg and board the train for Paris. I stand in the corridor, just outside our compartment, watching the gentle green landscape out the window. An older man is at the next window, and as I look up at him, his face breaks into a warm smile.

"Tu parles Francais? Do you speak French?" he asks.

"No." I'm not about to have my school French tested.

"Ah. American?"

"No. Polish."

"Polish! Your first time in France?"

"No. We've traveled through here before." I wave a hand back toward the compartment, indicating that "we" means all of us sitting back there. He doesn't question why a Polish girl would be speaking the English language. Instead, he turns back to the window.

"This is a very pretty area of France. And look! See those horses? White horses. You know they bring you luck." Perhaps I look like I may be in need of it.

"They do?"

"Yes, but you must lick your thumb, touch your other palm with it, and smack it down with a fist. Like this!"

I imitate his gesture.

"But you must not do it unless you see a white horse. Remember that. Very important."

In Paris, my father picks up a car that will be our family vehicle for many years to come. It is a silver four-door Peugeot, and for the first time, he confronts driving a stick shift. Leaving the city in afternoon rush hour traffic is difficult, and the car stalls more than once.

"Bogdan, please watch the car in front!" My father is confident—perhaps too much so—but that confidence gets us out of the city and eventually onto the country roads. We are to drive south to the coast of France, then to Florence and Venice in Italy, then up through Austria to Poland. My mother talks about how this is the last chance to see some of Western Europe. Eliza and I settle into our back seat world of clammy vinal and the hazy air of my father's cigarette smoke.

The days are a blur of traffic congestion, inadequate hotels, and tourist-packed cities of the Mediterranean region. It is my first real taste of vacationing in Western Europe, and like an Americanized child, I miss the more familiar motels, the hotdogs on a white bun at Howard Johnson's, and pop music on the car radio.

"Can't we stay in a motel?" I ask for perhaps the tenth time. "Look! There's one just ahead!" I point to an indifferent side of the road building that is squat and long. My parents aren't happy with the selection, but they have found that a road trip through the south of France in July is not the same as a road trip across America. Available, affordable rooms are scarce. My father sighs and pulls the car to the office door. We are assigned a small room facing the highway. There, we experience a restless night, listening to the uninterrupted roar of cars and trucks outside.

"Never again," my father grumbles the next morning. I sit silently in the back seat and offer no more advice on where to stop.

Our last night in Western Europe is just outside Vienna. We are gawkers, hugging the peripheries of the grand cities. We come in, admire the architecture, the art, the shops, and then retreat to sleep in humble rooms in the outskirts, some with wobbly and sticky tables and chairs, one with a profusion of bedbugs, and here, outside Vienna, in a guest house with pretty lace curtains and dainty pictures of edelweiss on the wall. And it is in Vienna, a city of grand music and Sacher tortes, of white stallions and cafés with hot chocolate always on the menu that I fall in love—with a dog. We are at an outdoor table of a café where my father takes a break for a cigarette and a cup of espresso. Next to us, a woman is enjoying a drink with a white poodle at her side. The dog is beautifully behaved, smart, and friendly.

I begin the usual sing-song pleading. "Can we please, please have a poodle when we get home? You said we could someday have a dog!"

I never really expected my mother to say yes. Asking for things is what kids do. But she, too, is smitten with the sweet-natured dog at the next table, and to my shock, she nods. "Alright. If you promise to take care of it."

And so it is established that there shall be a dog, and it shall be a poodle, and it is to be my responsibility. I feel as if I have inherited a new family member in a matter of seconds, and at this early pre-adoption stage, this feels just fine.

We are at the Polish border now, and the line is long. My father gets out and speaks to one of the guards. He shows papers to the man in a military uniform. We wait. My father returns to the car now, and we move to another shorter line. I ask why we have been given this break, but I already know the answer. It is our last moment to benefit from travel on diplomatic passports.

As we wait, I look out at the grim faces of both the searchers and the searched. The men in military uniform move slowly from one vehicle to the next.

"What are they looking for?"

"Illegal imports. Smuggled goods." It feels threatening. I don't want to witness a confrontation. I hope no one finds anything. But wait, whose side am I on? Who is the victim here? Who are the good guys?

Once across the border, we notice the road deterioration immediately. We are on a major artery linking the south of Poland with the nation's capital. The road is narrow with two lanes, no shoulder, and no chance to pass safely, even though you must, because trucks and cars share space with villagers biking home, horses pulling long farm wagons, cows, chickens and other animals, and school children. Sometimes, my father seizes an opportunity to speed ahead, weaving menacingly from our cluttered lane to the one with oncoming traffic. The chorus of backseat complaints begins.

"Daddy, please don't pass now. Please! There's a truck coming!" As if wanting to reassure himself that he is in command, he ignores us. A Trabant is puttering along in front of us with a lot of noise but not much speed. Tatek's muscles tighten, and he swerves into the lane of oncoming traffic. We groan. I look down and cover my ears as if protecting them from the noise of a sudden impact. When I look up again, we are again in the proper lane. We're safe this time until the next passing episode and the one after that. I cannot wait for the car trip to be over. Soon we will be home.

But where is home now? We are not returning to Ulica Nowowjejska. A year ago, during our summer return to Poland, my mother and father had set the goal of finding an apartment. Early on, my mother had grown impatient with what she thought was my father's lackadaisical approach to the project. As soon as we arrived in Warsaw, she called friends. And friends of friends. Eliza and I had not yet left the city hotel during our month in the village, and we were growing restless. My sister was thirteen, and I was twelve. We were used to our independence in New York, but in Warsaw, we had no outlets, no friends, no real reason to venture out on our own, so when my Mother suggested one afternoon that we accompany her on one apartment showing on Koszykowa Street, we were glad to go.

The building was older but in good shape. The gray concrete facade was unremarkable, but the unit had large, south-facing windows, offering a pretty view of the quiet street below. Tree branches provided some shade to the second-floor space. The parquet floors were in good repair. There were two large bedrooms and an area that could serve as a living room. To us, the place felt spacious and luminescent.

"It's nice and bright!" I comment. "I like it!"

Eliza agreed with me.

My mother frowned. "Maybe. I'm still hoping for another place, just around the corner from here."

She doesn't show us the other possibilities, but I quickly grasp that my father's stint at the UN has placed us in a different category of apartment hunters. More than perhaps any perk bestowed on our family, this is the largest. The unit that my mother just frowned on is a prize by Polish standards. It would be a nothing apartment in a not too attractive nothing building in America. The entrance leading to the stairs is dark and dank, like other Warsaw buildings, unlike the entrances to so many Manhattan apartment buildings with their canopied doors and large hallways on the ground floor. A proper kitchen has not been built into the unit. The new residents will put up shelves and install an oven. They'll tile the bathroom, and the few lucky enough to have a washing machine will find a nook in that bathroom to fit it in. Elevators are not common, but if there is one, it will surely be small, aging, and loud. But the measuring stick is different here. By Warsaw standards, this unit on Koszykowa Street is indeed fine. It's not necessarily larger than those of my future classmates but definitely on the clean, well-tended end of the continuum. There is no smell of urine in the entrance, no broken corridor lamps, and chipped steps. We are surprised that our mother appears dissatisfied.

By the end of that summer month in Poland, our mother tells us that she has obtained her first choice apartment on Aleja Roz. The "Avenue of Roses." There are no roses on this short block in central Warsaw, but it is indeed a great location, and I can tell she is happy with this outcome.

"Can we see it?" I ask.

"Not now."

Many, many years later, she tells me the story behind the pursuit of the apartment. This is her story, summarized now by me:

I met him [Jozef Cyrankiewicz, then the prime minister of Poland] through my friend Marysia. They had been great friends for years, you know. He came to visit me at the Grand Hotel, during our return trip to Warsaw, while you were in the country. He liked me, you know. He wanted to kiss me. I invited him upstairs, and eventually we made love. It was insane! From then on, I couldn't get him out of my head! We saw each other constantly. He wanted me to leave your father. He promised me fine clothes, trips to Paris. At the beginning, I asked only for help finding a good apartment. He found it: right there on Aleja Roz, across the street from where he lived. A beautiful place by Polish standards. We continued to see each other for several years. Sometimes in an empty apartment just above where we lived. I didn't love him, but I was obsessed with him! After several years of these surreptitious meetings and his repeated assurances that we would make a fine family, the four of us, without your father, whom he called "little man," I really thought—this is nuts! But we kept on seeing each other. And then it ended. Just like that, and I never saw him again.

It is deeply ironic that the apartment, apparently procured through my mother's secret love affair with Cyrankiewicz is gifted many years later by my father to his girlfriend. My father eventually separated from my mother, and toward the end of his life, he signed over Aleja Roz—by far the most valuable family possession—to a woman who had been his lover for many, many years.

Our new Warsaw apartment with three rooms, a hallway, a kitchen, and a bathroom, secured by my proud mother without my father's knowledge as to the circumstances of the plum offering, is empty now when we arrive after our long car trip. The shipment of our belongings will reach Poland later in the month, so my father drives us straight to my grandparents' house in Gniazdowo.

"We'll be back when the furniture arrives."

"Can we get the dog then?"

"Yes, yes, we'll find one for you."

They return to Warsaw to the Grand Hotel, conducting their business privately and for the first time, without the unity of spirit and purpose that seemed once to be theirs, at least in the early years in New York.

When the crates and trunks do arrive, my mother has her hands full. During her periodic visits to Gniazdowo, she tells us of the slow progress with apartment renovations.

"I'm having carpet installed. Like in America, wall to wall in the bedrooms. And there will be cabinets in the kitchen. Your room will have an entire wall of bookshelves."

Sometimes I think of her as having boundless energy, but at other times I recognize that she has a fragile edge to her. During this transition period, she appears tired and tense. At the time, I knew nothing of her ongoing affair with Cyrankiewicz, but I knew that my father was a source of at least some of her stress. He is without a job.

How could that be? He had had a splendid run as ambassador to the UN. And in the summer of our return, he is just forty years old—not even near his professional prime. He doesn't discuss it with us now. I do not know if he is worried or waiting for a particular position to open up. It isn't until he is an old man that my father is willing, indeed, eager to talk about his past, including his decisions on where to work after we returned from New York. He explains it in this way: "In the mid-1960s, there was already a strong and growing undercurrent among the Polish political elite of extreme nationalism and anti-Semitism. Those affiliated with security were taking over the Ministry of Foreign Affairs. I went to the foreign minister—a decent man, a real progressive intellectual, Adam Rapacki, and asked him, 'Don't you see what's happening?'

He laughed and said, 'You exaggerate.' But I knew I was right. I resigned from the ministry and started to look for other work."

To an outside observer, it is ironic that he eventually found work right in the belly of political power in Poland at the Central Committee of the Communist Party.

"Of all places, why there?" I ask many decades later.

He answers almost defiantly, "Well, where do you go? They hated me at the Foreign Service. We had almost no money saved—something like $600. I needed to work. And remember, I had ties to Gomulka."

I did not remember. In fact, I hadn't known this at all in my early years. My father was completely silent about his political life. But I certainly knew of Gomulka. As the head of the Communist Party, Wladyslaw Gomulka was considered the person in command in Poland. He rode to power during the post-Stalin thaw that took place in the country in 1956, and he stayed in command until he was pushed aside in 1970. And I learn now that by coincidence, my father met Gomulka right after the war. Through family connections, he was asked to tutor the son of the future Polish leader. Apparently, that contact with the Gomulka family held him in good stead during the 1960s, when the security forces may have otherwise drummed up reasons to put my father, with his extremely close ties to America and western democracies, behind bars. Just as my mother could have been made the scapegoat during the tense McCarthy era in America, my father, by his own account, could have been made a scapegoat during the suddenly tense times of acute nationalism that gripped Poland in this decade.

For six years, my father works as a deputy to the foreign affairs section of the Communist Party. He oversees relations between the Communist Party and international organizations. In my later conversation with him, he continues his explanation:

"And I was right about what was happening at the Foreign Ministry. In 1968, a list of Jews at the ministry was presented to Foreign Minister Rapacki. He was to fire them from their work. When he saw the list, he put his name at the top and resigned. Whereas, Gomulka thought he could save himself by forging alliances with the anti-Semitic forces even though he had had a Jewish wife! But even his outspoken anti-Semitism didn't help him. He was kicked out in 1970. And I knew sooner or later the nationalists would come after me, so I worked hard in those years to reestablish my connections to the UN."

But none of this was known to me then, in 1966, when I came back as a freshly turned teen to Warsaw. What was evident was that in the summer and fall of that year, both my parents were looking for work.

Despite the instability in their lives, my mother and father do not back down on their promise to bring a dog into our home. Toward the end of summer, my mother arrives in Gniazdowo with the following news: Ciocia Janka, my father's old friend, a woman who loves dogs more than almost anyone I know, has located a breeder outside the city, and we are to go there to pick up our poodle.

Ciocia Janka comes with us to the dog breeder's farm. The place is chaotic and not a little run down, but dogs are running everywhere, and they all seem playful and spirited. She points to one especially energetic and friendly puppy among the litter.

"He looks a little sick," I comment. His eyes are watery, and he seems to be sneezing a lot.

"Don't worry," Ciocia Janka tells me. "I have a good vet. You'll take care of him."

And so Mickey, our medium-sized black poodle, comes back to Gniazdowo with us. He never stops having health issues, but he remains the enthusiastic, friendly dog we saw that first day at the breeder's farm. He is with us until the day I am an adult and leave Warsaw for good.

Nina Lewandowska Camic

2.

September marks my reentry into the Polish school system. The last time I began a new school year in Warsaw, I was about to start first grade. Now, seven years later, I am beginning ninth grade, which is the second year of high school, at the Lycee Stefan Batory—the same lycee that my father attended just as the war broke out.

Batory is a regional high school, and it enrolls children with some degree of academic ambition. Those who finish elementary school with lackluster grades often bypass lycee qualifying exams, opting instead to go to a vocational high school. Kids who want a lycee education know they will need a university degree afterward to land on the desirable, though not necessarily more lucrative professional track.

Since our return to Poland, I haven't seen much of my father. He has a car now but rarely comes up for a visit during our stay in the village where my grandparents live. But when he does appear on one such visit, I can tell he wants to talk to me. We are sitting at the verandah table. The lunch dishes are cleared, and I am about to take the last slurp of fruit compote before getting up to go outside. He is leaning back in his chair across the table and looking at me as if trying to decipher something. His gaze comes with a crinkle in his eyes. He often looks like he is secretly smiling, even when perfectly serious.

"Can you talk to me for a minute? I wanted to ask you some questions about UNIS," he begins. He is speaking in English. In the middle of our years in New York, our family switched to English at home. We never returned to Polish.

My father's curiosity about UNIS catches me by surprise. I think back to the school I left behind. They're good thoughts, but already the New York school seems remote.

"What about it?" I ask. I can't recall the last time we talked about school. Maybe it was three years ago when he expressed dissatisfaction with the social science textbook I had been using.

"What did you study in math? And in science?" he asks.

I don't know how to answer his questions. My memories of schoolwork are even fuzzier than the other details of school days in New York.

He is patient. "Tell me, did you have biology?"

"Yes, we learned about frogs and cell structure. And in math, we did equations. Solving for x."

He takes out a little notebook, unscrews a pen and writes down a few words. "What else?"

I'm nervous. Is this a test? I want to appear learned before my father. "We did some chemistry too!" I boast. I'm sure some of that general science had chemistry in it. I think.

He puts down his pen. "It's like this. You started school in Poland at age six. You were a year younger than the rest. When I went to the Ministry of Education to enroll you and your sister in school now, I was told that we are right at the brink of educational reform. Your cohort—the group of kids you started school with in first grade—are entering eighth grade now, but they will be the first to have another year of school added. So if you went back to school with those kids, you would have to stay in school through twelfth grade. That's five more years of school for you. Right now, in Poland, there are only eleven grades. Eliza's cohort will be done after eleventh grade. But they are willing to put you ahead one more year if I can show them that you did advanced math and science in UNIS."

"Do I have to take a test?"

"No, I just need to write a paragraph effectively stating that you had science and algebra."

"Well, I did!" I say this without fully understanding the consequence of my words.

"Alright. So then maybe we can put you in ninth grade come September. You would be two years ahead of your age group, but you're smart. I told them that. You were tested."

Ah, here comes that IQ test that seems to matter so much to him. I had indeed been tested in UNIS, and the results made an impression on my father. He never forgets it, returning to my test scores sometimes with pride, sometimes with competitive envy. "If you got such a high score on that IQ test, you should be able to understand what I'm telling you now," he'll say. Sometimes, he'll credit himself for recognizing my cleverness. "I always knew you were smart."

"If I go to ninth grade, I would graduate after eleventh?"

"That's right."

"But wouldn't that mean that I'd be in the same grade as Eliza?" Her former school friends would be going into ninth grade.

"We would have to move her up one year. You can't be in the same grade. So, do you want to go for it?"

I don't hesitate. Even though I would never have considered myself a diligent and industrious student, I do work harder if that work will push me to the head of the pack. I'm competitive. To be placed at age thirteen in a class of fifteen- and sixteen-year-olds seems so splendid that I never once think about the burdens that come with that kind of a leap.

"Yes!" I nearly shout it. My father smiles. It is the first time that I feel him to be proud of me.

Looking back, I am amazed that anyone thought this type of advancement was a good idea. After six years in New York, I spoke Polish, but my written language skills were next to nonexistent. The students in the ninth grade will have had a year of high school—a year of Polish literature and history. I left the Polish school system learning how to read *Ala* and *As* in first grade. My classmates will have been writing long essays about literary giants and medieval uprisings in Europe. They will have had a year of physics and separately chemistry and biology and a year of advanced math. And perhaps, most importantly, a year of working in a high school environment. I worried about none of this. I thought, instead, about the social benefits of having older friends. And having agreed to move forward, I am forcing my sister to skip a year now. It may be just one year for her, but she will have only two years of high school left—a very short span of time to make up all that she had missed by going to school in the United States.

The petition requesting that I jump two years ahead is granted, and on September 1, 1966, I begin ninth grade.

The Lycee Batory is housed in an attractive cream-colored old mansion, just at the northern edge of the string of the great parks of Warsaw. It is a two-story U-shaped building with a sloping red-tiled roof, and it stands behind large gates in a small courtyard, giving it an appearance of a grand manor house. Classrooms extend along the corridors of both arms of the U. There are three ninth-grade classes. I'm told to go to 9A.

I know to bring slippers to school, and I am familiar with the uniform requirement, which includes a navy overcoat that girls put on in the cloakroom before entering class. I go upstairs to my homeroom slowly. I don't want to be early or late. I see that everyone is hovering near the closed class door. At eight-thirty, the door is unlocked, and we all go in.

It's a formidable room if only because the parquet floors are polished to a deep shine, and the ceilings are high, consistent with older architecture. I look around me. How odd that some things are just as they were in first grade! The inkwells are gone. Students use ballpoint pens now, but the seating arrangement is the same—two students to a desk, three rows of desks. I'm assigned an empty seat in one of the side rows. A girl across the aisle looks at me with curious eyes. She has short, ruddy hair, carelessly cropped, and a pale complexion that makes me think of Irish kids I knew back in New York. I notice that she shuffles when she walks from one spot to the next. It comes from walking in loose slippers across those wooden floors.

She leans over toward me now.

"I'm Danka," she says stealthily. "I sit with my friend Aneta."

"I'm Nina."

These high schoolers have been together since the beginning of lycee studies in eighth grade. Some have known each other since grade school. To me, however, they are all strangers. I say nothing more. We wait for the homeroom teacher to arrive. A tired-looking man of about fifty enters just as the bell rings.

"Good morning. Nice to see everyone after vacation. Welcome, welcome. We have a new student this year." My face becomes flushed as I hear this reference to me.

"Would you stand up, please?" I do so. He looks down at his papers. "Nina Lewandowska has lived in America for the last several years. Well now ..." He pauses as if to insert an editorial comment on that fact but then changes his mind. "She will need help in understanding what is expected of her. I hope you will assist her."

There are some things that I learn very quickly. You stand up when the teacher is talking to you. You show respect, addressing her as Pani Profesor and him as Panie Profesorze. You do the work and come prepared for class. Every day, teachers will call on students randomly and ask them questions about that assignment. The students will answer orally in front of their peers. They will be graded on their responses. At the end of the year, the subject grade will be determined by these recitations and any written work that may have been required.

I learn, too, that students help not only me but also each other. Student solidarity is strong here. Friends whisper correct answers to the poor kid on call that day. They pass slips with the right information. When I pause one day, not knowing the correct response, I glance up and see a student across the room frantically waving her hands, giving me hints. I understand her message and provide the right answer. The kid grins.

At recess, Danka takes me by the arm. Aneta is hooked to her other arm, and the three of us walk up and down the corridor arm in arm, up and down. This is what girls do during break. Danka asks, "America, eh? So is it different there?"

"Yes," I answer truthfully.

Danka nods her head as if expecting just that answer. Perhaps thinking that I'm apprehensive, she gives my arm a light squeeze. "You'll like it here. I'm sure you will. We have fun in class. Only you cannot ever please our Polish literature teacher. She's mean. But you'll like the others. By the way, some kids are saying that you're young. How old are you?"

"Thirteen."

"Thirteen? I'm going to be sixteen in December! You're a baby!" She says this affectionately. Instantly I hope that she will be my friend.

Aneta is frowning. Her hair is pulled back tightly, pinned in a way that is more common for a woman three times her age. There is no smile on her face. "Why are you in our class?"

"I've studied some of these subjects before, I guess."

Aneta shrugs and pulls at Danka's arm. "Let's go to the park after school."

"Want to come?" Danka asks. Aneta grunts audibly.

"That's okay. I have to go home today right after school."

I am lying. My father is at home, but he has no idea when I'll be back. He is still in the process of looking for work. As far as I can tell, he spends most of the day reading a stack of newspapers and periodicals. My mother, on the other hand, is immersed in her translation and editorial duties at Interpress. The job is new and is not full-time, but she often brings work home and shuts herself in her bedroom until suppertime. Yes, one big change at home is that my parents no longer share a bedroom. Our apartment has been divided in ways that I don't yet fully grasp. My sister and I share one room, my mother claims another, and the third, furnished as a living room, holds a single bed for my father. None of us view this as a place to hang out. It is his room.

"Why don't you sleep in the same room anymore?" I ask soon after we move into the apartment.

"He snores and keeps me up," my mother answers in a tone that implies she will be offering no more explanations. My father is silent, and his face shows no emotion. He grunts slightly and clears his throat. This is his trademark, whether or not he wishes to speak. He picks up the paper again and sits in the big leather chair that seems to be there for him alone. If they discussed this new sleeping arrangement, I don't know about it. Nor am I aware that my mother continues to see Jozef on the side. "Passionate encounters!" I am repeatedly told in later years.

The addition of our puppy, Mickey, is another change for us. Our young and energetic poodle needs to be walked three times a day, and the chore belongs to my unemployed father and me. I'm assigned the after-school walk. My father does the morning walk. We alternate evenings, though eventually, my father is the principal walker then, too. I don't know how this arrangement came to be put in place. Initially, I offer little protest, but over time, I realize that the walk after school is a chore that cuts into time typically spent with friends. If I plead long and hard, claiming a special social event, my mother fills in for me and takes Mickey out for a quick walk in the afternoon, tiding him over until I come home, but she never likes doing it and makes this obvious enough that I shy away from asking. My high school and university years are spent with a pup that needs my daily attention.

3.

My mother was the diplomat's wife in New York. In Warsaw, she is part of the labor force again.

"I am under a lot of pressure," she says now as she comes home in the early afternoon. The door to her room closes behind her.

My mother's new job causes her anguish. She is hired as the editor of books translated into English for publication by Interpress. The material spans a range of topics on Poland, from cookbooks and travel pamphlets to historical texts and art catalogs. Though she has editorial assistants, she feels them to be incompetent and not hard working. From her telling of it, I gather that the social chatter in the office is incessant. My mother is either unwilling or incapable of effectuating change in the work habits of her subordinates, and most often, she simply packs up her papers and brings them home.

As she becomes increasingly preoccupied with her editorial tasks, my mother wants to adjust her home obligations. We have someone come in to clean the apartment once a week. And now my mother is raising the issue of meal preparation. Cooking has never been pleasurable for her, and if she wants to shed household duties, it is all too predictable that this one will be the first to go.

"I cannot cook daily for all of you," she tells us now. We say nothing, waiting for the new rules to be set. "It's time you took on some responsibility." I want to tell her that all my friends' mothers work full-time, even as her job is only part-time, and that their children are not serving family meals. Still, I know too that many Poles eat their main meal at the workplace cafeteria and that several friends have grandparents living with them. The afternoon lunch—the main meal of the day for most of my classmates—is not infrequently prepared by the grandmother.

My mother has a new schedule in mind. "Sunday, we'll eat at Babcia and Dziadek's, in the village. Monday, we'll have leftovers. I need one of you to cook Tuesday. I'll do Wednesday, the other one can do Thursday, and you can go to the milk bar on Friday. I'll give you an allowance for a plate of blintzes or dumplings. Saturday, we'll be in the village again."

The big, hearty lunch is suddenly a big fiction in our home. On some days, if there is prepared food in the refrigerator cooked for that day by one of the three designated cooks, Eliza and I will stick a fork in and take a few bites straight from the pot. It seems a bother to heat it up. On the day that I am to cook, I look to see if there are scraps of leftovers from the previous day. If there is enough for my parents, my sister and I will skip the meal altogether. Better to eat a piece of apple cake left out under the dishcloth on the counter than to spend time cooking. No one seems to pay heed to the gradual deterioration in our eating habits. In the evenings of this first year after our return, my father will ask if anyone will be eating sandwiches for supper. Typically, we are plenty hungry, so we throw in our requests for one or two open-faced sandwiches, most often with Gouda or Edam over bread and butter, sometimes kielbasa and ham on rare occasions. Meats remain scarce in Poland. My father will call out that supper is ready. This will be the one time the four of us will see each other all in one place. We sit at the kitchen table and eat. To an outside observer, what may stand out is how silent our suppers are. No one wants to talk. No one asks questions about the day. Even though our house is always full of newspapers and journals, current events are never discussed. My father reads the papers, then my sister and I use them to line the trash bin. Dealing with the trash, too, has become our responsibility.

Is it odd that, for having such politically engaged parents, I never hear them talk about politics? And it's not just a ziplocked silence in front of the kids. Their paths rarely cross, and they remain mostly silent with each other. It's as if my father's professional interests and my mother's political views have turned private, only to be shared with trusted friends or colleagues, not with us, not during suppers at the kitchen table.

I ask my father much later, "Why did you never explain what was going on in Poland after we moved back here as teens?"

"I wanted to protect you."

"From what?"

"From the crap that was taking place then."

"Did you want to protect Mom too?"

"I have a lot going on at work," my mother says again as she picks up her empty sandwich plate and walks over to the sink to rinse it haphazardly and place it in the tower of cleaned dishes that rarely gets put away. Eliza and I look at each other. My father does not respond. He coughs slightly, and we wait to see if he is clearing his voice to speak, but in the end, he remains silent. We hear the door close to her bedroom. She has disappeared for the day. He, too, retreats to his room, though his door remains open.

4.

At Batory Lycee, I forget about UNIS. I'm facing a different school culture here, which seems rule-based and rigid, but I'm starting to wonder if that's only a first impression. Dig deeper, and you'll find something far more intricate and complicated. Take, for example, the simple matter of school uniform. We are required to wear it, but I see that many girls keep the length of the cloak at seven-eights so that a part of a skirt will show. Boys can escape the uniform requirement by wearing a white shirt or navy sweater. At recess, girls will unbutton some of the buttons so that a blouse may also be visible. Some students adhere to the rules. Others push boundaries.

Recess time is time for everyone to leave the classroom. During these years, daily showers and deodorants are not yet commonplace. The classroom smells of adolescent sweat, and the norm is to air the room at least every two hours. "Open the windows. Open the windows!" the girls shout when the recess bell sounds, and the class monitor (we take turns at this) does so, no matter the weather outside. We are not permitted to stay in the room then. Arm in arm, girls up and down the corridor. Boys cluster in small groups. The crowded halls reverberate with talk and laughter.

A longer recess in the late morning is a break for a "second breakfast." We take out our home-packed sandwiches and eat them at our desks. After, we go out to air the room once again.

Social norms are fairly easy to grasp, but somewhat predictably, Eliza and I are swimming in the sea of the unknown as far as our schoolwork is concerned. She is in tenth grade, and she is left with only two years until graduation. She has far more material to make up than I do. Neither of us knows anything about Polish composition or writing. When reports come back home about our gaps and deficiencies, my mother hires a tutor for us, a university student named Teresa.

"What's your homework?" she asks on the days that she is with us.

I quickly learn that if I say "not much" and "it's easy," my tutoring session will be short. On most days, I resist working with Teresa unless I do not know how to approach an assignment. But if I can make a guess and wiggle my way toward an answer, I'll plunge ahead and hope for the best. Perhaps this is a true sign of my immaturity. My work at home focuses not on reaching a full understanding of the subject matter but on trying to predict what the teacher will ask during recitations. I'm spot on most of the time and deliver a reasonable response when called to recite.

Eliza is less lucky. Her history teacher has taken a dislike to her, and she comes home with failing grades in that subject again and again. My mother is worried.

"Do you need more tutoring?" she asks.

"It won't help," Eliza answers sullenly.

My mother confers Irena, her old friend and Jerzyk's mother. Ah, Jerzyk! I remember him! I tied his laces during English lessons back on Ulica Nowowiejska!

"Oh, take her out of that school!" Irena tells my mother. "Put her in Zmichowska, where Jerzyk is. It's a lycee with a French language concentration, and the director is superb. The teachers are good too. I know because I serve on the parents' committee." Irena is a woman who knows how to work miracles within the constraints placed upon her.

"I don't know that we can switch." My mother doesn't really understand the rules at play here. Who can blame her? Her own high school years were in New York.

"Sure you can. You live on the border of the district for our school. Petition for it!"

If there are rumblings about our switching schools, I am unaware of it. I view Batory as my new UNIS, and I am growing very fond of my new friend, Danka.

Early in December, Danka asks me to come over to her house after school. "We'll bake a spice cake together!"

I am so happy with the invitation! I am a scrawny kid with pimples on my face. Danka is smart, older, and kind. I can't always be sure of what she is thinking, but this is not only Danka's way. Polish young people are less blunt in their dealings with one another. You don't fully reveal yourself. American kids are, for better or worse, quick to speak their minds. In Poland, after hours of conversation, there's still a layer tucked away for another day. Or never to be revealed at all. What you present is very deliberate and controlled.

Danka lives a short ten-minute walk from my home. It's my first visit to a high school friend's house, and I am a little nervous as I cross Plac Konstytucji and look for the number of her building and the letter to her stairwell. Often the entrances are tucked away in a courtyard. It takes me a while to understand this. In New York, the entry portal always faced the street, with fanfare or sometimes a degree of modesty, but always visible to all.

There it is: Plac Konstytucji 5B. I walk slowly up the dark stairwell to her family's third-floor apartment. I'm sure there is a light switch, but I am afraid of pushing any buttons. As I reach her door and ring the bell, I hear the familiar shuffle of slippers. She cracks open the door, smiles broadly, and ushers me in.

"Good morning, good morning, *witamy* (we welcome you)!" She uses a mock formality that is at once a tease and full of sincerity.

The parquet floors in the apartment are well worn, and the rooms are dim, with windows opening to the narrow street that leads away from Warsaw's large square. I take off my shoes and follow her to the kitchen. She has already begun sorting ingredients. She pours me a glass of tea, and I smile to myself. There was a time when tea in a glass felt so deliciously adult.

Danka goes back to her recipe. "I don't think I have enough sugar. Well, no matter. It's too sweet anyway. Let's pour in a little honey and see what happens." I watch her combine things in ways that aren't called for. All the time, she explains to me what she is doing.

"Do you ever bake?" she asks as she slides the pan with the batter into the oven.

"Yes. My sister and I both like to bake things."

"Like what?"

I hesitate. How do I explain that I have never baked a traditional Polish cake or pastry? That our list of favorites includes brownies laced with Philadelphia cream cheese or Boston cream pie?

"Cakes."

"What kind of cakes?"

"More like cookies." But I realize that's going to be misunderstood. Cookies are an American item. Cookies in Polish are little cakes—little *babkas*, squares of apple strudel.

"And cheesecake! We bake cheesecake!" That's safe ground. Poles love cheesecake.

Danka smiles. "You know, I have something for you. It's a little music box. I have had it for a long time, and now I want you to have it." She takes it out and plays it for me. It's a tiny little metal square box, and the melody is a familiar lullaby. If you put it against another metal surface, the sound is louder, more insistent. I grin broadly. Our friendship has just been sealed with a gift.

A week later, I am in the kitchen of our apartment, lifting cotton dishcloths covering foods on the counter, looking for something to snack on. I hear the front door opening. It's my mother, coming home from grocery shopping. She has been to the delicatessen, a store that bears no resemblance to a deli in New York. In Poland, these stores are more likely to sell sweets, coffees, and what are regarded as luxury items. She places a box of tea leaves in the cupboard, then reaches into her net grocery bag, taking out a square box wrapped in paper and tied with a string. She places it on the counter by the window. So, she has been to a bakery as well.

"What did you buy?"

"Cheesecake, apple cake, and some doughnuts." I'm pleased and not pleased, all at the same time. I am going through a particularly pernicious spell of acne, and my New York reading of such bibles on skincare like *Seventeen* magazine has led me to believe that sugar and chocolate and sweets, in general, are bad for your skin. I've completely eliminated chocolate from my diet, but I can't shake the urge to eat baked goods. My sister is less troubled by bad skin, but she is forever

Nina Lewandowska Camic

groaning about getting too fat. She is a petite, slim teen, and I have to think that this, too, is a holdover from our days in New York, where weight talk was rampant. She is likely to be unhappy that there are fresh cakes now on the shelf.

Having unpacked her shopping bag, my mother begins to leave the kitchen but then pauses in the doorway and comes back. She stares at me for a while, then blurts out, "What do you think about switching schools in January, after Christmas break?"

"No!" And in throwing down this one word, I realize that I have grown to like school. I'm used to my class and teachers, and I adore my new friend, Danka.

"Well, Eliza has to switch, and we thought it would be best to keep you in the same school as her. It's easier to do it that way. I've been talking to Irena. You'd be in Jerzyk's class. She tells me he has a wonderful set of friends."

Jerzyk? I suppose that makes sense. With my leap forward, I would catch up with my sister's old cohort.

"Mom, I like my class at Batory!"

"You'll like your new class too. You had no trouble adapting to Batory. Zmichowska will be an easy change for you."

I go to our bedroom looking for Eliza. I want to ask her if she knows of this change, but she isn't home. I close the door to the room. I can only think about Danka and the music box on my shelf.

In late fall, our class goes on a field trip to visit an old manor house several hours away by bus. I am a touch apprehensive about the trip. My last class excursion was to the beach with my twelve- and thirteen-year-old UNIS classmates. We thought it was great fun to sing songs with an undercurrent of pre-adolescent naughtiness.

Mother give me one of those!
One of those girls without no clothes!
I don't want no fire truck!
I want one that I can ooom tarara!

On the bus ride to the park and manor house, Danka makes sure that I am sitting across the aisle from her. And it isn't long before this group of teenagers is singing too, only the songs sound to me more like the ones I had heard in Russian camp than those from the UNIS beach trip.

"Do you know this one?" Danka asks, launching into a song that I will hear at every outing, hike, and campfire during my years in Poland. Others immediately join in.

Zal, zal za dziewczyna,

Za zielona Ukraina..

(Pining for my girl and for the green of my Ukraine ...)

Many of their songs sometimes date back to the First World War. Mournful melodies, with lyrics depicting the loneliness of a soldier fighting in the trenches, far away from his homeland. Sometimes, they'll be about the beauty of the Polish mountains. *Bieszczady, gory mych marzen snow! (Bieszczady! Mountains of my dreams!)* Other times they will exalt excessive drinking. *Wina, Wina, Wina Wina dajcie a jak umre pochowajcie! (Wine, give me wine! And when I die—bury me!)* Most every child will know all the lyrics of the songs. You get the feeling that they grew up with these tunes and that their parents know them too.

Danka smiles as I join in. I am flooded with gratitude for her friendship.

On the last day of school before winter break, I am strolling arm in arm with Danka and Aneta up the school corridor, then back again.

"Do you want to come over tomorrow? We have some new magazines to look at," she coaxes me.

"I'm leaving for my grandparents' village for Christmas," I tell her. I take a deep breath. "And I won't be coming back to Batory after the holidays." I try hard to hold back tears.

"What?!"

"I'm switching schools."

"But why? I thought you liked it here!"

"My parents thought it would be better." I don't trust myself to say more. I am very near crying.

"Alright then." She grows silent. Aneta comments on the assignment and then talks about a movie coming to town. "You and I should go," she tells Danka.

I walk silently back to class.

Over Christmas break, I write Danka a letter. I tell her how much I loved being her friend. I explain why my parents thought it best that

I switch schools. I play the music box and cry. "You're *always* crying," Eliza tells me.

"You're such a *sunshine kid*," my mother often tells me. Which one am I?

5.

I grew to love the storybook images of an American Christmas that I came across when we lived in New York. So often, these images included a rural landscape buried under a blanket of heavy snow, with stars twinkling, sleigh bells jingling, pies and cut-out cookies baking, and thick, perfectly formed fir trees waiting for artfully crafted decorations. Images of music and merriment, of families gathered for the holidays. And of course, there was the guy from the North Pole and all his named reindeer. Now, on my first Christmas after my return to Poland, I look outside, and I see a winter landscape that is not dissimilar to those that I remember from American Christmas cards and television commercials. We are at my grandparents' village home in Gniazdowo, and every picture book element is in place. Well, minus the Santa, the tree, and the merriment.

There is electricity in the house now, and Dziadek has even installed a toilet and a tub with an electric pump that brings the water right to the house. He and Babcia still use the outhouse, though. "For the fertilizer," he grins when I ask why.

———

The downstairs part of the house is warm, heated by coal and wood-burning stoves. My sister and I share the tiny room off the kitchen, my parents claim the spare room on the other side of the house, and Dziadek and Babcia continue to use the room with the two huge beds—his and hers. I remember hers so well from my earlier years here. I spent many nights in it, fighting nightmares and anxious moments wrapped in her warm and patient embrace.

The village house is so familiar, yet it has been a long time since I've spent winter days here. We keep a few T-shirts and pairs of shorts in the chest of drawers in the little room. Clothing that's useless for this cold season. We've added now thick cotton nightshirts, and as I pull mine out and bury my face in its clean smell, I wonder what it is about this country home that makes me feel so safe, even as there is no phone line, no easy access to stores or other services. And still, as I slip under the thick quilt, I think about how lonely it must be to live here year-round.

Since the verandah is without heat, we eat all our meals in the kitchen. Babcia has been working hard to prepare for our visit. The wooden board has rows of nut cookies and poppyseed cakes. There are pots, some filled, some ready to be filled on the cast iron stove surface.

"Too much food," my mother tells her. "Ma, you make too much. No one can eat all that." Babcia says nothing and gives her full attention to the task of moving the kettle to a hot place on the stove where she can boil water for tea. The kitchen oven is warm, and the room has the smell of burning wood and yeasty bread.

Outside, you can hear the occasional sound of bells as farmers navigate the slick roads in wagons that now have sleigh runners instead of wheels. The air is brisk, and the fields, forests, and farmsteads are buried under a deep layer of snow and look indescribably serene and beautiful. Nonetheless, replicating the holiday mood inside the village house is not easy. Dziadek and Babcia do not observe Christmas, and our own mimicking of Christmas rituals, even in the thick of American commercial holiday activity, has always felt fragile and tentative. So far as I know, no one in the entire house adheres to any Christian beliefs. Perhaps Babcia does, but she keeps her thoughts on this to herself. Many years later, I'm told that her aunt was raped by a man of the cloth, resulting in the birth of a deformed and unwanted child. I would guess that it was not hard for my grandmother to accept Dziadek's disdain for organized religion. This year, without even the external commercial prod, the holiday feels especially insignificant.

I ask my mother if we could have a tree.

"Go ahead, find one," she tells me, almost defiantly. Neither she nor my father seems happy to be spending the holiday away from Warsaw. I turn to Dziadek. He is eighty-one years old now and not in great health. But, he tells me I could ask one of the farmers. "They'll cut a tree down for you for a few zlotys." He suggests the farmers just on the other side of the great forest down the snow-covered road. I put on my warmest cap and my winter coat and set out.

The farmer, Pan Krysik, knows my grandparents well. Babcia buys all her dairy products from him, and Dziadek has great respect for his farming practices. When I come here to pick up cheeses and eggs for my grandmother, the farmer's wife, Pani Krysikowa, always coaxes me into her kitchen for a brief chat. She does so now, on this cold December day. I sit on a wooden chair by the warm stove and answer her friendly, curious questions. "How long are you here for?" "How is Dziadek's health?" "Is Babcia cooking up a storm now that you're here?"

Looking around me, I notice that Pani Krysikowa's kitchen is different than Babcia's. Yes, they both use similar coal-burning stoves, but Babcia puts all her effort into keeping the house clean and her wooden trays of food full. She doesn't give any attention to decorations or adornments. I see embroidery on shelves of the Krysik farmhouse, a religious cross hung on the wall, a picture of a somber-looking Jesus and plastic flowers in a vase. You'll find none of these in Babcia's home. Too, the Krysiks are true farmers. Their home faces the farmstead courtyard, and their house abuts the stable where horses, cattle, and pigs are kept. Babcia feeds a cat to keep the mice away. Except when my grandmother brings in a chicken for slaughter, there are no farm animals on my grandparents' property.

Pan Krysik smiles when I ask him about the tree. I can't help but notice how different a smile is here. Most Americans have such good teeth! A Pole, especially one who lives in the country, will have at least a few missing. Still, Mr. Krysik's smile is genuine and kind. Yes, he'll help. A small tree? He takes off his cap and runs his hand through his thin hair as if he were giving my question a full review. He nods then and tells me that there are many just up the road, in the forest by our house. He'll get his son to cut one down and bring it over before it turns dark.

And so we have a tree. Because the room Eliza and I share is so tiny and the kitchen is so crowded, the tree stands in my parents' room. And the radio plays holiday music, and we listen to it. My father occasionally puts down his book or newspaper and hums along. He may have been raised in an atheist home, but these Polish carols appear to have meaning for him, and his eyes crinkle into a private smile. Once more, I find myself missing the more familiar to me American music. I take out a pen and a piece of paper and concentrate on writing letters.

Dear Jackie,

I hope you can come visit this summer. I'm switching schools again, but maybe the next one will be good too. How is Michael? How is Jonathan? Write soon! Love, Nina.

The holiday comes and goes. Christmas in Poland is celebrated on Christmas Eve. The traditional dinner, eaten at dusk, is large and lasts a long time. It includes borscht with dumplings, herring, vegetable salad with thick mayonnaise, baked fish, boiled potatoes, and many cakes. Most Poles regard it as the most important meal of the year. But there is no fish in the village, and if our own Christmas dinner is special, it's because all meals prepared by Babcia are cooked with care and effort. The day after Christmas, we return to Warsaw. My parents will not ever suggest that we spend Christmas in Gniazdowo again.

Chapter 5

1.

In January 1967, everyone in my family experiences change. We have been back barely half a year. I am still thirteen years old and worry more about the acne on my face than about the sudden shortness of winter days or the unsettled political climate in Poland. Eliza and I are about to begin a new school semester at the Lycee Zmichowska. My father starts work at the Communist Party headquarters, and my mother signs a new contract with Interpress. My parents maintain a very light social schedule. Every few weeks, they visit neighbors—a speechwriter for First Secretary Gomulka and his wife who live in the building next to ours. Like my parents, they lean left, if I may borrow that term to describe those who have no stomach for the resurgence of nationalism and anti-Semitism in the government.

Also, at this time, my father strengthens his friendship with Mietek Rakowski, the editor of *Polityka*, one of the few news journals that, despite the presence of censorship, publishes political commentary that does not parrot the increasingly hard-line positioning of the governing elite. Rakowski comes over frequently, and when he does, the door to my father's room closes. The door to my mother's room also closes as she isolates herself and struggles to meet publication deadlines for the manuscripts before her. Her room is quiet—his, less so. I hear animated voices late into the night. Occasionally my father will emerge and pick up a few glasses from the kitchen before returning to his room.

Mornings remain dark. Light switches flick on as we arise, positioning ourselves in line for the inevitable bathroom queue.

"Are you done? Can I use the shower now?" In the bathroom, I peer long and hard into the mirror. I cannot get rid of the acne on my face. If I turn to the left, I see fewer blemishes, but I know it's only a temporary reprieve. Horrid stuff. And my supplies of American Clearasil are dwindling. What now? Polish face creams? I tried one. It's greasy! How can you put grease on a face that is too oily? I know that my mother feels sorry for me. As I stare at my profile, she comes up behind me, and for once, her manner is gentle and upbeat.

"I'll get you an appointment with a cosmetologist. Every woman here seems to go to one regularly for skincare. But really, it doesn't look too bad now."

My hair at least looks better than it did in UNIS. I'm learning how to cut my own bangs with greater care. I look down, away from my face. I'm of average build for a thirteen-year-old. Long-limbed, though not especially tall. Still, my face feels flushed and pouty. I turn away with a sigh. It's the first day in a new school all over again.

The Lycee Zmichowksa stands at the opposite end to where Batory was in relation to the chain of city parks, a block away from the southern corner of Lazienki. Whereas Batory felt like a self-contained campus, Zmichowksa is housed in one building of a block-long row of apartment houses. If you didn't notice the plaque announcing that this indeed is Lycee Number XV, you might mistake it for another residential building, similar to its neighbors. Once inside, we have our badges inspected by the attendant, and then we veer left, taking the stairs down to the cloakrooms. Each class has its own space, partitioned by a chain-link fence, which is locked during the school period to guard against theft. We leave our coats and outdoor shoes inside the gated enclosures. My classroom is on the European second floor. I walk up and look for my assigned room. I'm in 9B this time.

Jerzyk comes up to me the minute I enter the classroom. I barely recognize him. His curly hair is cropped short, and his face has lost the roundedness of a little boy. He has very kind eyes and a pointy nose. "I broke it skiing," he tells me later.

"Hi! Let me introduce you to the kids. My pal Marcin, our friends Grazyna, Basia, Malgosia ..."

I smile in the way that one does when one can't quite connect to anyone in the room. The names are swimming.

The homeroom teacher, Pani Profesor Zydkowicz, comes in. She is a thin, wiry woman who is also the Polish Language instructor. She assesses me quickly with no more than a glance, and then as if making up her mind about me in ways that aren't necessarily complimentary, she tells me to sit in the side row next to a student who has not been introduced to me.

"Happy to meet you. I'm Joanna." Joanna with the full head of thick, long, ashen blonde hair. Joanna with the pale blue eyes. Joanna, who up to now, had been perfectly content not having to share her double desk with anyone at all.

I study the schedule. Polish Language. That would be literature and literary criticism. Grammar in its own right had been taught earlier, in eighth grade. It's a shame. I could have used the boost. History, Geography, French and Russian. I'm not attending Russian yet. Petitions are floating as to what should happen to my study of Russian. Physics, Chemistry, Biology. Physical Education, Workshop. What's missing here? What does an American high school have that's not in my schedule? Music, Art. Choice. Once you enroll in the Polish lycee, you study what everyone studies. You have a choice of a third language (after Polish and Russian), but the rest is set for you.

The week is irregular. Sometimes classes end as early as one. Other days end at two-thirty or even three-thirty. There are no extracurricular activities afterward—no athletic teams, no drama, dancing or debate. Some students study additional languages or music privately. Most do none of that. There is homework, but rarely does it consume all the evening hours. And for people like me who look for shortcuts, it can be done reasonably quickly, certainly within two or three hours. My study habits grow even more irregular and unpredictable. When a subject doesn't interest me, I do the bare minimum. I am quite independent but childish, too. I have no real passion for schoolwork. When the bell rings, and we file out to the cloakroom, I think about the walk I want to take or the novel I had to put down earlier, just as the story was heating up. Eventually, as the evening progresses, I remember that I have homework assignments to prepare.

2.

It is my first winter in Poland since I left the country as a seven-year-old. Now, as a teenager, I look at Warsaw in a new way. If it was once dark and brooding, now it feels more open and easy to navigate. It hasn't the crowds of New York, and it hasn't the snarl of constant traffic. If I get on a bus at point A, I can almost always count on getting to Point B in the same number of minutes every day. I use the buses and trams a lot. And I walk. True, the shoveling of snow on the sidewalks remains sporadic in the winter. Finding a way to cross through a piled mound of snow can be a challenge at some intersections. I understand why women love knee-high boots here. It's not only for aesthetics but necessity.

I stare at women's boots in a shop window. Back home, I tell my mother that I would like a pair. I rarely ask for an article of clothing. The stores don't offer anything I would need or want. The boots are the exception. She is distracted. "Yes, yes, alright. I suppose you need them. Where did you see them?"

"In the shoe store on Piekna Street."

"How much?"

I tell her the price, and she hands over the bill needed for the purchase. I go back to the store where the boots were on display. They have a simple, straight line, but I like the slight heel and the deep chocolate shade of brown. Inside the store, I get those famous two words that every Polish person knows so well. "*Nie ma.*" We don't have any.

"But I see them on display!" I haven't fully embraced the way business is conducted here.

"Those are for display only. There'll be another shipment coming in."

"When?"

"We don't know."

The sales clerk shows complete indifference to the whole matter. I realize that she does not care if the shoes come, if I return, if I hate her, love her, hate the store. None of this matters. If I am lucky, I'll encounter a clerk who will at least offer a grain of hope. Please come tomorrow, or next week, or next year.

"Are you getting some this month?" I persist.

"We don't know when they will be delivered."

There is an interesting intonation to the Polish sentence. It always sounds unnecessarily assertive to my ears. The pitch of the sentence rises quickly. The words come out in a rush and then drop precipitously as if the speaker wants to dismiss the whole exchange as ridiculously unnecessary. If I say in English, "I'm a very good speaker of Polish," it will usually be even-toned, with perhaps a deflection on the last word, indicating the end. If I say the same words in Polish, I will race through the words, climbing in pitch, so that "good" comes out on top and the rest plunges into an abyss of irrelevance. After years of listening to only English, I suddenly feel attacked by the spoken word around me. Everyone sounds defiant. If language hints at a nation's insecurities, I'm sensing that spoken Polish hints at the Pole's struggle for recognition and positioning on the world platform.

Where does this feeling of being undervalued and pushed aside by the rest of the world come from? When I was in New York, I felt hostility to my Polishness, but I attributed it to Poland being labeled a communist state. Now I'm discovering that Polish people have thought themselves to be kicked around dismissively long before their leadership embraced a communist agenda. During my years at the lycee, I learn about the two seismic and brutal attacks on the Polish identity.

First came the partitioning that led to the erasure of Poland. That split of Polish territories between Austria, Prussia, and the Russian Empire lasted throughout the nineteenth century until 1918. And then came the Second World War. The vivid memory of the horrific destruction of Poland during that war only magnified the gaping wound left by the partitioning in the previous century. I had grown up with images of war, reconstruction efforts, rubble, and commemorative candles burning on street corners where Poles were executed at the hands of Nazi occupiers. And now, in my Polish history texts, I'm learning the details of warfare and erasure, of attacks and destruction, and the indifference of others to the fate of the Polish nation-state.

But perhaps it is equally important to understand what I'm not learning. My books stop short in detailing all the events that transpired after German forces dropped bombs on Polish soil on September 1, 1939, signaling the beginning of the Second World War. It isn't that what I am reading and reciting before my formidable history teacher, Pani Szalkowa, is incorrect, but it is incomplete. It omits the role that the Soviet Union played in the near destruction of my country. Even as a young teen, I am savvy enough to suspect that anything written about the Soviet Union will be sympathetic to that country. But it isn't until many decades later that I begin to understand that the textbook's omissions were not merely sympathetic shadings of the kind that I read daily in the Polish press, but they were glaring and deliberate exclusions, creating a pockmarked narrative that was in part correct, but also intentionally misleading and deceptive.

At the lycee, I learn of the bombing of Poland by the Germans. But we do not discuss the invasion of Poland barely two weeks later by the Soviet Armies. In reality, in 1939, Poland was assaulted by two neighboring states. Warsaw, where I lived, was indeed occupied by Germany from 1939 until Poland's liberation in 1945. But my schoolbooks do not reveal that to the east, and the Soviet Union occupied Polish lands. For two years, until the Germans pushed back the Soviet Army and took control of eastern Poland, the Soviet forces conducted executions and deportations of more than one and a half million Poles who were thought to be a threat to the Soviet Union. They destroyed, pilfered, and looted Polish towns and villages, all under Stalin's watch. I knew enough from reading western texts that Stalin was responsible for the murder and deportation of people in his own country. But even western texts were curiously silent about Soviet executions and deportations of Poles. And so, World War II, in my school-girl eyes, is a war waged by

Nina Lewandowska Camic

the Germans. Nearly a quarter of Polish people perished, half of them Jews. I learn that the destruction of Poland as a nation nearly repeated itself. Even as a young girl, I understand that this war will have left its mark, and that mark will not be buffed and minimized in my time and probably not in the time of the generation that came after me. But I did not know then what those who lived in the eastern provinces of Poland knew, that the goal of destroying Poland as a sovereign, independent nation was shared by Germany and the Soviet Union.

How much of this history was understood by my parents? As a low-level bureaucrat working his way up the diplomatic ladder, my father knew all too well that his early associations with the anti-communist Polish government that went into exile in London in 1940 would cost him his job if they were to be exposed. He became a government employee by happenstance, but once he embarked on this career, he clung to it, perhaps desperately, and at times defensively. Even in his later years, when he was more willing to talk about his views on communism and Poland's troubled relationship with the Soviet Union, he scoffed at what he thought was simplistic finger-pointing. The Soviets stood passively to the side during the Warsaw Uprising? And what help did the West provide? Communism is evil? "What's communism?" he would retort. "The only true communists I ever met were those in Berkeley. And maybe your grandfather."

3.

Jerzyk invites me to a party at his house shortly into the semester. "Just for our small group of friends," he tells me. I'm thrilled that I have at least a foot into a group of classmates. Isn't it odd—bizarre actually—that just nine months earlier, in New York, I had had my first boy-girl birthday party? We were twelve and thirteen then. I'm still thirteen. Do they know that? I'm clueless as to what to expect at a party. These kids, Jerzyk's set, they're strangers to me. Jerzyk himself is not the boy I knew when I was just six. I note that he has a habit of looking straight at me when he talks. It's a sharp gaze but well-intentioned. Protective. I like that, and I think I like his friends, too. His best pal Marcin is cheerful and chatty. And the girls are friendly, not unlike my Batory classmates. Always entwined with each other at recess, they smile when I pass by. They're polite toward me. I notice, too, that they care about their appearance, and even though makeup is not permitted in school, they style their hair with great exactness. None of them reach out in the way that Danka did at the Batory High School, but I try to reassure myself that it is only a matter of time.

On Saturday, the day of the party, I am apprehensive and curious. I walk the four blocks to Jerzyk's house. The route takes me past our elementary school, and I think how little I remember about it now. I continue on with a tug of sadness. School memories shouldn't pass this quickly. I shake off these thoughts. I'm heading to a party!

Jerzyk's apartment faces the busy Marszalkowska Street. The entrance is through the back courtyard. I walk up the stairs slowly, not knowing if it is normal to be late or on time. I ring the bell, and Jerzyk opens the door immediately as if he had been waiting for me, the last guest, to arrive.

"*Czesc!* Come on in. Nasty out, isn't it."

I hadn't noticed, but I acknowledge that it is cold.

I step into a long hallway. Wasn't it here that I lined up to receive my vaccination from his father? Jerzyk's dad no longer lives here. Irena, his mother, divorced her husband when we were in the United States. I see her now, hovering in the background. She appears large and matronly and somewhat stern until she opens her mouth to speak. Her words roll out with a full laugh, and her formidable look recedes. I get a big, double kiss of welcome (as is the Polish style among people who know each other). I see that girls are taking off their winter boots and putting on party shoes—small heels, some patent, some plain leather—over a stocking foot. In America, pantyhose are coming into fashion. In Poland, women are stuck with garter belts and stockings. I'm just learning how to hook them properly so they stay up.

I hang my coat on a rack and follow Jerzyk and his mother to the room that clearly serves as a living and dining space. Large pieces of furniture are pushed against the wall, creating room for dancing. Marcin, Grazyna, Malgosia, and Ewa are all there. Obviously, I am on the late side. I wave my hand in greeting and then follow Irena to the table of food. She has baked cakes and made sandwiches, and she explains in great detail what there is for us to eat, even though there is no need to explain. She is giving me time to feel comfortable. My classmates are extremely polite to her, and she banters freely with several in the group. But after a few minutes, she retreats to another room. The record player is turned on, playing French music, Adamo, and Polish rock groups. There is a tape recorder as well, and someone plays songs recorded with a microphone from the radio. I hear the Beatles.

I think of my own Beatles record collection at home that I know by heart. We all knew them at UNIS. Here, when a Beatles song, taped from the radio, comes on, there isn't the same instant recognition. You cannot purchase Beatles or any other western music in Polish stores. And not surprisingly, no one is paying great attention to the lyrics, and why should they? English is familiar to some, but not to all. The songs played at parties are in a variety of languages. Moreover, I can already tell that western pop music is important to some kids, but not everyone. In school, earlier in the week, we had been drawing models of automobile engines in a workshop class. We are studying the mechanics of cars, and sketching the engine parts is tedious work. The teacher, an older, squat woman with graying hair and a droning voice, permits a modest amount of chatter during these drawing sessions. One of my classmates, a girl I barely know, turns to me and asks, "Do you know the Beatles songs?"

"Yes, sure."

"Can you sing one for us?"

"Which one?"

"Anything. Your favorite."

It is 1967, and this winter, the Beatles have just released "Strawberry Fields." In a stroke of luck, a friend of my parents had traveled to the United States. The kind man asked what we would like from New York.

"The new Beatles record! And a tube of Clearasil," I say without hesitation. I sing "Strawberry Fields" now in class as we put the finishing touches on our auto engines. A cluster of girls who are clearly pop music enthusiasts pulls up chairs to our table. Others continue to chat in small groups at tables around the room. At first, the teacher pays little attention, but a minute into the song, she comes over and looks at our sketches.

"Maybe you should focus more on your work," she tells me without emotion.

"But Pani Professor, she's singing a new song for us!" one girl protests. Some teachers are feared and respected, and others are challenged.

"Get on with your work."

"Eh, Nina, finish the song!" I look at the girl who is so earnestly prodding me to continue, and I shake my head. In UNIS, I was often the rebel. Here, I prefer to blend, to stay quiet.

The girl comes up to me after class and asks if I would be willing to let her borrow some of my records for a party. I hesitate. There is probably not a thing at home that I value more than my Beatles collection. She notices my hesitation.

"It's okay, I understand."

"No, go ahead. Only please don't let them out of your house."

At Jerzyk's party, the preferred music groups are from France. And, to my shock, the preferred dance style is rock and roll. The boys spin the girls in ways I have only seen in American movies depicting an earlier era of music and dancing. I think of it as a dance step that belongs right there with twirly poodle skirts and sock hops. And I'm clumsy at it. No one has ever spun me around like that before. Slower dances are more predictable, though here, too, they follow a set pattern—two steps forward, one back. I am a little relieved when the party draws to a close by midnight.

Jerzyk offers to walk me home. Even late at night, the streets are safe in Warsaw, but I know he is doing what other boys routinely do after a party. They make sure all the girls have escorts home. It's a norm rather than a necessity.

"Did you have fun?" he asks me on the short walk home.

"Yes, sure. Thank you."

"They're good kids, and you seem to fit in at school too."

He's right. Batory is already fading in my mind, and I am very focused on this new set of classmates.

If I were to describe the social configuration of our class of thirty-six students, I would say that there are no cliques, but instead, there are clusters. I am with Jerzyk, and he affiliates himself with one cluster of friends. For the most part, these are kids who try hard to pull in good grades. My mother would call them clean-cut.

"Such clean-cut friends you have!" she says this with obvious approval, so much so that I almost want to protest, as if that label paints my set in the blandest of colors. But I stay silent. I prefer to be on her good side so that I do not have to feel the scorn that she occasionally displays toward my sister's friends. Eliza's classmates are never present in our house, as my sister avoids parading them before her family. And still, my mother is suspicious of her choices, much as she was during our last years in UNIS. And even though my mother mostly distances herself from our social lives, every once in a while, she emerges and speaks her mind, as if it strikes her that she ought to be more attentive to her daughters' lives. With "clean-cut" friends, her caustic comments are reserved for the kids we play with during our summers in Gnizadowo and only much later do they target the young people who would become my friends and lovers.

Apart from noting the social clusters, I also discover that these clusters are neither hierarchical nor exclusive. I am, for example, not limited to Jerzyk's set. There is Joanna, my seatmate, and I know from the beginning that she is a loner. She prefers to go off by herself when our class takes walks in the park during a good weather physical education session. And she gets on the bus quickly after school, heading home, rather than lingering with us over a cream-filled waffle from the creamery across the street. She and I do become good friends, though, and she dutifully comes to parties I have in my home, even though she doesn't like the dancing and is fairly indifferent to Jerzyk and his pals. She and I spend many hours in cafés alone, endlessly talking. In my mind, she has a level of anxiety that I find remarkably similar to some of the New Yorkers I had encountered. "Neurotic," a label used broadly and perhaps too inclusively back at UNIS, but Joanna surely fits the bill.

"I get so upset with my mother and father's pandering to my grandmother!" she explodes with indignation one day. Like in so many friends' homes, a widowed grandparent lives in the apartment with the younger family.

"They enrage me! I go to my room and close the door when they come home from work."

In most families, the presence of one or both grandparents is accepted without visible rancor. Indeed, the grandparents serve a useful role. They stand in line for foods. They cook meals and look after the young children while the parents work. It is not surprising that the "Polish grandmother" is a common term. You see her often on the streets, in the park, holding a child's hand, pushing a stroller, always available, always there to offer care, to advise. It is understood that, for better or for worse, she will step into this role. Most every young mother is employed. Babysitters are unheard of. And so, there is Babcia. In our family, Babcia and Dziadek are important to the unit. I surely remember when Babcia lived with us in New York. She was a great help then, and you could not say that she was ever in the way.

But intergenerational struggles plague some households, and irreconcilable differences are particularly noxious when these families are forced to share housing. The shortage of available apartment units in Warsaw remains pronounced, and you can rarely move out if your living situation is not to your liking. In that sense, my parents were lucky from the very beginning. When my mother moved to Warsaw to be with my father, they first shared a small apartment with my father's parents. That proved to be cataclysmic. My mother then, and even now, nearly twenty years later, cannot get along with her in-laws. From her comments, I surmise that they needle her every chance they get. Is it because she is only faintly Polish in her approach to family life? Do they resent the intrusion of the somewhat different social dynamic that she introduces into whatever home she enters? By all accounts, I understand my father's parents to be cantankerous, difficult people. Upon arrival from the United States in 1948, after a few months of living with his Polish-American girlfriend and his parents, my father appealed to the Foreign Ministry for his own space. Fortunately, he was granted a small, independent apartment. He and my mother quickly moved out of his family home. The move did not improve relations between my mother and his parents, but the physical separation enabled my parents to develop their social and family lives away from the penetrating gaze of my second set of grandparents.

Nina Lewandowska Camic

Helen and Bohdan,
married (1948)

Helen: arrived from
Washington to a
destroyed Warsaw
(1948)

Front: Nina, Babcia Lewandowska, Dziadek Haracz;
Back: Eliza, Helen, Babcia Haracz (1956)

Nina with Johnny, in Gniazdowo
(1957)

Nina, Eliza, in front of Palace of
Culture (1958)

Nina: nursery school photo day
(1957)

Nina and Eliza: nursery school
photo day (1958)

Class 1A, Elementary School no. 43; Nina with arm band of class monitor
for the week (1959)

The 36 students of class 1A, Elementary School no. 43;
Nina with arm band of class monitor for the week (1959)

Vacation in Bulgaria (1959)

Nina and Janek: holiday party
(1959)

Nina Lewandowska Camic

Eliza, Nina and a department store
St. Nicholas (1959)

Eliza, Dziadek Haracz, Nina: a
visist to Kamionka in southeast
Poland (1960)

Jerzyk, Eliza, Nina: in Zakopane (1960)

Eliza, Helen, Nina: sailing to New York, RMS Queen Elizabeth (1960)

Bohdan Lewandowski: Polish Ambassador to the United Nations
(1960 – 1966)

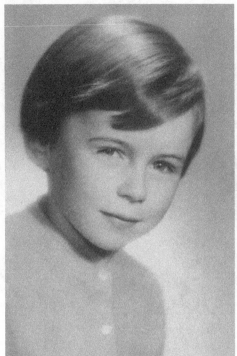

Nina: passport photo (1960)   Helen: a diplomat's wife (1961)

Nina in Bunk 1, Camp Robinson Crusoe (1961)

Eliza, Helen, Babcia Haracz, Nina: saying good bye to Babcia (1961)

Gniazdowo house, with finished additions (1965)

Helen, Nina, Babcia, Eliza in Gniazdowo (1968)

Jackie and Nina (1964)

Nina, strumming, as usual. Gniazdowo (1970)

Friend, Eliza, Helen, Nina in Sochi, Soviet Union (1968)

Babcia and Dziadek
Haracz (1971)

Jerzyk, Marcin (1969)

Nina: passport
photo (1971)

Apart from Joanna, who always remains just a little separated from the social groupings within class, my other classmates appear to be in stable, solid friendship circles. Some are larger, and some are smaller. Two girls sit up front in class, and I quickly learn that they are extremely ambitious and hardworking. Dorota speaks French fluently, and Malgosia is a dedicated chemist. I later learn that Malgosia's father is an old colleague and acquaintance of my parents and that Dorota's father works for the Polish government like mine. Though the two girls form a separate social unit, they are on friendly terms with the rest of the class. I see no animosity or bullying behavior among my classmates in all my time at the lycee. We have two rowdy boys named Leszek and Andrzej in the back, and they get low grades and smoke cigarettes after school. On one field trip, as we pile into a train compartment to sing songs, I ask them why they aren't joining us. In my mind, more singers would add to the fun. The tallest, lankiest boy and perhaps most noticeably disinclined to be prepared for class looks at me inquisitively, as if asking with his eyes, "Don't you know? We are not like that."

After a brief pause, he shakes his head and responds, "Ninka, I don't think so." I catch the word Ninka. Few people ever use it toward me. It is at once endearing and informal, and I wonder why I never once heard it at home. "We've long ago outgrown group singing during train rides, especially songs about Polish patriotism and politics."

Patriotism and politics? Do we sing about politics?

I have already learned that singing together during travel time is routine for Polish teenagers. We had done it during the Batory field trip, and my new Zmichowska class is inclined to group together and go through a range of ballads and folksongs when the opportunity presents itself. Marcin strums the guitar, and we sing. Much of it is old Polish music, romantic, from the battlefields of a war-torn nation. Then there are the gypsy ballads or the one I remember from Batory about Ukraine. So why do the boys of the back row mention politics? I think about the song we had just finished a minute ago: *"It was bad before, it'll be worse now, in Poland and elsewhere ..."* It's a song that mocks the deeply rooted Polish pessimism so ingrained that even young people recognize it as part of daily life here. You see it, and you sigh deeply.

Life has been harsh for Poles. A country that is a thousand years old, with a thousand years of battles, wars, cruel partitions, and most recently, unspeakable loss during the war. And now this! Whatever it is that we have in Poland at the moment causes the people to shake their heads in dismay. Or is it mock dismay? I can't tell.

But if a brooding pessimism has permeated every crevice of the Polish psyche now, this feeling of being always on the wrong side of history is something that I recognize more in my parents' generation than among my lycee friends. Jerzyk and his group of friends appear impervious to it all—the shame, the soul searching, the inevitability of suffering. And I feel drawn to the zest of these new friends, to their passion for camaraderie and adolescent fun.

Very soon, however, I begin to sense that not everyone is on the same page with respect to school, family, religion, politics. Joanna is cynical about school and people in general. Malgosia and Dorota, I learn, are politically engaged. They are best friends, even as they are ideological opposites. You can tell that they disagree, though not through their overt statements. Rather, it comes out in how they sidestep certain controversial topics. Sidestepping and reverting to indirect allusions is an art, and it's practiced by almost everyone I know here, but they are clearly adept at it at some higher level. Dorota is active in the Young Socialist Movement (ZMS). Malgosia is, as best as I can tell, scornful of such political activism. She is Jewish, and her father is going through the difficult process of deciding whether to leave Poland (her mother died of cancer a few years ago), a country facing a particularly intense period of anti-Semitism in the late 1960s. Ultimately, they choose to stay. Only decades later do I learn about how tough these years are for her. In my time at Zmichowska, I know nothing about their angst or indecision.

"You know Malgosia's family, don't you?" I ask my parents when she hints one day in school that her dad has mentioned my parents to her.

"Yes, we do." That's it. I hear no more on the subject. Decades later, I found out that Mr. Melchior had been instrumental in helping my mother get a supply of milk formula for her firstborn when there was a shortage in the stores. But if my parents' social contacts were intense and personal in the early years of their marriage, right now, they appear sporadic and fragmented. Neighbor visits. Her tea with Irena. His late-night talks with Mietek Rakowski. I have the impression that their past social circles have long dispersed.

On at least one occasion, Malgosia invites me to her house. She lives in an old apartment building with tall ceilings and a heavy wooden entrance door. The minute I enter the stairwell, I notice how quiet it is inside. The thick stone walls shut out the congestion and the tramcars that crisscross the nearby Plac Zbawiciela. I am a little intimidated by Malgosia and shy about the visit. She is one of the oldest in class and almost three years older than me. And she is the most serious about all aspects of school.

Her studious manner is, perhaps unfairly, announced to the world by the very thick glasses she is forced to wear. Her hair is cut short, but you can tell that it is thick and curly even as she appears to pay it no heed. She opens the door now, and I follow her inside. I enter a room that also serves as a hallway, much like we have in our Aleja Roz apartment. Like in my home, doors lead to several bedrooms from this room. And just like in our apartment, the doors are closed, though you can see enough through their milky rough glass panes to know if a light is on or off in that room. As we cross the hall, a door from a dimly lit room opens, and her father comes out to greet me. If Malgosia seems serious with her steady voice and almost adult mannerisms, her father appears even more so. One solitary wisp of hair falls halfway down his thinly wrinkled forehead. He is tall and looks as if he has just been interrupted from reading a terribly complicated set of documents.

"A pleasure to meet you. Please give my warmest regards to your parents." So, he knows about me. Malgosia must have talked of my visit, and now she doesn't have to offer introductions. I think about how little information I hand down to my parents about who is coming and who I am visiting on any given day. My parents never ask, and I rarely volunteer.

"I will, thank you," I say to him meekly, and I follow Malgosia to the kitchen, knowing that I will most likely say nothing about this visit to my preoccupied parents, and his greetings will never be conveyed. In the kitchen, she sets the kettle on the stove and pours me tea essence from the little teapot. We all use these small pots to brew strong tea essence, which we then dilute with hot water when we're ready for a cup of tea. Malgosia has an easy conversational manner, and she asks questions about the group of friends, Jerzyk's friends, that I have come to accept as my own.

"Who is your favorite?" she asks. I think about this. I'm really not close to any of the girls. We have met occasionally for tea, and conversations have been fleeting and inconsequential.

"I don't know. We do things as a group."

"Well, they're not my type. None of them," Malgosia tells me.

"Would you come to a party if I invited you and maybe Dorota too?""Sure. But I'm most certainly not interested in any of the boys. They're so much in their own world! Childish. Still, I'll come."

My group is candy, a confection, but not anything that touches her life in a significant way.

I am intrigued by Dorota's political activism. She and I share that we both have fathers who have made their careers in politics. My father is now at the Communist Party, and though I am never invited to see the inside of his office, I know where his windows are in the enormous, block-long building that houses the party headquarters in Warsaw. Initially, I am proud of him. What a relief! He's employed. He is in charge of the work of others. I'm proud that people appear to respect his talents. But with time, I sense that a shift has taken place. Whereas before, my father was the one who represented Poland in that great international forum, the United Nations, now he is patently part of "the system"—a system that most of my friends regard as being, at the very least, corrupt and dishonest. No one speaks of this or gives even a hint of any disdain. Perhaps my father's continued close ties to the United States cut him a break. Or it could be that a young person's deeply rooted respect for members of an older generation trumps feelings of distrust and disapproval. But even though none of my friends will ever say anything to my face about this, I understand that my father's work for the Central Committee of the Communist Party is thought by many to be a descent into a devil's playground. And yet, Dorota, who surely knows that there is at least some wisp of mockery directed at those who are members of the Communist Party and, by extension, toward members of such organizations as ZMS, has chosen to participate in this socialist youth group.

"What do you do in ZMS?" I ask Dorota after school one day. She is an outspoken girl—a hot redhead, we would say back in America. Her angular face is peppered with freckles, and she tosses her head for emphasis so that her long, full, strawberry blond ponytail swings viciously from one side to the next.

"We have meetings, and we get involved. We work on projects. We have discussions. You should join!"

"Maybe," I tell her. I miss political engagement of any sort. In New York, I had just started reading *The New York Times* and *Newsweek*, and I was captivated by the evening news. I had believed, in those days, that I wanted to be a journalist when I grew up. Tracking stories and pushing for interviews once seemed thrilling and intensely exciting. But in Warsaw, all that has changed. We sometimes watch the news program on TV, but we watch it differently. We make fun of a good portion of it. There is inevitably a news announcement about a factory or a company exceeding their production goals, and we smirk at this, and I'm sure most audiences do the same. It's a show, a spectacle. A portrayal of success that may or may not be accurate, but it most certainly does not translate into any improvement in the daily lives of most Poles, as marked by the presence or absence of consumer goods in stores. Why do we listen to this TV blather? We listen because important world events will be noted, even as local affairs will be presented in this intentionally biased fashion. In the Poland of today—the Poland that was wiped off the face of Europe—it was and is very important to find meaning between the lines. Truth is very elusive. It is not evident in the spoken or written word. You have to dig to get closer to it.

But this surely is not my first glimmer of a biased presentation of fact. In New York, I heard that communists killed babies and continued, even after Stalin, to send moneyed people to prison. On the other hand, in New York, these were hushed speculations. The stories on the news appeared to hold on to the pursuit of journalistic truth rather than the fabrication of convenient fiction. Still, I can't help but note the parallel. In Warsaw, I'm hearing the flipside of the American vision of world economies. If for Americans, communists took away your hard-earned cash. For Poles, capitalists robbed the poor to line their own greedy pockets with unfettered wealth. None of this surprises me. I'm getting hardened against the idea that facts are easily discernible, especially through the quick soundbite of the media.

"So you have discussions." I return to the topic of ZMS with Dorota a few days later.

"Come to our meeting," she repeats.

I consider her suggestion. I don't think of myself as being political, nor do I object to the ideology at the foundation of socialism. If asked about the downsides of communism in Poland, I'd probably retort that we don't have communism or even socialism at this point. We have a corrupt political system, a successful power grab by those who align themselves with the Soviet state because it is in their interest. I can imagine that socialism can proceed along a different path. It hasn't here in Poland, hamstrung by our neighbors to the east, but at least in theory, it could. A youth group where this can be sifted and sorted through spirited discussion appeals to me. And so I agree to stay after school with Dorota. The ZMS meeting is in one of the now-empty classrooms. Dorota is smart and sharp. The dozen or so other students are unknown to me. No one from my group of friends belongs. As the discussion turns to world events, I find myself perking up. This could be interesting! I sign up and become an official member of ZMS—the Socialist Youth Organization.

That evening, over an open-faced sandwich of bread and cheese, I break the silence at the kitchen table. "I joined ZMS."

"You did what?" It's as if I had announced I'm leaving home and never coming back. I notice a look of alarm on my mother's face.

"Yes, my friend Dorota and I went to a meeting. It was kind of interesting. Shouldn't I have joined?" I study my mother and father carefully. Both my parents belong to the Communist Party, though the move to join came at a different time and was surely motivated by a different impulse. Still, I know that, at least in theory, they are not opposed to principles of socialism. But to what extent does this translate into support for the Communist Party? I do know that my mother, especially in recent times, is deeply cynical at every mention of the party, but at the same time, she speaks with reverence about Dziadek's past work for the benefit of the labor movement in the United States. And if she scoffs at communism now, isn't it in part because she and my father are both scoffers and critics of much that I see as benign? This was the case in New York as well. I remember long car rides where my mother's stream of negative commentary would drift in waves to us in the rear of the car, much the same way as we listen to her now take pot-shots against the trivial and mundane during our car rides to and from Gnizadowo. Still, now I'm hearing something else.

"Sometimes it's difficult to un-join once you belong." My mother shakes her head as if to let everyone know that she can't quite fathom how anyone can be so impulsive.

"But I think I may like it!"

"Well, now. Good for you!" This comes from my father. He dismisses my mother's reaction. If I wanted to make him take note, I seem to have gone in the right direction. I know I've done something without full knowledge of what I did, and I'm not going to understand anything more by merely asking my parents about it.

And so I ask Jerzyk the next day. "Why doesn't anyone from our group of friends belong to ZMS?"

"Are you kidding me? We think it's a farce! It's for ambitious kids who want to get ahead. That's why they join! Did you know that Pani Zydkowicz (our Polish literature teacher) has a counter group going? She and a bunch of kids, including some of our friends, gather together at her house regularly to discuss politics. But I shouldn't tell you this. It's a secret."

I get it. The real conversations are taking place somewhere else. Not at my supper table, not at the ZMS meetings either. Soon after, I stop going to ZMS meetings. I explain to Dorota that I just haven't the time. She accepts my explanation with barely a shrug of her perky shoulders.

4.

Spring explodes with the freshness of new growth. Pussy willows and crocuses yield to pansies and forget-me-nots. By May, the landscape is lush with the young green colors of near summer. In the middle of the month, our homeroom teacher announces that there will be an overnight field trip. It's an escape from urban life, a chance to walk a dirt road and take in the fresh, sweet smells of a rural landscape. Jerzyk's mother is one of the organizers and chaperones.

We travel by public bus to the village of Hojnow and hike to a farmstead where we have been given the nod from a farmer to spread sleeping bags or blankets in his barn on the prickly hay. Farming families in Poland are cash-strapped and land-poor. If you fly over Poland, you see ribbons of farmland so thin and minuscule that you have to wonder if they could ever produce enough for anyone attempting to make a living there. It is no surprise that farmers are happy to pocket any additional money, including from a group of school kids wanting to secure a place to throw down their bags for the night.

The girls are to one side in the barn, the boys to the other. When the light fades, the girls trickle out in groups and pairs, and the boys follow less quietly. Someone has built a campfire. Marcin is there with his guitar and, as always, we sing.

During a lull, as Marcin picks randomly at the strings of his instrument, a girl looks pointedly at me and asks, "Can you sing an American song? Marcin can play for you. Or maybe you can play?"

I hesitate and look over at Marcin's guitar. He catches my glance. "Here, go ahead."

I'm not nearly as good with it as he is, but I do strum it a lot at home. What can I play for this group? Maybe "Donna Donna." That's a Joan Baez song. To me, she is an American legend. I begin the song

On a wagon, bound for market, there's a cow with a mournful eye,

High above him, there's a swallow, winging swiftly through the sky.

How the winds are laughing ...

The repetition in the refrain *"Donna, Donna, Donna, Donna"* is so close to the Polish folk lyric *"Dana Dana"* that many find themselves joining in. Encouraged, I continue.

Cows are easily bound and slaughtered, never knowing the reason why,

But whoever treasures freedom, like the swallow, has learned to fly ...

Donna, Donna ...

"What is it about?" someone asks. Not everyone studies English. Again I hesitate. Though I know the song well, I have never thought much about the lyrics. Suddenly they seem complicated. I offer the most basic translation. "It's about swallows who are better off than cows. Swallows know when to take flight."

"Very nice, Donna, Donna. You must write out the words for me," the same girl tells me. "Another one!"

They like "Where Have All the Flowers Gone" as well. I put down the guitar then.

"Can you dance American dances?" I don't know myself to blush, but I feel my cheeks grow hot when I hear the question. It's been one long year since my UNIS classmates and I partied to the beat of the Rolling Stones, jumping, waving arms, stomping rhythmically. In that year, I've let go of many memories of New York, but now, quite suddenly, here on this serene and remote meadow of rural Poland, a chance question opens the latchkey. I am flooded with images of my UNIS days, of the dance parties we were just beginning to host, of preadolescent crushes and flirtations—all of it as fiercely present before me, as if I were back in our New York apartment instead of watching the embers of a campfire spit and hiss and throw sparks into the night air.

"I can't do it without music. I need a beat." Someone picks up the guitar and uses it as a drum. I get up slowly, and I start to move. I dance as if I were dancing with Ashok or Michael. My Polish classmates are encouraging. Some of them clap along, and a few girls giggle at my exaggerated movements. I close my eyes, swing my arms, and jump fiercely from one foot to the next. Crazy and a little wild, dictated by nothing, constrained by no one. And I will come back to my American dancing again and again during the high school parties, even as most of my friends will continue to spin each other in rock and roll and dance in the more orderly way of two steps forward, one step back.

Dawn comes early in May in Poland. By four in the morning, the skies are picking up the hues of a cloudless day ahead. There is a faint rustle of leaves as a breeze passes through the wheat fields and nudges the leaves of poplar trees that grow to the side of the barn. I am awake, perhaps because there is another noise—scuffling and grunting just a few feet away. I look up and see Jerzyk. He is stealthily crouching where the girls are sleeping. The stealth ends as other boys join him, and they all swoop down on the sleeping girls and lift and carry a few to the wet grasses of the meadows, releasing them and releasing me into the morning dew. It's a prank, and I see that Jerzyk's mother is in on it because she is now standing to the side, arms folded, bosom heaving in laughter. She catches my eye and winks. I get it. I'm included because she nudged them in my direction. No matter. I'm included. The girls are squealing and giggling. I am too. Jerzyk carried my feet, and Marcin had grabbed me under my arms. And it is at that moment, dangling precariously from their grasp, that I have a flash of a new awareness: I am in love with Marcin.

At home, I tell Eliza. "I am in love."

"With whom? Jerzyk?"

"No, Marcin."

"Which one is that?" "He plays the guitar and wears the loose navy sweater. Short light brown hair, thin. Tells jokes and stories all the time."

She thinks about this for a minute. "Does he know?"

"No. I'm thinking that maybe he's interested in Grazyna. But I can't tell. And I have no idea what she thinks of him."

It is remarkable to me that in this tightly bonded circle of friends, none of them talk about or even mention feelings of attraction or love.

Eliza is mentally shuffling through the catalog of friends she has met during a party at our house. She is good at remembering people, and she is a good listener. She is the quiet one, while I am the one who will rush to blurt out my emergent feelings of love. Within the year, everyone will know about my infatuation with this boy—everyone except Marcin.

I prop a pillow on my bed against the wall as I settle in to tell Eliza about the field trip. My sister and I have always shared a bedroom. I like having her there, even though now, in our teens, we have to step gingerly to allow each other greater privacy. When a friend comes over, she will always leave the room, most often retreating to the kitchen to sit and do homework at the table there. Or she will go out for a walk.

(I will do the same if the visitor is one of her friends.)

In Poland, rules of polite conduct appear to be firm. My friend and I will have a brief conversation, but it has to be interrupted with an offer of food. For this, we retreat to the kitchen. It is in serving food that parents and even grandparents meet and greet the friends of their children or grandchildren. And very quickly, I realize that my parents are different. If, by chance, they pass through the kitchen when I am there feeding a friend, they will pause, but that's because the young visitor will have jumped up to greet them properly. The boys will kiss the back of my mother's hand and shake my father's hand. The girls may lightly curtsey. They'll wait then for the polite conversation, which, at my house, will never come. My father is wholly uncurious about my friends, and my mother is lost in her own world of people and problems. Perhaps she can be excused. She is stuck with the belief that teenagers do not want adults in their midst. When she was a teen in New York, that's how it was. My parents' social customs are a confused mixture of American-style habits, Polish circumstances, and personal predilections.

Both my parents appear to be stuck figuring out how much of their Polishness they want to reclaim. My mother is especially conflicted about this, and it seems to me that over time, she retreats more and more from feelings of Polishness rather than warming up to what life offers her here. When she and I are out hunting down food or looking for schools supplies, she works hard to demonstrate that she is not like the people she brushes against on the streets of Warsaw.

"If we stop in at the delicatessen on Marszalkowska Street, we can pick up some coffee for your father and maybe some honey cake for all of us," she'll say to me as we make our way back from an errand together. Inside the store, where the air is hushed, and the line is very long, she'll exclaim, in English, with the proper amount of exasperation, "Oh, just look at how inefficient the sales clerk is! Talking to her friend as if there wasn't a line waiting for her attention!" My mother is, of course, correct. The clerk is inattentive, indifferent, and insolent. And it is unlikely that she or anyone else could understand my mother's words. But those very Americanized words make a statement. They are audible and foreign. My mother does not want to blend with the snaking throng of Polish women in their heavy wool coats and their fur-lined caps and their empty nets, waiting, always waiting in line. She is one of them, but I know she feels far removed from them. She belongs elsewhere.

Over the years, both my parents' inattention to our social lives has become so pronounced that I like to joke that they do not really remember which school Eliza and I go to, let alone whom we encounter there. Nevertheless, both quickly pick up that I am smitten with Marcin. They can hear me talking on the phone about it to my friends. There are two telephones in the apartment. One is in what was to be the living room but now is my father's space, and the other is positioned centrally in the hallway. It's not easy to escape being overheard. I have long conversations with Joanna about what Marcin did at recess and what impact this had on me. He spoke to me. He didn't speak to me. He teased Grazyna. He teased me some. He teased me more! Do you think he knows? Surely he must know. "Nina, get off the phone already!" The phone is close to my mother's bedroom door, and my chatter disturbs her need for quiet.

As if long phone calls and endless speculations aren't enough, I am now immersed in journal writing. I began keeping a daily journal in UNIS days when I was just twelve. Now I add pages and pages in book after book, mostly on the subject of Marcin. I've thrown away adult journals, but I've kept my childhood ones, and it is remarkable how little information they contain beyond my endless annotations on Marcin's attention or, more often, inattention toward me.

I am not incorrect in thinking that Marcin favors another girl, Grazyna. She is undoubtedly pretty, with wide brown eyes and perfectly even, American-style white teeth. She is also very smart. Certainly one of the top students in the class. A grade grabber. But, too, she has a delicate voice and a girlish smile, and she wears her hair neatly teased, with a tiny flip of a ponytail in the back. Pani Zydkowicz, our literature teacher, muses out loud about her. "How is it that one person is bestowed so many gifts!" Grazyna smiles demurely. She knows how to do that too.

My parents have a very large collection of books. Many are biographies or historical accounts of political events. But my mother has also collected a fair share of paperback novels. I ask her to recommend some for me now. She pulls out *A Tree Grows in Brooklyn, American Tragedy, Marjorie Morningstar,* and *The Group.* These are my sources of information on relationships between men and women. I read them with a greedy appetite, and I worry that I'll eventually work through all the good books on her shelf. You cannot find American novels in Poland. Where will my education into adulthood come from then?

And still, I remain without great ideas on how to get closer to Marcin. The novels and the occasional American magazine don't address the nuance of relations between girls and boys in Poland. And because girls here are less eager to reveal their emotional worlds to each other, I can only guess from what meager signals I pick up around me. Are Marcin and Grazyna a couple? I cannot tell. On some days, but not very often, Marcin walks Grazyna home. She lives close to me, and when I see them walking side by side, my world crumbles, and I fall into deep gloom. I go home, pick up my guitar, and strum it for hours, homework untouched, chores left undone.

"Nina, take out the trash," my mother tells me. Taking out the trash is a real bother. Eliza and I alternate weeks. The person on trash duty has to take the bin down to the courtyard, empty it into the receptacles and then line the bin with old newspapers back in the apartment.

"It's not full yet. Eliza lets it fill up much higher before she goes down with it." I push on the waste to demonstrate how much space remains.

My mother leaves the kitchen, visibly annoyed. My father ignores the exchange.

I go back to guitar strumming.

On other days, Marcin will completely snub Grazyna and spend time talking to other classmates after school. If I am included in his demonstration of friendliness, I am overjoyed, and I think hard about what I did to warrant this trickle of attention.

My constant mood swings are mostly private. Eliza has taken to spending a lot of time outside our home. She never invites anyone to our house, and I know next to nothing about her set of friends. The house is eerily quiet. My parents stay in their rooms, and long months pass when neither one speaks a single word to the other. This gross silence between them spills over, perhaps inadvertently, into silence toward my sister and me. A triggering event between them often starts a fresh period of shuttered communication.

My mother will complain that my father drank too much at the rare social gathering that they will have attended. Most likely, she is not incorrect. My father does drink excessively, and his behavior quickly changes when he consumes alcohol. He slurs words, and his eyes appear watery and unfocused. I would agree that it's not a change for the better. We remember this from our years in New York. But my mother has now lost interest in discourse with him on this or any other serious topic, and after an evening of what she sees as an embarrassingly high level of drinking, she lapses into a tough-as-nails silence that envelops the entire household. There will be many consecutive months when she will not speak to anyone at home, and my father will not try to break the cavernous quiet.

———

How do you run a household in total silence? How are decisions made and problems solved? We live behind closed doors. I never hear my parents argue. I never hear them discuss anything at all. They have entered a phase in their marriage that does not include words. In subsequent decades, as the chasm in their relationship widens, the words come back, both spoken and written, and they are harsh and full of accusation. Much later, my mother hands me a thick folder of letters between them, written when my father eventually resumes work-related travel to the United States. Hers are filled with bitter snipes at his enduring preference for political discourse with his friends over family life ("to understate a fact, neither your family nor buddies added to my joy of life, so forgive my lack of enthusiasm on their behalf …"). His letters are long and certainly equally unsatisfying. In reading their back and forth, I also pick up on the disenchantment that my father has now, after his time at the UN. If in the decades after the war, he took pride in Poland's postwar reconstruction and in his role in that effort, decades later, he entered a survival mode. He worked out of duty and to pay the bills. In response to a particularly accusatory letter from my mother, he seemed incapable of and disinterested in fixing anything satisfying at home or in his line of work. And he is filled with regret about his chosen profession. "I wish ... that I could start my life again and not to ... be entangled in what is called rightly in derogatory sense bureaucratic work or, in more sophisticated terms, executive responsibilities.... I'd rather be an actor, a painter, a writer, a musician, even a doctor, but not a bureaucrat."

Chapter 6

1.

Marcin, now my friend, if not my boyfriend, joins me on my path home after school. The weather is brilliantly sunny and warm, a spring gift. He suggests we take a detour through the Royal Park Lazienki, Warsaw's treasured green space. It's a labyrinth of grand avenues and winding paths shaded by European ash, larch, poplar, and a dozen other species, many growing here for one or even two hundred years, offering a respite from city chaos. The park unfolds at the street level, then continues down a hill toward a carefully reconstructed summer palace that stands serenely next to a small lake home to flocks of swans and ducks. The alleys and pathways are so densely plotted that even a native of Warsaw can get momentarily lost, distracted by a red squirrel, a peacock, or a swarm of yellow finches. Walking through a park is a common way for friends to socialize in Warsaw, especially on fine weather days. I'm happy that I happen to be Marcin's walking companion today.

"A small group of us is going to the movies tomorrow. *Oliver* is playing. Want to come? And my parents will be there. Maybe yours can join us too?"

"No, not them. Actually, they're not speaking to each other." That's an easy excuse. I do not say that neither parent would want to go to the movies with my friends and their families, even if they were on speaking terms. That Polish social contract, where your friends know your parents and their parents know you and your entire family, is not something they have ever felt compelled to take on.

"Why? Did they argue?"

"I actually don't know this time. She's mad at him. He just lets this go on for as long as she needs to be silent."

"Can't you facilitate them coming together?"

"How?" I do not like the direction of this conversation. I try to avoid my parents when they are in their silent phase.

"Ask him if he would speak to her, and then ask her to talk to him."

I would shrug this off as an unworkable idea, but the suggestion comes from Marcin, and painful as it may be, I am willing to follow his plan of attack.

I take a breath and enter the living room—my father's room now. "Daddy, would you talk to Mom if she talked to you?"

He looks at me over the newspaper. "Why do you ask?' There is a pause. "I suppose I would." There is no anger or dismay in his voice. It's as if he were evaluating going out to get a loaf of bread.

"So, if she came in, would you listen to her?"

"I don't see her coming in." He goes back to the paper.

I knock on her door. "Mom ..."

"What is it?" She looks preoccupied. Harried. If he showed little emotion, her voice is tinged with annoyance.

"No, never mind." I leave.

Marcin asks me the next day. "Did you talk to them?"

"It didn't work."

"I can't believe that!"

"Well, it's true."

"At home, we talk about everything! We sit down, and everyone expresses their view, and we come to resolutions."

I'm silent. Marcin seems to me to be always content with his situation. It's as if he lives by a deck of cards that always turn up kings and queens and aces. It becomes hard for me to explain that what happens at home is beyond my control.

Family movie outings, so common in the last years of our stay in New York, ended with our return to Poland. Indeed, we no longer go to concerts, the theater, or musical events as a foursome. Willingly or grudgingly, our friends move seamlessly between socializing with friends and attending family events. Eliza and I have only the occasional overnight trips to the village. In Warsaw, we are left entirely to our own devices.

2.

One evening, during that first spring after our return, my father comes home with a small piece of news. Eliza and I are in the kitchen, trying to decide which pastries to attack. My mother has placed cardboard trays of baked goods from our local bakery on the counter, and we're eyeing both the apple cake and the poppyseed roll as possible substitutes for a more conventional supper. My father is clearing his throat, but we ignore him. His years of smoking must have done their damage because he is forever grunting, coughing, or clearing his throat. This time, however, he wants our attention. "Hey!" he says rather loudly, looking directly at us. We turn around, surprised. "I have a piece of news that I think you will like." What he says then completely stuns us. The Rolling Stones are coming to Poland. They will be giving a concert in Warsaw.

"For real? The Stones are coming to Poland?" No popular rock group from the West has ever traveled to an Eastern Bloc country. It's exhilarating to learn this, even for a diehard Beatles fan.

"Can you get tickets?"

"I already have them. Three, in fact. You can invite a friend."

The concert is at the Palace of Culture in the Congress Hall. To me, it seems a funny choice of venue. With nearly three thousand red plush seats, the hall is more suitable for a parliamentary session than a rock concert, particularly one with the Stones, who are anything but staid by 1967 standards. And who should we invite? I do not feel especially close to any of the girls in my social group. Eliza, too, hesitates in sharing this event with a classmate. In the end, we decide to invite Joanna, my seatmate in school.

"Are they good tickets?" I ask my father when he brings them home.
"Third row."

It is not hard to figure out why he has them. They came as a perk of working for the Communist Party. His job of overseeing relations between international organizations and the party makes him an especially good candidate for this handout. But is the privilege of securing comp tickets specific just to Poland? I remember how my friend at UNIS secured for me an invitation to participate in a children's TV game show because her father was high up in CBS.

On occasion, my parents would go to a Broadway show or a Metropolitan Opera performance because they were on friendly terms with the publishers of *The New York Times*, who, in turn, had access to all the hard to get shows and musical events in the city. And now my father brings home tickets to the Rolling Stones because he is high up in government foreign relations. Still, if your parents' work mattered in the allocation of perks and prizes in America, in Poland, your place of work determines so much more, from vacation options to apartment choices, and now I see that it matters, too, in the allocation of prized concert tickets.

I'm very excited to see how the concert will unfold. I have never been to a rock concert, not here nor in the United States, but I remember the impact the Beatles had on the audience when the group first traveled to New York. Wild, screaming mobs packed every place they went. On the day of the Stones concert, a cold and wet April Thursday, I purchase a small bouquet of violets. I'm still thirteen, the same thirteen that I was nine months ago when I traveled from New York to Poland one final time. On an impulse that surely is a sign of my very young age, I scribble a note and attach it to the flowers. Maybe the Rolling Stones want to meet their Polish fans, especially English-speaking ones. I explain in the note that I am an English-speaking Polish fan. "Here's my phone number, in case you want to call."

We come to the concert early, with plenty of time for the preshow—a Polish group of little significance here, let alone abroad. The audience is dignified. Respectful. And then, quite suddenly, the Rolling Stones thunder onto the stage. Their sound is tremendous—ten times that of the previous group, as they blast into their hit song, "Satisfaction." *And I try, and I try, and I try, and I try! I Can't get no! Pah pah pah! Satisfaction! Pah, pah, pah pah pah!* Polite applause follows. Someone whistles loudly, and there is laughter. The Stones continue. And now comes their current hit, "Ruby Tuesday"—a real tear-jerker, at least to this one young fan in the third row. Eliza is waving her arms, singing along. Joanna gets up, sits down, gets up, sits down. A number of men in the audience take off their jackets and circle them above, like flags in the air. It is, overall, an orderly crowd, but there isn't a doubt that everyone is engaged.

The concert is over. I throw my flowers on the stage and spend the next three hours at home hoping that maybe the phone will ring.

Many years later, I read that tickets for this concert were distributed primarily to Communist Party officials. Few, if any, were made available to the public. The tickets came with instructions to behave in a dignified manner. We never received such directives from my father. Maybe his imagination could not contemplate anything but good conduct on the part of his daughters. Or maybe my father simply could not bring himself to pass such directives on to us.

3.

It's the summer of 1967. A year has passed since my return to Warsaw. I know that I'm rapidly losing my connection to my New York life. I learn that Jackie, my UNIS friend, will not be visiting me this year as planned. Her mother writes to explain that the trip is too complicated. I shrug my shoulders. I'm sure it's the Poland factor. It scares people to travel here. It was fine, for some, to mix with communist kids on the safe grounds of a New York school. Even as Jackie is now freshly fourteen years old, sending your child to Poland is another story. I think that maybe it's just as well. The expectation had been that Jackie would spend the summer with me in Gniazdowo. But what could I do with a friend who is used to Flushing, Queens, here in this remote village of rural Poland?

As Eliza and I get ready for our summer with Babcia and Dziadek, I get a happy twinge of relief at leaving Warsaw. I'm hoping that a summer without Marcin will cure me of my growing infatuation with him. I recognize the wasted hours strumming guitar chords even as I continue to strum, pluck, and wait for a call, a visit, an acknowledgment that he likes me.

June arrives and the city parks explode with color. In good years, this is one of the most beautiful months. The air can be balmy and warm. The markets begin to reflect the growing season's early harvest: lettuce, radishes, fraises de bois, sour cherries, and rhubarb. On the streets of Warsaw, old women set up their selling stations. They come in from the villages on buses and trains to sell spring flowers alongside their usual eggs, white cheese, and butter. June can also be wet, cold, and decidedly unpleasant. But this year, we're having a sweet and fragrant early summer in the city. A heady time of blooming chestnuts and lilacs. Nonetheless, Eliza and I are glad to be leaving Warsaw.

We are not alone in abandoning a city home for refuge in the country. Eliza and I have made a number of friends in the village over the years, though not with the children of the farm families who live in the area year-round. Rather, we have met a handful of urban kids who come to stay with their rural grandparents or with families who take in children for school vacation. There is a clear distinction in our village. You're a local kid or a townie. Socially, there is no crossing over from one set to the other. In fact, we don't even see the local kids much. They don't play in the forests and meadows like we do. If we do see a village child in the meadow, it's because they will be sitting herding a handful of black and white cows there. If the cow ventures into a segment of the meadow that puts her too close to the cultivated fields or private fencing, the child will use a twig or whip to get her back on the meadow grasses. Otherwise, the village child will sit alone, without amusement or distraction. If we walk by, the child's eyes will follow our movement. When we get older, a modicum of politeness sets in. We say good morning, and the child will often respond with a good morning. No other words are exchanged.

The vacationing kids that do become our friends are from all over

Poland. Across the road from us, an older woman boards children from Lodz, the city where her own granddaughter lives. Her house always has at least a half dozen children of various ages. It becomes a ritual to walk over at the beginning of summer to see who is there and greet the kids we know from previous years. We spend nearly every summer day in their company. High on the list of favorite activities is a walk to the riverbanks for swimming and spreading towels on the sandbars. On more ambitious days, we take hikes to the larger villages with a grocery store or an ice cream stand. On rainy days, we paint with watercolors and draw together. Like in Warsaw, we are unsupervised. We have an evening curfew and are expected to be home for lunch and supper, but otherwise, we are free to roam and ride our bikes and follow our own ideas of where to go and what to do.

But we are not free to bring the pack of kids home to Babcia and Dziadek's house or yard. Babcia has a reputation in the village for being strict about hygiene and fussy about everything else. Most certainly, she is not very welcoming of anyone who is not family. She is suspicious of the children of strangers. And, more generally, she would prefer that the rooms of her house remain as spotlessly clean as she likes them to be. When we were little, Eliza and I were not permitted to play during the day in our bedrooms. These rules have been relaxed now, but we know that noisy, dirty kids disturb her sense of order, so we spend most of our time leaving her house and yard to play with our friends elsewhere.

And, perhaps predictably, we get into trouble. Initially, when we are still young adolescents, it is small trouble. After supper, we are out on the meadow, passing a volleyball in a circle. The evening is soft and mellow. We watch the sun set behind the pine forest to the west of the field. The river picks up some of the colors of a pink and orange sky. As dusk settles in, one of the older children suggests a campfire. We hesitate, though not because this is a forbidden activity. Most of our guardians and grandparents permit it, so long as they are notified. The meadow is long and wide, stretching all the way to the riverbanks, and there is little danger that the fire will spread or cause damage. On this particular evening, most of the younger kids, who have earlier curfews, are no longer with us. The hesitation is there because a fire requires work. But as darkness sets in, we grow more enthusiastic. Evenings can be chilly. A fire would be a wonderful way to prolong our time together on the meadow. We spread out and collect brush in the nearby forest and have a nice blaze going within an hour.

"Should we bake potatoes?" someone asks. If you bury them in the embers, the smaller potatoes will be done by the time the fire has run its course. We go to the fields at the meadow's edge, where local farmers grow their crops. Poking in the dirt produces a nice batch of young potatoes, and we gather enough for the seven or eight of us. We don't notice the flashlight until it's too late. Hearing our voices in the fields, the farmer saunters over with his torch.

"Get out of my field, you cholera-ridden shitheads!" he is shouting, using the most common Polish curse words. "Who is there? Who is digging up my potatoes?" His light hits my face, and I know he recognizes me.

"I'm sorry, I'm sorry. It's just a few. We'll pay. We just took a couple." It is, in fact, a small amount. Pennies' worth. But, they are his potatoes, and there's no denying it. We are guilty of stealing them.

As a kid, I was not a real troublemaker. I am often reminded that I misbehaved in fifth-grade music class, but apart from that, breaking the rules knowingly and purposefully was, for me, a rare event. But not a never event. I remember pocketing pieces of hard candy from Woolworth's a handful of times. And now this, the stealing of potatoes. I know Dziadek will be disappointed.

The next morning, news of the potato rifling travels back to my grandparents. Dziadek looks at me with a hard but not unkind gaze. He's not angry. But nor is he indifferent to what happened.

"Maybe you should stay home in the evenings for a while. And please, go back to the farmer and give him some money."

Nothing more is said about the event. I don't think my mother and father are ever told of it. In future summers, kids continue to steal potatoes for campfires. But I cannot. I violate rules, I break curfews, but I cannot go to the fields anymore. Dziadek is getting old. Often, he is bedridden, and I see him only fleetingly if the bedroom door is open. I cannot do something that I know he thinks is wrong.

Evenings are quieter for us after the potato incident. Since Eliza and I stay home now after supper, we have to amuse ourselves without the company of other children. When the light fades and dusk takes hold, Babcia finishes her kitchen work and often comes outside. There is a bench just by the front door, next to an old wooden table. During the day, she transacts her affairs with villagers here. If someone brings cheese or eggs to her house, she'll go through the purchase at the wooden table rather than inviting the farmer or the farmer's child inside. In the evening, she sits on the bench and looks out on the quiet dirt road. She wears dentures, and now and then, I can see her face muscles working to clear some bit of food sticking in her mouth. It's a habit that I hear my mother replicate, even though my mother has terrific teeth—probably the best of us. I come over and sit next to Babcia now.

We watch as two village girls come to the gate. They're moving from house to house, hoping that someone will buy the wild blueberries they had picked that day. The berries are in a bucket, and Babcia asks them to put it on the bench so that she can inspect them more closely. The older girl lifts the bucket and stands back. Babcia runs her fingers over a few berries. She reaches into her apron pocket, takes out a leather pouch with money. She picks up the bucket deftly and pours all the berries into a white enamel basin that she keeps by the well at the side of the house. She doesn't say a lot, just "How much?" The girl mumbles a hopeful price, and Babcia hands over the exact amount. Both girls are delighted to be rid of all the berries. They thank her and saunter off.

"I can make blueberry juice from these. Pierogi, too," Babcia says. We sit on the bench together and pick through the berries, looking for green ones, leaves, and forest debris that would have fallen from the bushes. This is a rare time that I remember having Babcia to myself. It is, therefore, the perfect time for me to ask the questions that I have about her. How was it to raise kids in Poland, then the United States? After all those years away in the big urban centers across the ocean, how was it to travel back here? "Babciu?" I start. She looks up at me and waits. I'm too shy to continue. "It's a nice evening," I say, returning to the berries, picking out one leaf, then another.

4.

In August, my parents drive to the village to pick us up for a two-week family vacation in the Polish Tatra Mountains. We'll be staying at Antalowka, a guest house perched on a hillside at the edge of Poland's popular mountain resort of Zakopane. I know the two of them have stayed there during previous summers when they would take their vacation weeks without us. This year, however, they include us on their trip.

Antalowka is a vacation place for families of government employees. Dom URM (Urzad Rady Ministrow), or Guesthouse for the Council of Ministers in English. The place reminds me just a little of American motels—a long, two-story structure with a row of windows looking out on the mountains in the distance. It's a clean and comfortable guesthouse. Eliza and I share a room, and my parents share another. Is Antalowka better than the other vacation places in Zakopane? It looks modern and well-tended, even as the conventional wisdom has it that miners stay at the best vacation resorts. Writers and artists have their own houses, and these are often the most coveted for the enviable quiet and the atmosphere of a literary culture. As if by staying there, you could reassure yourself that you have succeeded in your writings or your art. In his later years, my father will stay in Zakopane's guest house for writers even though I've never known him to write, at least not anything that would be published or widely disseminated. A friend arranges an invitation for him, and from then on, at first alone and then with his girlfriend, he returns to the writers' house, again and again, never looking back at places and people that filled his life while he worked for the Polish government.

I come to love Antalowka. And surprisingly, both of my parents appear to be pleased to be there too. *It's just like Howard Johnson,* I think to myself. We eat all our meals at the guest house. Everyone eats the same food, and for Eliza and me, it is a rare encounter with real Polish cooking. Sausage, cheeses, brown bread for breakfast. Milk soup again! I haven't had that since nursery school! Soft boiled eggs scooped out into a glass. Tea. For lunch and dinner, there is always soup: sorrel soup, mushroom soup, beet soup. Meat sometimes, though not very

Nina Lewandowska Camic

often, and never beef. Pierogi other days. Chicken. Dry, ubiquitous, no-thank-you-pork. My father is pleased. He was raised on these foods, and at Antalowka, he eats everything that's put before him. At home or at Babcia's, he'll fuss about the skin that forms on his milky tea and push away foods that he claims are too starchy, but he seems not to mind here. My mother, Eliza, and I are pickier. We eat things that we think of as good foods similar to what we would have had in the United States. Yes to a piece of bread with farmer's cheese (so much like cottage cheese!). No to beet and horseradish relish on slices of pork. Not too much sausage, please. We push away the cubes of lard from the pierogi and spoon off the cream and sugar from blintzes.

"Too fattening," my mother comments as a plate with fried cutlet is placed before her. I don't know my mother to be a fussy eater, but here she appears to have strong preferences. Perhaps it's because the food is so very Polish. Nothing like what she is used to preparing at home. Our meals in Warsaw are simple. No one fusses when it is my turn to cook. It is a meat and potatoes diet, but the meat is more likely to be boiled chicken or baked veal from the village, and the potatoes are boiled and left naked. None of the richer Polish foods like noodles with butter, blintzes with heavy cream or sour cream, potato dumplings with more sour cream, or soups with even more cream make an appearance in our kitchen. We stick with the cooked meats and potatoes, followed by or sometimes substituted with cakes. Plenty of sweet, baked goods from Gajewski, the pastry shop around the corner. My mother's favorites are cheesecake and apple cake, but she almost always gets a little paper tray loaded with other cakes, too. Poppyseed squares. Polish doughnuts—fried balls of dough filled with rose or plum jam and dipped in a glaze. And invariably, Eliza and I eat all of these, often in one sitting.

"We need to even out the edges," Eliza will say, taking a knife and a fork to the cheesecake.

"I'll help." We sit at the kitchen table and break off pieces of cake until we can eat no more. We'll skip dinner then, feeling bloated and too full of sweet cakes to take out the pot of boiled meat and potatoes.

Neither Eliza nor I ever grow plump from our poor eating habits. Perhaps we are too active. And, unlike in the United States, eating snack foods in front of the TV is not a Polish habit. In this way, we are quite like our Polish friends. Television is minimally interesting and therefore rarely turned on. Ours stands in the corner of the hallway. A few wicker chairs can be pulled up to accommodate us for the rare show we may want to catch, like *Bonanza*. It's usually a voiced-over American series or some other mildly amusing older program. Sometimes, we'll turn on the news. And after, it is not uncommon for us to go out for an evening walk with a friend or, in my case, to retire to the bedroom and strum the guitar, waiting for the phone to ring.

In Zakopane, we spend the time between meals on hikes at the base of the mountains. This is not strenuous mountain climbing. My parents prefer the steady pace of a walk without great elevation. Eliza and I often join them, walking behind or in front, keeping to a steady stride without pause. We are like a marching foursome. Here they go, the Lewandowski family! Two in front, two in back.

Though Eliza and I eat and hike together with our parents, anyone looking our way would say we are a quiet bunch. And we don't throw others into our mix. My parents never socialize with the other guests at Antalowka. They walk briskly through the reception area and head straight for their room. I have the impression that they don't know most of the people there and would like to keep a distance from them all. Is it that meeting people who are so utterly Polish has become a chore for my mother? Or is it that my parents have chosen a more reclusive lifestyle since returning from New York? After all, it isn't only in Zakopane that they shy away from meeting people or from socializing together, as a couple, with friends. In New York, their schedule was full and included a significant number of dinners, receptions and, for my mother, the so-called "ladies luncheons." However, their dinner entertainment dwindles to no more than two or three a year in Poland. No one drops over for tea and cakes or a more informal meal with the family.

The rare evening dinner party they host is an orchestrated, planned affair, and I have the impression that it is something that they approach mechanically and without great enthusiasm. My mother asked me to help serve the food and clean up afterward. "I'll pay you for the evening," she tells me. I don't need the money. There's not much that

I want to buy in Warsaw shops, but I readily agree to help anyway. I find these evenings to be an interesting departure from the usual quiet of our home. The food preparation isn't complicated, but great care is taken with the table setting. The silverware is polished, antique plates bought at New York auctions are set at a table that stands in my mother's bedroom and that she uses during the day for her editing work. It is somewhat odd to watch guests move halfway through the evening from his bedroom, which also has the more formal living room furniture, to hers, where the dining table is set and waiting. At the end, they retreat to his again for coffee and after-dinner drinks. It's as if they're moving between my parents, never quite connecting one with the other.

My mother does also have a handful of friends, mostly wives of men who were in professional contact with my father, but when she sees them, it is rarely in our house. Quite possibly, she continues to see Jozef on the side. My father's extramarital romantic interests, if they exist, are never fully disclosed to me. I learn more than I ever want to know later in life about his strings of affairs, but it is my impression that this period is romantically quiet for him. He concentrates his social time on meetings with Mietek Rakowski, the editor of the quite popular Polish weekly *Polityka*, even as my mother is not especially keen on having him at the house either.

"You talk to him for hours. You won't stop. It's as if you can't live without spilling your guts to him," she'll say with a frown. I sense that she feels excluded. My father looks blankly at her and says nothing. Eventually, he moves his discussions with Mietek outside our home. It's as if neither parent can imagine that our apartment is a place where their friends are welcome.

Though few of my parents' friends indeed stop by for a visit, there are two occasions where Eliza and I do find ourselves in the thick of our parents' social life. Both are unusual in that they aren't with people we know or would consider as close family friends. Nor do they take place in our home. The first is a Sunday outing to Jablonna, and the second follows shortly after. We are all invited to spend a weekend in Natolin. Both places are historical landmarks, and both are used now for government functions. Jablonna is mainly appropriated by the Polish Academy of Sciences, and Natolin is a compound where, when he is not in Warsaw, the prime minister of Poland lives. Both invitations come from the prime minister himself. Does my father understand that this man is having a sexual romp with my mother? And that the invitations may reflect Mr. Cyrankiewicz's attempt to get a greater foothold into her private life? Most likely, my father, like Eliza and I, simply believes that his past diplomatic life is behind the invitations.

Though you could argue that my father's position has fallen from that of an ambassador to a bureaucrat in the not altogether popular communist government, nonetheless, his United Nations stint seems to have bequeathed upon him, at least in his mind and perhaps in my mother's imagination as well, a lifelong elite status. I don't know this, but in these years, he is already scheming a return to the UN, and he will succeed. In the 1970s, he will be returning to work for the United Nations, this time as under-secretary-general. For now, he keeps the title of Ambassador. And he likes it!

Even when he is unemployed, and even when he will have been long retired from any work, he'll never fail to suck any last advantage out of his former ambassadorship. "I am calling to make a dinner reservation for Ambassador Lewandowski," he will say into the phone. He is never embarrassed by the obviousness of this ploy for stature, even as it seems like such an embarrassing brag to Eliza and me.

The Jablonna invitation includes a meal and a chance to horseback ride at the stables there, and I am excited by this possibility. It turns out not to be a long ride but several rounds of bareback in a circle, but I love my memories of horseback riding at the YMCA camp in New Jersey we attended during our last American summer. The smell of a horse, the rhythmic movement of strong muscle next to my small frame feels heavenly now.

"Can we go back to Jablonna?" I ask my mother after our day there.

"You liked it?" she asks with genuine curiosity.

"I did!"

"We'll see."

But we never do return there, and I am left wondering if it is because my parents have fallen out of favor with whoever invited them in the

Nina Lewandowska Camic

first place or because they never really were intimately connected, and the invitation was a chance event. Or, is it perhaps that they are slowly falling out of favor with each other and lock themselves away from any occasion to do something pleasurable together?

My mother tells me many decades later: "Jozef invited us those two times so that he could show me how good he was with children. He so wanted to convince me that he and I could be together!" Is it true? I surely didn't know this at the time, even though everyone in Warsaw talked about how our prime minister, married man that he was, had a keen eye for women.

The second outing, to Natolin, is a significantly bigger event. Once again, Prime Minister Jozef Cyrankiewicz includes our family on his list of weekend guests there. And again, I am slightly curious as to why we should be invited. When I ask, I am told that the invitation comes to us because we are "friends of friends" of the prime minister. This is how it is. You know someone who knows someone, and then suddenly, you are on that person's list of invitees.

As my father drives the short distance home at the end of the Natolin weekend, I sit back in the car and try to bring up one good memory from our time at the compound. I cannot. The weekend was exceedingly dull. Eliza and I had stayed to the side as our parents mingled with other people whose faces were as meaningless to us as ours were to them. It is the weekend when I get rid of any last vestige of admiration for government luminaries.

For many decades after, my father and mother will refer to the famous people who filter in and out of their lives. Name-dropping is like a hobby with them. They think nothing of it, probably because most of their friends and acquaintances share in this conversational habit. I grow indifferent and often outright hostile to talk of politicians and government leaders. Even as my childhood proceeds in the shadow of my father's political career, I come to regard talk of famous acquaintances as terribly depressing. As if you can do no better in life than to get close to people whose prominence you hope somehow will reflect on what you have accomplished. Anticipating our weekend in Natolin is the last time I remember being excited about coming face to face with someone with political clout.

Even though my parents appear for the most part to be retreating from a social life, during our mountain vacation in Zakopane, they do once (and only once) decide that we should pay a social visit to the Rodzinskis, friends of theirs who have a summer home nearby. It's a pretty place, styled in the manner of a small mountain chalet. Mr. Rodzinski is, like my father once was, part of the foreign service. He and his wife have known my parents for decades. They, too, have two daughters, both just slightly older than Eliza and me. We spend a quiet hour at their house, as my parents talk lightly of various people they know in common. After the visit, I ask my mother if the Rodzinskis take all their vacations in the remote mountain cottage.

"Probably. They like nature, and they like quiet. And they're always doing things together as a foursome. It's odd. Girls that age should have their own friends!"

I accept my mother's definition of the oddity of being a close-knit family. I cannot imagine being without my friends. I cannot imagine being that close to my mother and father.

If there is a message that my mother wants to convey during our adolescent years, it is that message of independence. "I want you girls to be independent!" she'll say repeatedly. Well, that's great! It means making my own decisions, choosing what I do, what I eat, where I go, and choosing to play the guitar on my bed, day in and day out, thinking despondently about Marcin.

5.

It is September 1967, and I enter the tenth grade. My mother continues to edit texts in translation at Interpress, and my father remains in his position at KC (Komitet Centralny) or the Central Committee of the Polish United Workers Party, Poland's dominant political party that will remain in power until 1990. My sister is entering eleventh grade and her last year of high school.

As I walk to school on that first day of the new academic year, I think about how tightly integrated I was into the social fabric of the class back in June. Will it change now, after a two and a half month break? School friends went their separate ways in the summer months, dispersed under arrangements made by parents. In truth, I had no idea where most of them had gone. My grandparents' village home has electricity now, but there is no phone line. My sister and I were completely cut off from our Warsaw friends.

But as I step into the hallway of my school building, I am at once in the thick of a social frenzy that I recognize as being not unlike the one I had left in June. Nothing has changed. And there is another element in my life that remains unchanged. The minute I see Marcin, my insides flip over and back again. He greets me with his usual easy grin and speaks enthusiastically about a summer kayak trip he had taken with his family. His cheeks are flushed, and his hair, freshly cut for school, has taken on tones of dusty hay. Damn it! I am completely weak from being near him now. A couple of months away did absolutely nothing to steady me.

I am now fourteen years old, and my classmates are upwards of sixteen. Despite the age difference, we intend to build a rich social life for ourselves. Are we unusual in this? On the one hand, I know that friends also mattered to me at UNIS. My childhood diaries are full of anecdotes about who did what to whom. But now, in Poland, the intensity of social life accelerates, and I have a feeling it's not just because we are that much older. Banding together in social groups is all that we have. Organized extracurricular activities are missing here. Stores and shopping are not real options either. We have little spending money, and there isn't much you'd want to buy anyway. If you're hunting for a coveted pair of jeans or a record album, your best bet is to have a friend or relative abroad who'll think of you and shop for you there. Polish stores offer none of these things. And eating out, which is so common in America, is another empty choice here. The few restaurants here seem to be reserved for foreigners who come to Warsaw as tourists. That's my guess. I really don't know, as we never go to one. A Pole's time away from school or work is wholly devoted to time with family and friends in these years. People thrive on hosting gatherings in cramped apartments, with clever foods prepared with scant ingredients and plenty to drink at later ages. We banter, with men often taking the lead in this. We take walks together, and we visit coffee shops. We are not a quiet nation. Animated conversations abound. In my social circle, boys try hard to outwit each other. Girls are often the listeners, though not necessarily deferential listeners. If the story isn't clever enough, they'll shrug and retreat into their own gossip sessions. We are a band of giddy adolescents, in love with laughter and camaraderie, seemingly oblivious to the political reality we find ourselves in.

———

In early October, our class is going on a three-day hiking trip to the highlands. We're taking the overnight train south, and we'll be climbing all day until we reach one of the public shelters at the mountain ridge. Though I have never really climbed mountains, I think of myself as being athletic. I'm enthusiastic about the hike.

But my seatmate, Joanna, balks. "I like the highlands," she tells me, "but I don't like being with the class the whole time. I'm not going."

"We can hike together!"

"You'll be with your set."

"They're not my set!" There's a shade of truth to this. None of the girls in Jerzyk's group are close friends to me. Friendship in Poland isn't easily begotten. In my first high school, Danka was exceptional in her eagerness to get to know me. Joanna, too, became my friend within a year, which was a very speedy bonding when measured against the Polish norm for establishing a true friendship.

"Yes, they are your set. That's exactly what they are!" Joanna is also correct. Even though I haven't a deep-rooted friendship with the girls, the entire group has welcomed me into their collective fold.

"You said you'd come to the party I'm having next month. That's the same group of people!"

"I'll come to the party, but I'm going to get a doctor's note to get out of the mountain trip." Her mother is a doctor. Notes are easy for her to obtain.

At home, I wash my hair twice on the day we are to leave. I'm not sure what the hair washing opportunities will be like on this trip. Unlike the typical Polish teenager, I have kept the American habit of showering daily and washing my hair equally frequently. It feels perpetually greasy, and I worry that it will be unbearable by the end of the trip. At the very least, I plan on washing my bangs in the sink daily. I tuck a small container of Polish nettle shampoo into my backpack.

At the train station, the two teachers and a chaperoning parent check off who is present, but otherwise, their oversight is minimal. It strikes me that everyone in my class is very familiar with train travel. I see confusion and chaos at the crowded platform, but all this is normal to the rest. As the train approaches, we swarm toward the door of one wagon and quickly climb on board. I suppose other passengers, viewing a pack of teenagers, know to seek out other wagons where they will have a quieter ride. The train cars are old, and the hallway that runs alongside the compartments is suddenly straining with the movement of energetic girls and boys. Miraculously and with only slight engineering on my part, I find myself in the eight-person compartment with Marcin. We find seats on the hardwood benches, and as the train picks up speed outside the city, we begin to sing our usual repertoire of folk songs and ballads.

It's near midnight when someone finally suggests that we turn off the light and get some rest. I am sitting next to Marcin, and he pulls me closer to him, his arm loosely around my shoulders. I am immensely happy. I close my eyes and take in the smell of him, of his thick sweater. I wiggle slightly. I want to say something, but he quiets me. "Rest," he tells me.

The hike the next morning is long and hard. I have freshly scrubbed white sneakers, and Marcin teases me about climbing steep trails in shoes meant for gentler play. Many of my classmates have well-worn hiking boots. I take the tease with a happy little dance around him. He laughs and we join the rest of the class in our steady uphill trek. But if I was hoping to have more of Marcin by my side on this trip, I am to be disappointed. The love of my life spends most of the hike moving affably from one group to the next, and I note that he is holding hands with Grazyna at the end of the day.

"A perfect couple," Pani Zydkowicz, our chaperoning teacher, comments. I sulk. There is a coy girlishness about Grazyna that is deliberate and natural. She works on her appearance, not with the makeup and accouterments that are so familiar to an American teen, but with a careful styling of her hair, puffed up then drawn back with a simple black ribbon, and with an attention to the fit of her school white blouse and navy skirt. And whereas the other girls are variously proportioned or, like me, have traces of that cursed acne, Grazyna has skin that is as milk and honey as they come. She is trim and fit, ready to beat your socks off in volleyball. She'd likely do it with a demure smile, accenting the slight dimple in her cheek. As if that weren't enough, she is at the top of the class in all academic subjects. It must be teen stubbornness that keeps me so fixated on Marcin even as our teacher so perceptively links him to Grazyna.

November comes, that dark, dreary month where the few green patches of grass are now mud strips with dog waste in various stages of decomposition. Oh, how I hate to walk Mickey in November! And this dreadful, dismal month comes too quickly this year. With the holidays around the bend, my mother tells me we will not be going to the village for Christmas, and I don't question the reason for this. I'm happy with her decision. I'm completely focused on the social life of my school. I would have hated to miss weeks of contact with my peers.

In these years, I have mixed feelings about going to Gniazdowo, even for a weekend overnight. It's a routine family trip, but we are a family of four people who right now have very little to say to each other. My great desire is to stay in Warsaw and hope for a *potancowka*, a dance party at the home of one of my friends. Missing this Saturday social gathering is, for me, tragic.

"Mom, I have a party at Jerzyk's! I can't go to the country!" It's a tough sell. My mother likes to keep to the schedule of leaving Warsaw on Saturday and returning Sunday after lunch. She likes eating meals prepared by Babcia on two of the days there, and she is a walker, so when the weather is good, she takes long solitary walks along the dirt roads that crisscross the countryside. She relents on some weekends. We cut the village visits then to just a Sunday outing. But on other weekends, she is firm.

"How many parties do you have to go to each month? This weekend, we're going to the country."

When we do go to the village, everyone quickly disperses and follows their own directives. My mother walks, my father reads the paper, then washes the car. Babcia, as always, stays close to the kitchen. Dziadek often works in the yard or occupies himself with a construction project either in the house or the shed. I do not know this, but he is intensely lonely. When in America, he rarely was without like-minded men in a room, discussing and planning community projects or strategies for organizing labor groups. Here, his activism has fizzled. Though he has made valuable contacts with the orphanage administrators just up the road, he has not managed to bring together the village men in any productive manner.

As our family visits to Gniazdowo decrease in frequency (though perhaps not as a cause of this), he decides to go back for an indefinite visit to the southeast of Poland, where many of his relatives still reside. Babcia has mixed reactions: "Good riddance. I'll have less work with him gone," is tempered significantly by trepidation. Keeping the house and yard heated, in good repair, and ready for her family takes its toll on her, especially in winter. As 1967 draws to a close, my grandparents' interest in keeping Gniazdowo begins to wane. It will be another four years before the house is sold, but if anyone would look closely at the current arrangement—the lack of access or transportation to town, the coal furnace that requires stoking several times each night, the danger of river floods in the spring, the absence of a phone line or medical facilities nearby and now, the occasional disappearance of Dziadek, who could attend to most of the structural problems that begin to plague the house—it would be clear that given the opportunity, Babcia would very much like to move out.

6.

Yes, winter in Warsaw can be cold and dark. The days are too short, too gray, too punishing on those who venture out. There is a moment of serenity when the snow comes down. Bare trees, mud patches, and dark park benches are hidden under a glistening layer of fresh snow.

Monuments to military heroes, cultural icons, and political dignitaries are suddenly decked in white, momentarily prettifying their somber, stoic shapes. Everything feels fresh and strikingly beautiful. But as in any city, and perhaps especially in this city, the moment of magic fades quickly. The snow is never shoveled properly, and the carelessly pushed aside piles remain hard to navigate. The days have too few hours of light, and soon enough, the snow becomes dark too. It is a punishing combination. This year the season seems especially interminable. Eliza is in her final year of high school, and she is in the process of deciding on her next step after graduation. She is uncertain. My mother presses her to study English.

"After you finish your university studies, you can translate, like I do."

Eliza balks. She sees herself as interested in the arts. Though she hasn't more than a set of watercolors, she is a talented painter and has not a small amount of regret that she was never given a chance to study arts in a more dedicated fashion. My parents, always vociferously preferring the pragmatic over something perceived as frivolous, chose an academically rigorous schooling track for her. Eliza, at this point, is thinking that perhaps she should have been more adamant in choosing to study art. However, she is not inherently confrontational, and toward the end of winter, she agrees to take the university entrance exams for English language studies.

In Poland, the time to deliberate your academic track is during your years at the lycee. After lycee graduation, if you want to continue with your schooling, you must submit to entrance exams in the field of your choice. If accepted, you stay with your selected discipline. There is no room for indecision or a change of heart. As I watch my sister struggle with her selection, I quickly decide that I will not study English. I don't want to be a translator. I find my mother's work dull, and she appears greatly distressed by it every day. Anything but English studies, I tell myself.

But there is another reason why this winter is especially tough and fractious. It is the winter of 1968, the winter that precedes the March Uprisings at Polish universities and other academic institutions. These are the months when actions by the government, described much later

Nina Lewandowska Camic

as nationalistic, increasingly anti-Semitic, and perhaps even despotic, are being scrutinized and discussed, still tentatively and quietly so that I have only scant knowledge of what others are saying. In a country where there is no dominant, reliable, and independent news source, no trusted voice heard by a majority, each person's understanding of a political drama is differently shaped. We are a people of thirty-two million stories, some of them following wildly disparate trajectories, depending on what you did and where you lived since the Second World War. Distrust of not only those who hold political power but, too, of anyone whose story varies from your own means that there is little airing of political beliefs. For a young person, a conviction, at least initially, is formed at home. Stories about relatives, persecuted or rewarded, demoted or promoted, gain a foothold in the trusted inner circle of family life. But my own family rarely speaks at all, let alone about sensitive political matters. Just by inference and the occasional snide comment, usually delivered by my mother, I know that my parents have a healthy disdain for the political propaganda offered on television or in the two national daily newspapers. I pick up other bits of information from various written sources, Polish and American. But most fact-based accounts remain elusive.

Still, I do know some things. I know, for instance, that the theater performance of a nineteenth-century Polish classic *Dziady* by Adam Mickiewicz has been stopped midseason by the government body engaged in censorship because of the perception that the words of the great author are being interpreted in ways that are damaging to the idea of a socialist state. I know, too, that there are student uprisings in neighboring Czechoslovakia. And slowly, I learn that there are emergent protests now in Poland. I know of this because the western media, which I occasionally find on the kitchen table, references the unrest now and then. Poland isn't frequently mentioned in western news sources, but when it is, the story is almost always now about the tensions rising within our borders.

And I know that the protests, initially just about the Dziady play, speak to a far deeper unrest in my country. You need only listen to the Polish news to recognize that a new wave of propaganda is being aired, targeting "the Zionist elements that are a threat to Poland." If the act of government censorship triggers the protests, they are now extending to other issues confronting Poland, at the same time that suppression of political speech and the scapegoating of a religious minority accelerates. The anti-Zionist public statements are rampant. There is a power struggle in Poland, and the language of "perceived threat to socialism" is being used to suppress any pockets of opposition.

As we yet again listen to a TV news report that targets "Zionist elements" in Poland, I ask my father if the criticism of Zionist expression means the government views all Jewish people as a threat. I do know my parents have no stomach for the anti-Zionist propaganda heard on the air. My mother has talked about turning in her membership to the Communist Party several times. My father is much more cautious. He is walking a fine line now. At once embarrassed in front of his western friends by the repeated anti-Semitic statements by public officials, he nonetheless makes his opposition to the campaign known only to some, and even his response to me is guarded.

"Not all Polish Jews are Zionists, and those who are Zionists have little to do with what's going on in Poland right now. What you hear on the news is just a way of blaming others for problems this country is facing," he answers simply.

The few Jews still living in Poland after the Holocaust are now leaving the country in large numbers. Several of my parents' good friends who had survived the war or had come to Poland after the war from the United States or Canada in the hope of joining the nascent socialist movement here are now making plans to go to England or Israel. In school, none of this is mentioned. In fact, apart from Malgosia Melchior, I do not know who else in my class is Jewish. Years later, I learn that at least one or two others probably have Jewish parents, but they do not admit to it. Malgosia's family chooses to remain in Poland largely because she is doing well in school, and she and her brother are reluctant to start again in a completely new environment. But I know none of this now. All I understand is that as we approach the first whiff of spring and the air turns balmy and unusually mild for March, spontaneous protests are erupting around town.

One especially windy afternoon, I walk home from school the long way past the market and bakery on Polna Street, where I occasionally stop to pick up warm, freshly baked bread. I button my sweater. I hadn't taken a heavier coat, believing that we were at the heels of spring. I wait in line for the bread, and after paying for it and breaking off the end piece for a snack, I make my way toward Ulica Nowowjejska, the street where we first lived when I moved to Warsaw at the age of three. I am about to cross Nowowjejska so I can veer right and make my way toward home when I see people running. I am by Politechnika, the Engineering School of Warsaw. Students, with coats flying, are scampering across the street, darting between buildings, like mice released in a city of cats. So this is the protest that we have been hearing about! I come closer so that I can watch. Though I know few details of their demands, I am rooting for the demonstrators. In my mind, there are no complexities here. It seems obvious that the student concerns are legitimately felt, and it is equally obvious that their voices are not being recognized. As I stand there, facing the Politechnika building, mulling things over in my own framework of right and wrong, a militiaman chasing a student looks over his shoulder and sees me. Perhaps out of frustration or because he is in a state of rage, he rushes at me with his club and strikes me hard several times across my back.

I am completely taken by surprise. I fall forward, then quickly get up and start running. He chases me, repeatedly striking at me from behind. I outrun him. Or maybe he decides it's time to move on to someone else. I continue running home, sobbing now, all the way up the stairs to our apartment. As I let the door fly open, I careen straight into my mother.

"What is the matter? Did something happen to you?"

"I got beaten by a militiaman."

"What? What were you doing?!"

"I was just standing at the side! Nothing really. Watching." My back is sore, and I am tired from running. I wipe my nose and my eyes, and I look at my mother, Mamusia, hoping a little girl's hope that she can say the good words: The militia officer didn't mean it. He made a terrible mistake, and we'll make it right. It won't happen again. But how can she? It is not true, and it is not in her nature to load color into a blustery black and white March day.

She picks up the phone and calls my father.

"We're going to the doctor," she tells me. "I want your back examined. I want there to be a record of this!"

I tell her I'll be fine, but we go to the clinic anyway. The doctor looks at me, listens to my mother's rage, and says calmly and quietly, "Just a little sore, a little bruised. She'll be alright. She is lucky. Some of the other students, good young people, did not get away so easily from the brutality."

"Why did this happen?" I now have a reason to confront my father with questions about the protests when he comes home from work.

But his answer is brief. "This is how they deal with protest. In their eyes, you were one of the opposition."

I can't sleep that night. I know Poland is changing, but I don't fully grasp why or where it's heading. The people who were at the helm in the years of my childhood had been moving Poland away from postwar authoritarianism in favor of a more open society. But if you listen to these same government officials speak now—Gomulka, Cyrankiewicz—you'd surely be confused. They do not sound very open or democratic in their struggle for political survival. The western press refers uniformly to the communist dictatorship in Eastern Bloc countries. Still, we know that there is no communism in Poland or the other countries of the Warsaw Pact, nor is there uniformity of thought among those in power. For westerners, nuances may well be swept under the carpet, and we may all seem like one package of totalitarianism, but surely that is a very poor description of who we are. Nothing in Poland resembles what you'd find in East Germany. Nothing in Czechoslovakia resembles Hungary or Yugoslavia, and this doesn't even begin to describe the ideological honeycomb within each of these countries. Still, it surely is starting to feel like any continued movement of Poland toward a more open society will be countered and suppressed with the help of the militia and by certain fractions, notably those supported by the Soviet Union.

Politics rarely make their way into the conversation among my group of friends. Nevertheless, I ask Marcin soon after, "How is it that your parents are successful if they don't belong to the Communist Party?"

I remember what was said about Dorota's membership in the Socialist Youth Movement. *She joined because she's ambitious. She wants to get ahead.* Is it the only way to get ahead?"My parents are scientists," he answers. "They are good at their work. They don't need to participate in politics. They're proud, and I'm proud that they got where they are without joining the party."

I know, too, that Marcin's family is deeply Catholic. They favor organizations such as the Club of Catholic Intelligentsia (KIK). But I do not question him about this. Marcin has long figured out that our family is not Catholic. Perhaps, for this reason, religion is a topic we avoid—one of many that we sidestep without admitting that we are sidestepping anything at all.

7.

In April, I turn fifteen. Not even two years have passed since I left New York, yet I have lost all contact with my UNIS friends. I rarely think about my years in the United States. When I do, the images are of pizza that I miss, of A&P, the grocery store where food shortages are unheard of. I miss that. Here, in Warsaw, we don't stack toilet paper like Babcia does in the village, but we do hoard some strange items. Our hallway, that same space where we occasionally watch TV, has a wall full of closets. I don't really know what's inside them, except I've seen my mother reach into one to retrieve packs of underwear for us when ours began to wear thin. Our food supply is supplemented by what comes in from the village—poultry and cheese and whatever Babcia has prepared for us. My mother also has a connection through work to an old woman from another village who brings veal into town for her handful of loyal customers. And so we have veal once a week. During the growing season, produce like berries, apples, and cucumbers are in good supply in the markets. Poles love what food stores lack: meats, sausages, hams. I miss the variety of specialty items. Prepared and processed foods appear irregularly. And prices are high. I learn about average pay scales in Poland, and it does not add up. How can people afford cars? Washing machines? Coffee? Chocolate?

When I ask my mother about this, she shrugs her shoulders. "I don't know how they manage. They probably get help from relatives abroad. Or they sell things."

Yes, I've heard about people selling things. Polish cosmetics, for example, do well in the Soviet Union. And she has to be right in her explanation because wages are just too low to pay for appliances, let alone any luxury items, even as many of my friends' families have small, functional cars. All have refrigerators, and a few lucky ones even have washing machines.

My parents, I know, are managing in part because of their time spent in the United States. Our car was purchased with American dollars, as were our washing machine and refrigerator. Babcia and Dziadek, too, benefit from western income streams. They live on American social security checks that pay insignificant sums by American standards but which are valued tremendously here because the monthly payment is made in hard to come by dollars. And Babcia provides real help by caring for us during vacations and finding foods for us year-round.

And what about other shopping? Is it improving? Can we look for the items that would pop up on the list of any American teenage girl? Are clothes, records, and makeup available? The answer is that it's a mixed bag. We steer clear of clothes. What little you see is so dull and without style. You can tell just by looking at the displays as you pass by. No one gives a second thought to how they may appear or whether they tempt you to come inside. You want the skirt, the blouse? Fine. Not interested? Fine as well. The sales clerks don't care. And are we drawn to cosmetics? Most girls my age rarely apply makeup. Polish creams are thought to be good, but they're for older people. They promise some relief for dry skin, and I'm sure older women use great quantities to fight the onset of wrinkles. But none of this is marketed for the high school crowd, if it's marketed at all.

———

If I do spend money, it is on the occasional record album. Nothing from the West comes to Polish stores, but like so many of my friends, I am drawn to Polish vocalists who infuse their modern music with Polish folk elements. The group No To Co releases a song titled "Nikifor," and I am in love with its soft melodies. It's not your typical western hit parade song. The lyrics are about an artist, a painter who was adored for his simple, primitive pictures of scenes from the highlands and old churches in the south of Poland. I feel completely Polish here, listening to music that originates here rather than in the West, knowing that none of my New York friends would understand what draws me to these lyrics and melodies.

But I am not exclusive in my preferences. I also listen to the "top ten," a compilation of Polish and western music presented once a week on the Polish radio station. We have a big clunky German tape recorder, which snags and snarls tapes, but when it works, it gives us the songs we tape directly from the radio, often with a voice-over from the Polish announcer. "And now, let's listen to the number one hit this week, 'Build Me Up, Buttercup,' by the American group the Foundations!" And of course, we continue to listen to our old records, supplemented once a year by the newest Beatles album when my father travels to the West. If I need money for anything, it is only for a tea at a café or an ice cream scoop after school, purchased as an excuse to linger with friends before heading home.

It is fortunate that we haven't grown much since returning to Poland. We can stay with the sweaters and skirts we brought back from America. It's a small stash compared to a western closet. Eliza and I have just a few hangers in a narrow space and four narrow shelves each. We can easily fit all our clothes for all the seasons into these. When I finally wear out my one pair of American Wrangler jeans, my mother reaches into her rapidly disappearing dollars and takes me to Komis, the dollars-only store in Warsaw.

"How can people shop in this place?" I ask her. I know that she guards her saved dollars, but at least she has this handful to help her out when she decides it's warranted.

"Like us, they have traveled abroad and have some saved foreign currency. Or they have relatives abroad who send them money. Or they convert Polish money on the black market."

In front of Komis, a young man paces and stops shoppers who are going in. He's looking to buy dollars. My mother tells me that another person is just around the corner selling western cash, probably at a higher price than what this man can afford. It is true that I don't know of anyone who would change western currency in the bank. The official rate is perhaps ten or twenty times below the street rate. And, the exchange in the banks is a one-way street. You can let go of your dollars, but you cannot buy any. This keeps most Poles out of stores like Komis and keeps them from traveling abroad. For the vast majority of Poles, getting a passport is fairly straightforward. I know of no one among my friends who has been denied one. But if you want a trip to the West, a passport is only the first step. Next, you have to obtain a visa. In your visa application, you must demonstrate an ability to pay for your expenses abroad or list someone living there who will sponsor your stay. Having a friend or a relative in the West is like having a goose that keeps on laying one golden egg after the next.

8.

In the summer of 1968, just as Eliza learns that she has passed her entrance exams and has been accepted into the English Language program at the University of Warsaw, we are told that we have a trip abroad before us—the first one for Eliza and me since leaving the United States. My father has accepted an invitation to vacation in the Soviet Union. We'll spend a few days in Moscow and Leningrad and a week at the Black Sea resort of Sochi. Perhaps to give us a broader range of experiences, we will also be visiting Tbilisi, the capital of the Soviet Republic of Georgia.

Is it a coincidence that my father has signed us on to travel to the Soviet Union this year? We're in the thick of a spring of political tumult. Czechoslovakia, to the south, appears to be inching toward democratic reform. The Soviet Union is taking the position that it must react to these reforms, as they are, according to what we might read in the press, instigated by the West to undermine a socialist state. Is our planned trip a demonstration of sorts? There perhaps to balance my father's other activities, which reveal his sympathetic ties to the western world? I don't know. But I am looking forward to the trip.

I am curious. What's it like in this country that is so despised, though for different reasons, by both Americans and Poles? I am not unhappy that I will see at least a fragment of it for myself.

But as it turns out, we see very little beyond what our hosts want us to see. We stay at hotels in Moscow and Leningrad, but we are provided with escorts—men with black cars who zip us from one place to the next, ushering us to entrances, bypassing lines and ticket booths. I don't think we ever come within a foot of a Russian who is not employed by the government in some fashion. We travel by train to Leningrad, but it is an overnight train, arriving in Leningrad at the crack of dawn. We are picked up at the station there as well, and our itinerary is sketched for us in great detail.

I have been studying Russian on the side with a tutor—a Russian-Lite course of basic grammar structures—but I can read it fairly easily by now, even as Russia's history completely eludes me. I know a little of it from the western textbooks, and I know some more from the Polish textbooks, but claims made in one are completely at odds with those in the other, so I am not convinced that I know anything at all. I walk with my parents and Eliza through the Tsar's palace courtyards in Leningrad, and I am at once appalled and entranced by the horribly derived beauty of the place. The Hermitage Museum has me gasping. Room after room after room of celebrated paintings. The audacious richness, the authenticity of the architecture—all of it is so excessive that it leaves me tired.

The restful portion of our trip in Sochi is eye-opening as well, but for different reasons. We are given a small villa for the week at a resort and spa designated for a certain group of workers. In this case, the workers are connected to the government in some fashion. But the Sochi resort is no mere guesthouse. It's a sprawling place, opulent and excessive at every turn. It is not an exaggeration to say that it is the most sumptuous vacation week I have ever had or am ever likely to have in the future. Lush, tropical vegetation grows at all sides of our two-story white stucco building, hiding it from the rest of the resort. Inside, the interiors are light-filled and sparkling clean. Floors are polished daily. Food appears periodically on the table. There is plenty of space for us to lose ourselves in our own quarters. Even by American standards, the accommodations feel rich.

Our stay here, by the Baltic Sea, comes with certain protocols. We are all given physical examinations at the beginning of our visit. The doctor is the first to detect that I have an asymmetrical bone structure, with one hip joint significantly elevated over the other. He explains all this to my father in Russian, leaving me shaking with trepidation. I am intimidated by the regime of tests, measurements, and diagnoses. The conversations take place without my participation, and I feel like someone has taken charge of me, my body, and perhaps my future. Didn't I read somewhere that random arrests, imprisonments, and institutionalizations are common in this country? I'm infected for a brief moment with fear. Might some bizarre intervention take place now? I shake off my panic. All this is just standard spa stuff. The doctor shakes hands with all of us and leaves the room. I suppose we pass some standard of good health because, after the examinations, we are left alone for the rest of the week. But there are limits on what we can do. We eat alone in our little mansion. Lunches and dinners are brought to the villa, and the food is not lacking in quantity. During the mornings, we sit by the sea. There is no beach, but a concrete slab extending to the water's edge has beach chairs, and there are tables with large chess pieces for people to play should the idle sitting get tiring.

Here, Eliza and I do make friends. Two Russian girls from cities I've never heard of are vacationing at the same resort. We speak broken Russian, and they speak a smidgen of French, and so we converse clumsily, awkwardly. But though I cannot have a sensible conversation with them, I like both girls. We exchange addresses, and on the first day after my return to Poland, I spend a laborious amount of time writing letters in Russian with a dictionary in hand. I don't know if they ever received them. I never hear back.

Our afternoons in Sochi are spent walking. My mother insists on it.

"It's too sedentary here," she tells my father. "All we do is eat."

We leave the compound (and it is a compound with gates, guards, and high fences, though no one interferes with our comings and goings) and walk up the road. It isn't really a pleasant walk. There is traffic, and Sochi proper is far enough from the resort that we would not be able to reach it on foot. Despite the difficulty in moving along the road, we continue to do this walk every afternoon. We like being outside the compound. Eliza and I have been instructed to be careful in what we say when we're in the villa. We know about listening devices in apartment walls. That was a lesson learned in the United States. We have no reason to believe that such devices are within this Russian compound, but we also have no reason to believe that they are not there.

Following Sochi, the trip to Tbilisi is a blur. Once again, we are whisked from airport to hotel then to the monuments and places high in the hills, with views of the city. Dinner is at the family home of a local dignitary. I remember platefuls of exotic foods, some eaten by hand, all accompanied by plenty of local wine. We are too young for it, but my mother and father both drink enough that they appear almost happy to be in each other's company.

The Aeroflot plane lifts off for our return flight to Moscow. I look down at this city of scrambled architecture sprawling along a river valley, and I'm left wondering—is this Asia? If so, it will have been my first trip to this continent. I ask my father, and he gives me one of his famously discreet smiles.

"If you want to think of it as Asia, go ahead." The man of half-answers or full-text expositions. There is no middle ground. I say nothing more. Later, I found out that Georgia, like Turkey, is on the border of the two continents, and opinions differ as to which continent should claim this strategically positioned territory. But even though we had spent almost no time walking along the streets, the city felt very different from any European city I'd ever visited. Chaotic and loud, it certainly felt very removed from Moscow. Perhaps the lesson from this trip is one for which I was not prepared. It becomes apparent that at this point in time, the Soviet Union, with a highly centralized Moscow government, is really a country of many nations, some of which likely had little faith in or even understanding of where the federation republics were heading.

Shortly after our return to Poland, we learn that the Warsaw Pact countries, which include the Soviet Union along with its satellite Eastern Bloc nations, have invaded Czechoslovakia. Earlier, there had been hope that a compromise could be reached between the reformist movement south of us and the Soviet Bloc. That hope has now dissipated. At least that's what the western press is telling us. On the Polish news, we hear that the Warsaw Pact nations provided security for the people of Czechoslovakia. No one at our house nor anyone else's believes the Polish media accounts. We know that "provided security" means invasion.

It's hard for me to discern what impact this has on my parents. It's exactly twenty years since they traveled from America together, sharing as they did then a great enthusiasm for rebuilding this destroyed nation. Yet surely, this year has demonstrated that the Soviets will not tolerate Poland's future as an open, socialist-democratic state. The invasion of Czechoslovakia is a sharp warning to all Eastern Bloc countries.

At home, on the surface, nothing changes after the summer of '68. My father continues to have long political discussions with his close friend Mietek, the editor of *Polityka*. That weekly literary and news magazine continues to not give in to the pressure to publish nationalistic or anti-Semitic rhetoric. A lot is left unsaid, but what is said is not distorted to meet someone's political agenda. My father has slid to the margins of political life. He is biding time, waiting for an opportunity to work for international organizations.

Mietek, on the other hand, remains confident that Poland will survive this political crisis, and in future years he will have an opportunity to play a central role in government. For now, the two men discuss the future of Poland privately, to the exclusion of others.

My mother, to my knowledge, speaks to no one about the political crisis that has intensified since we have returned to Poland. With the squelching of the Czech progressive movement, she seems even harsher in her occasional jabs at the status quo here. But is it that she is disgusted by the current political repression in our country, or is it that she feels quite hostile to the nature of her marriage and family life in general? Eliza and I would probably see her mood more closely linked to the latter.

Our autumnal class field trip is again to the southern highlands this year. And this time, as we sit around the campfire, there is fragmented talk about the invasion of Czechoslovakia. We are so close to the border! Some classmates are concerned that Poland is next in line, that a Soviet invasion is inevitable. Rumors are being shared now. Someone talks of there being a movement of Soviet troops at our borders. Another classmate says that's nonsense. I listen and I'm frightened, not even by the possibility of an invasion, but by how little I know. If my parents are reviewing the political events that are taking place now at our borders, they're not doing it at home, between themselves, or with us in the room. I remember watching TV in New York during the Cuban Missile Crisis. I was frightened then, but my father's presence in the room as he monitored the crisis was reassuring. As if he represented sanity and hope in a political world that seemed to me a tad insane. But in Warsaw, he says nothing to us on any topic that touches politics. And sensing his disinclination to talk, I never ask.

But I do ask him one day about something else that has been bothering me. We are in the kitchen together. I'm drinking tea, and he is fixing sandwiches for supper.

"Daddy, how is it that you can be dead and never again take part in life?"

"Why do you ask?"

"I just can't grasp that."

"Are you afraid of dying? That's not going to happen anytime soon."

"How do you know?"

"I can tell you with 99.9 percent certainty."

I'm reassured with that for about a day. I corner him again in the kitchen the next evening.

"But eventually, I'll be dead."

"Yes, but you've been alive. And your presence has made a mark on this world. You're a grain of sand, but it's the grains of sand that make up the ocean floor. So you are part of life now, and nothing will change that."

I persist. "It's weird. There wasn't a me before. And how do I know that there is a me now? Maybe life just stops when I close my eyes?"

"Now, that is a self-centered way of viewing life!"

"I'm just saying—we don't really know anything."

"Do you have to understand everything?" he asks now, and I can tell he is speaking more expansively. "You do not fully understand how phones work, how babies grow, but you accept both. It's okay not to know everything."

Sometimes, but very rarely, questions come not from me but from my father.

"So, how is that Marcin boy? You still like him? A nice kid. Always cheerful."

I look at my father with bewilderment. He doesn't know Marcin at all! I am now in eleventh grade, and I have made no inroads in connecting with Marcin intimately. In my mind, that boy has caused me more pain than any other person I've ever known. Why should my father like him? Tatek, Daddy, this man with the childishly affectionate nicknames has no understanding of my angst now.

"He plays the guitar, doesn't he?" my father continues.

"Yes."

My father hums an old ballad and then breaks into song. *"Zal, Zal, za dziewczyna, za kochana Ukraina ..."* It's that song about grieving for a loved one left behind in Ukraine. It is my turn to say nothing.

My mother is more sympathetic to my Marcin woes. I come home one day in tears. It's not unusual for me to cry when I am disappointed with the way things have proceeded with Marcin. There is a pattern, and it replicates itself again and again. Marcin will stop by my home and ask me out for a walk. We'll have a beautiful hike along the Vistula River or in a park, and he'll talk about his family or his weekend outings. He'll take me affectionately by the arm for a minute, suggest a movie outing, and I will be buoyed beyond belief. And the next day, he'll be preoccupied, focused on other things, other people, and I'll not have much contact with him again for a long while.

"Pig!" Joanna exclaims as we sit in a café, and I again recount a series of high notes followed by the inevitable low ones.

I often wallow in my grief privately in the room Eliza and I share. But this time, I am in the kitchen, weeping my heart out, and my mother is taken by surprise by the apparent depth of my misery.

"There'll be others. Your father will chase them out with a broom. There'll be others."

I am not consoled. She reaches into her bag and takes out a pill. She deftly splits it in half, handing me one little morsel.

"Here, take this. It's valium. It'll ease the pain."

I know that my mother occasionally takes valium. I think of it as a woman's stress pill. If you're an adult, a woman, feeling anxious, you have a cocktail or pop valium. Surely this is a sign that my mother now regards me as nearing adulthood.

9.

I am fifteen, but I am now approaching the time when I will have to decide what to do once I graduate from the lycee.

My parents ask me, "What subjects do you like in school?"

I'm good at math. We're studying calculus, and I enjoy the neatness of it all. There are problems, and there are solutions. I like getting to a point where I know the correct answer, but I am not a math superstar. Felek, a boy in my class, is. He attacks the most difficult problems with such ease that he leaves us gasping. I don't want to study math, knowing that I can never excel the way he does.

I hesitate. "Geography. I like geography." It's basic stuff—the economic geography of various regions around the world—but I find it interesting.

My father suggests that I talk to my uncle, his brother. Uncle Andrzej is a professor of economics at the University of Warsaw. My mother is dubious.

"Andrzej isn't a real scholar," she says bluntly, and for once, my father challenges her. "Why do you say that? He is a distinguished professor."

"Well, you know how you get to be an economics professor."

"How?"

"They kicked out the real scholars. He stepped into their shoes."

My father ignores this and suggests that Uncle Andrzej visit us for tea one evening so that I can talk to him about whether economic studies are a good match for me. My mother, I know, doesn't like my father's family. Since she first moved back to Poland immediately after the war, she has felt her in-laws' sometimes mild and sometimes not so mild hostility toward her. Now she feels especially pained by my father's newfound closeness to his younger brother. I have heard that Uncle Andrzej wanted to visit us in New York toward the end of my father's term at the UN, and he hoped for a possible lecture appointment somewhere in the United States. "He doesn't even speak English!" my mother retorted scornfully at the time. The visit never took place.

Now, in our Aleja Roz apartment, Uncle Andrzej encourages me to pursue economics. I am a little reluctant. I know that the field is riddled with political commentary, and I have no interest in majoring in something that is a mere rationalization for socialist economic order. I am not opposed to such an order, but I do not want to be engaged in scholarship so tinted by ideology. My uncle senses my hesitancy. "How about econometrics?" he asks.

"What's that?"

"It's when you use mathematical models to explain economic change. It's cutting edge, but we have a strong presence here because Oscar Lange, one of the fathers of econometrics, is a Pole. He wrote the book that set the discipline in motion. You might want to read it. It's called *Introduction to Economic Cybernetics*, and it was published in 1965, the year he died, unfortunately."

I'm intrigued. Here is something that appears to combine a handful of my interests.

"It's hard to get into econometrics. There are just a couple of dozen openings. But you can go for it, and if you're good enough in all other parts of the entrance exams but not strong enough in mathematics, you'll be accepted into standard economics. A backup plan!"

I am willing to consider this. And one day, I share this idea with my friends.

"I'm thinking of applying to the university in econometrics." Marcin looks at me with a grin.

"Really? So am I!"

It is a stunning coincidence.

Chapter 7

1.

At the end of lycee's studies come the baccalaureate exams. *Matura* in Polish, like maturation, as if you become suddenly mature and pass into adulthood. They are weeklong exams, and all Polish lycee students have the same questions and problems to solve. For me, Polish literature and language remain a challenge. I have too many gaps. I haven't caught up with my peers in reading, and my writing is still awkward. Once again, my parents hire a tutor to help me with both. Pani Modzelewska is a teacher herself, though she is not at my school. Whereas my world of adults is overloaded with dour faces at home and in school, Pani Modzelewska is cheerful. She is all smiles and encouragement, and though she never uses our work time for idle chatter, I get the feeling that she is very much aware of who her students are and what personalities lie behind the polite exchanges. She has clued into my impishness and desire to make light of topics that typically receive more serious treatment. For the first time since returning to Poland, I love a teacher and want to please her.

None of my other high school teachers have inspired me much, and most stayed with us for all our high school years. Our math teacher is, in my view, completely without personality. Thinking back now, I can't even recall his face. Our physics teacher is too old to notice if the world is turning, let alone what takes place in his classroom. He sits comfortably in his chair, and I watch his white hair slowly fall across his forehead. Sometimes he appears to be sleeping when students recite the lesson. His explanations are rote and dull, and I quickly stop following them. The boys' perky responses receive high praise. Mine fare less well, and I walk away from the physics class with the only C-level grade on my report card.

On the other hand, Pani Zydkowicz, our Polish literature teacher (who is also our homeroom teacher), is young and spry. Others think she is terrific, but I am convinced she does not like me. Her gaze passes over me dismissively again and again, as if she has long figured out that I do not belong in that class, that my advancement was an accident and something she has to accommodate but not admire. I am not insightful in my recitations. My essays are, at best, predictable. My knowledge of Polish literature is far more superficial than that of any student in class. And my father works for the Communist Party. I retaliate by not liking her right back. It is easy to do that. She is a slight woman with jerky movements and a terrific problem controlling her body odor. I do receive decent grades from her—*dobry*, the equivalent of a B. It's as if we compromise somewhere along the way. She will reward my competence but will go no further. And I will stop trying to reach beyond what is a good enough grade for a student with university ambitions.

Our history teacher, Pani Szalkowa, too, has a reputation for knowing her subject matter extremely well. She is a formidable woman with a bellowing voice and a monstrous bosom that shakes every time she shifts in her seat. She is in her sixties, and wisps of gray hair escape the loosely clipped, graying French twist. On some days, she will go off on tangents, relating textbook events to her own life, often moving well beyond the scope of the assigned chapters. One day, we are listening to her recitations on the bravery of those who participated in the Warsaw Uprising during the Second World War. Suddenly, she puts the text down on her table and folds her arms against her tightly buttoned gray sweater. Slowly, names begin to flow out of her mouth, one after the next, names of relatives lost during the war, as if she had before her a class list of the dead, lives crushed into the rubble of a destroyed city. She shifts then to talking about those who survived. We sense that she is no longer aware of us, of the classroom, of her lesson plan. Her mind is on her relatives. And now she is quiet. We are, too, unsure of how to respond. And then she bellows,

"I'm afraid of death!" She shakes as she shouts these words at us. She pulls out a linen handkerchief and wipes the deep dark crevices underneath her eyes. We listen in stunned silence, waiting for her to continue.

"Yes, I'm afraid of death," she repeats, more quietly now. Silence. She looks at her notebook for a long time, then points her finger to the name of a student and goes on to ask a question on the homework assignment.

I climb the stairs now in the modern apartment building where my tutor, Pani Modzelewska, lives. It's an unusually clean stairwell, with cactus plants on windowsills and glossy fresh paint in a cheerful lemon yellow on the walls. I open her door and step inside her flat. Usually there is a student before me, and I wait in the front hall until I'm told to come into the room where we have our lesson. But there isn't anyone on this day, so I enter the room and sit down at the solid wooden table. She is in an easy chair with a magazine and a pair of knitting needles before her. I like studying her face, her profile. She has blond hair, flipped up in what I think of as the Patty Duke style, and this only makes her look perkier and younger. Today she offers me a glass of tea. She has lemon slices for it, and I take one, remembering that only ten years ago, my mother was buying lemons just two blocks from where Pani Modzelewska lives. In New York, we never even noticed lemons. Abundance makes you gloss over the details.

"You'll have a choice of essay questions for the Matura literature exam," she tells me now. "Typically, there is a question from the early period, another one from the Romantics or further XIX-century authors, and one from the twentieth century."

"I dislike the early texts," I tell her. I had missed the year when they were studied in class, and reading them on my own was tough going.

"You need to be prepared. You might wind up preferring that question."

"I like the Romantics."

"Let's work through both."

I am finding great beauty in the Polish epic poems of the XIX-century writer, Adam Mickiewicz. I like to read portions of *Pan Tadeusz* out loud to myself. Wouldn't it be magnificent to memorize the whole book? To bring up passages in idle conversation? I have a storehouse of such ambitious fantasies, quickly imagined, even more quickly forgotten.

—

I am nearing my sixteenth birthday. Love, romantic love, and the physical expression of it are textbook concepts for me. I am still deeply infatuated with Marcin, but it remains a nebulous idea—a love that is not realized, not articulated. I have gone on dates with one or two other boys in my class, but I find the experience just a little gross and quite a bit boring. When Jurek, one of the tallest, lankiest classmates, ends a date with a declaration of love, I look at him with disbelief. I want to tell him, "You have no idea what love feels like! You're just playing games here!" My feelings for Marcin surely belong to another category altogether. After that, I stop going on dates.

If my real-world love is continuously stifled and frustrated, my fantasy romance is fired up and bursting with emotion. I am in love with a story and the characters within that story. Franco Zeffirelli's film *Romeo and Juliet* has come to the Warsaw theaters, and I am mesmerized by it.

I call Joanna. "You have to see this with me. You have to. I cannot tell you how fantastic the movie is! It's playing at the cinema at the Palace of Culture. Go with me!"

In the course of spring, I see the movie more than a dozen times. Alone. With my sister. With Joanna. With Joanna again.

I critically study the two young men in the leading roles. "He's too soft in the face! Romeo is not nearly as attractive as Mercutio."

Joanna agrees. The actor who plays Romeo looks very American, even though he isn't American at all. I am getting more used to the angular face and gaunt body structure of what I regard as the attractive European male. John McEnery, who plays Mercutio, typifies that look. But even more dazzling than John McEnery is, in our opinion, Olivia Hussey, who plays Juliet. She is my age, almost to the day, and I find everything about her flawlessly exquisite. When Zeffirelli depicts the sexual encounter between Romeo and Juliet, I think physical love never looked so good, so tantalizing and splendid as it does in that one fleeting scene.

I am studying hard now for the Matura exams. If I lacked the stamina for homework in the past, I am making up for it now. My break time is limited to *Romeo and Juliet* escapes and walks along an alley lined with tall elms. I had read in *Kobieta i Zycie*, the Polish woman's favorite magazine, that looking at the color green clears the mind. I stare at the trees and acacia bushes and hope my speed learning will serve me well. I am especially concentrating on my favorite Romantics. I'm determined to write a stellar essay on the XIX-century Polish literary giants.

The examinations take place in the offices of the Ministry of Education. The graduating students at Warsaw lycees are divided into rooms alphabetically, and I see few of my friends in the course of the week.

"Good luck," my sister tells me on the day of the Polish language and literature examination. I smile. I'm feeling confident. Pani Modzelewska will be proud.

The great room where I am to write the exam is crowded with students. We don't speak to each other. We're intent on finding our seats and getting our pens ready. We open the sealed exam questions together. I glance over the three essay choices. I swallow hard and look again. That's impossible! One early period question and two questions on the twentieth century! I can't do this! I feel only marginally comfortable with the twentieth-century authors and not at all comfortable with the early writers. I have looked at exams from the last ten years, and they have always had a XIX century question! Panic sweeps over me. I remember learning the wrong half of the French poem back in UNIS and getting a sparkling F for my gamble. Is this a replay, only with more tragic consequences? I had never worried that I would fail the Matura exams. Only those near the bottom of our class will fail. I swallow hard. I have to write something, so I begin to conceive an idea for an essay. What if I addressed the theme from the twentieth century with references to the Romantics and the Enlightenment authors? Surely that's permissible. Let me try.

I hand in what I regard as a quirky exam packed with references but certainly offbeat. They're going to love it or hate it. It is the best I can offer. I put the anxiety aside and concentrate on the remaining exams for the rest of the week.

2.

My friends and I convene when the week is over. We have a few relaxed days of classes left, where we do low-key assignments and spend not a small amount of time on non-academic class discussions. We have *bal maturalny* ahead of us, the equivalent of the American senior prom. Some classmates will pair up and have a formal escort, but at the bal itself, groups of friends will sit together at large tables, and if you come without a date, you won't stand out. As the school year moves toward the final week of classes, I start feeling restless. We'll have entrance exams for the university in another month. Marcin and I will be applying to the Institute for Econometrics at the university. My other friends are scattered across other disciplines. Jerzyk is applying to study medicine. Grazyna is trying for psychology, which has a very large pool of applicants and, therefore, a low acceptance rate. No one doubts that she'll get in. Joanna will be in biology, Malgosia in biochemistry. Dorota, to everyone's surprise, wants to be a veterinarian. Felek, predictably, will study mathematics. No one is leaving Warsaw. Does this mean we'll stay friends? I wonder about that.

It's three days before the end of classes, and I am feeling nostalgic and not a little sad. Jerzyk and I are lingering near the school doors. On an impulse, I ask him, "Does Marcin know that I love him?"

"Do you?" He looks genuinely surprised.

"Of course I do! I have now for several years! Isn't it obvious?"

Nina Lewandowska Camic

"No, not really." He hesitates, then asks, "Do you want me to tell him?"

"Yes!"

I don't know what led me to say that, but I do not regret it. The summer is before us. If he is going to be offended by my bluntness, I will not have to see him for a while.

The next day Jerzyk comes over to my desk.

"I told him."

My heart is racing. "What did he say?"

"He was surprised. He did not know. He'll talk to you about it, but not today. He wants to square things with Grazyna first."

Square things with Grazyna? What the hell does that mean? I try to avoid my group of friends that day. We have *prace spoleczne*, a mandatory physical workday that occurs once or twice a year, where we are asked to repair or clean up a park or a designated spot within the city. This time we're to work in the former Jewish ghetto, established by the invading German army to seal off Jews from the rest of the city. A new park is now being planned for this area. Nothing of the ghetto itself remains. An uprising of the ghetto's Jewish people led to massive executions and deportation, and the buildings where they lived were razed to the ground. Our assigned task is to distribute gravel along proposed park pathways. During the work period, I stay close to Joanna and try not to think about love, or Marcin, or anyone at all. And still, it's impossible not to notice that at the end of the day, Marcin is walking Grazyna home.

The following day, on the next to the last day of school, Marcin comes to my desk. He's cheerful, but that's not unusual. His face is never sullen.

"Can I come over to your place later this afternoon? I'd like to talk."

"Okay."

I have before me an afternoon of tense waiting. At home, I walk the dog, give a quick glance at the mirror and spend two hours on my bed, guitar in hand. It is nearly evening when I hear the elevator door outside the apartment slam and our doorbell ring. I answer it, and there he is, still grinning.

"Let's go for a walk."

We walk to the parks as we have done so many times before. At first, he chats about school, about his plans for the weeks immediately after school. But a few minutes into our walk, he grows momentarily silent.

"Jerzyk told me. The thing is, I wasn't sure about Grazyna and me. I don't know. Sometimes she acts as if we are together, but other times she acts as if we are not. I wanted to be fair, to give her a chance to explain herself. So I asked her yesterday. I told her I needed to know. I said I'd give her a day to think about it. If she wasn't going to treat us seriously, I wanted to date you. She burst out crying and ran inside her home when I said that. Today she was cold and aloof and told me I should leave her alone. So, do you want to date?"

I can hardly believe it! I'm smiling broadly in what I hope is a not too forward way. I read in *Seventeen* magazine that it's not good to be forward with boys.

"Yes, sure. But I'm going to the village in two days."

"Jerzyk told me that he has been there to visit you. Maybe he and I could come together for a few days?"

I think quickly about this idea. Babcia knows Jerzyk. My mother continues to be friends with his mother, and Jerzyk is a trusted presence. But how will she take to Marcin? I'll talk to her. I'll use my most reassuring voice. I will convince her he belongs to the category of what is referred to in my family as "clean-cut" young men.

"Sure, that would be great. Jerzyk knows how to get there by train."

School is over. We have an end-of-year ceremony. Several of us get prizes—books on one topic or another. Felek wins for math, and Grazyna gets the prize for her work on Polish literature and history. I walk away with the prize for "the most improved." Well, that can hardly come as a surprise. When I started Zmichowska Lycee two and a half years ago, I could hardly put a Polish sentence together on paper. My final grades are all good except for physics. In math and geography, they are quite excellent. The Matura exam results will be available within a week. Could it be that my lycee studies will have passed without a major snafu? I am hopeful.

3.

The village house is quiet. Eliza is in Warsaw, finishing her first year at the university. She occasionally comes to Gniazdowo to see Janusz, a young man who lives year-round in the village and with whom she has formed a significant and intimate relationship. When news of this trickles down to Babcia, she reports it to my mother, who voices her strong disapproval. Janusz is, in their eyes, a drifter. He lives with his mother in a small shack, and no one is clear on their source of income. Last year, he built a shed in the back of their yard and plastered it with magazine cut-outs of pop stars. The older summer kids have taken to hanging out in his shed, which we call *buda*. Someone painted a skeleton on the wooden door, and we like to take photos of each other next to it. Inside, we sit on the two cots placed against opposite walls and smoke cigarettes. Occasionally someone will bring a jug of homemade wine. Slugging it down quickly becomes a game. The one time I participate, I get so violently ill that I scare myself away from buda drinking in the future. Eliza sees in Janusz a sensitive soul. Babcia regards him as a man who is using my sister to up his station in life. The conflict over her associations with him is so intense that my sister increasingly chooses to see Janusz secretly when he comes to Warsaw for the day.

Dziadek, too, is spending time away from the village and Babcia. Again he returns to his reestablished contacts in the southeast of Poland, and he is devoting his fading energies to supporting community projects in that region. The house in Gnizadowo is so quiet that my arrival in the village in May to see Babcia is especially welcome.

"Babciu, Jerzyk and his best friend, Marcin, will be visiting me for a few days. Is that alright?"

She nods her head. She has grown lonely, and there is a sadness about her that I hadn't seen before. Two years ago, Eliza and I were still spending the bulk of the summer months with her. This year, I'll be returning to Warsaw for the university entrance exams. If I am admitted, I'll have a month of community service to keep me in the city. We expect to take the usual two-week family vacation as well— one of the last that our family will experience together. This means that my trips to the village will be limited to the occasional weekend and perhaps a few days in early fall, before the start of university classes in October.

I spot Jerzyk and Marcin walking from the station along the river's edge two days later. They carry backpacks, and they come with gifts of food for Babcia. She appears to accept their presence as the modest substitute for the family that is no longer coming to the space she had created for them. She prepares a supper of bread and *twarog*, farmer's cheese with radishes, cucumber, and chives, and pours mugs of *kompot*, stewed fruits in their juices. The three of us eat in the verandah, and then Marcin and Jerzyk help wash the dishes. I can see that Babcia is immensely pleased with this. In fact, in all my time in Gniazdowo, I have never seen any male help her with housekeeping chores.

After, the three of us retreat to the great attic space in the house, where my parents typically sleep. Marcin and Jerzyk have sleeping bags, and they find room on the floor to spread out. As the light fades, Jerzyk retires to his corner. Marcin and I are talking quietly, inconsequentially. I can hardly focus on his words. I have a sense of the unreal. I am in the most familiar place on earth, and here is Marcin, too. Suddenly I sense his hand reaching for me, touching my shoulder gently, leaning toward my face. I feel his strong, forceful kiss. He pauses then and looks at my face.

"Zabka," he says. "My little zabka." Little frog. I consider the nickname. Yes, okay. If you like, I will be that. I move closer to him, and we spend the next hour kissing under the exposed beams of my childhood home.

The next morning, I walk upstairs to wake Jerzyk and Marcin, but they are already up, washed, and ready for the day. Nothing is said about last night, but there is an almost palpable charge in the air. Marcin greets me with his usual grin. I return the smile, but I'm feeling shy about being near him now. Are we officially a couple? I suggest a hike for all of us after breakfast.

We set out toward Lochow, the small, provincial town, several hours away by foot. We talk amicably about school and the Matura exams. The day before I left for the village, we received the results, and all passed with high marks. I am, of course, greatly relieved. Our focus now is on the upcoming university entrance exams. These will be especially challenging for Jerzyk, as he'll have several tough tests in the natural sciences. Marcin and I have exams in math and geography and a foreign language of choice. Jerzyk tells us he'll be returning to Warsaw the next day so that he can settle into a studying routine.

"Can I stay here a few days longer?" Marcin asks me. I am completely happy. He wants to be with me. He really does want to be with me, alone. I never once consider the possibility that he and I may not be on the same platform. I've been hugely infatuated with him for three years now, whereas he approaches this as something new and untested.

I tell him I'll ask Babcia, but I know she won't object. She hasn't given any sign of disapproval of the visit. Perhaps she sees this as the natural progression of events. And to her, Marcin belongs to the group of young men who are "of good background."

The next day we walk Jerzyk to the train station. Over the years, not much has changed along this hour-long walk that I know so well. Follow the sandy road through the forest, cross the meadow toward the river until you come to the rail bridge. Take the bridge to the other side, follow the tracks, and arrive at the Urle station.

"When we were kids, we'd place coins on the tracks and keep them as souvenirs after the train flattened them. But over the years, the flattened coins got mixed up with other flattened coins. I've forgotten which belongs to what moment or even what year." I say this somewhat wistfully as if wishing that the best memories would never leave us.

Marcin is again grinning. "My family rented a cottage not far from here several years ago. We liked this river further upstream."

"It used to be a lot cleaner even a few years back. It's getting hard to find good bathing spots."

Jerzyk gives a wave as he boards the train. "See you back in Warsaw!"

Marcin and I retrace our steps past the meadow into the forest again. It's quiet here, disturbed only by the birds that make their home in the trees. Marcin takes my hand and pulls me toward him.

"Let's sit for a while." He chooses a sandy spot off the path with a trace of dry pine needles. His arm pulls me down toward him, and we lie down in the shade of the pines, touching each other with our bodies, unsure of what should come next.

The moment of uncertainty passes. Marcin is kissing me, not tentatively at all, and I respond. And then I pull away. Someone is on the nearby path. I am suddenly afraid that we will be discovered, and I will again be the subject of village gossip that will eventually make its way back to my grandparents. I jump up quickly and brush the pine needles off my T-shirt. Marcin laughs.

"Zabka," he repeats.

In the attic of my grandparents' house, we finish what began in the forest with the passion and fury of adolescence. I have just turned sixteen, and he is eighteen. I love him so intensely that I let the events unfold under his direction, without a doubt that I am doing the right thing, even as I do not fully understand what I am doing.

In reality, my knowledge of sex is spotty. It comes from novels off my mother's bookshelf and movies where couples seemingly make love whenever they feel aroused. I know there is a risk of pregnancy, but I push that thought aside. Marcin will be careful, I tell myself. Perhaps remembering her own love life prior to marrying my father, my mother had said several times that when we approach adulthood, we should make sure we had contraceptives on hand, and I tell Marcin later that I will be making an appointment in Warsaw to visit a gynecologist.

Again there's that smile. He pulls me closer. Running his finger along my forehead, he asks, "What percentage probability do you give to us being married someday?"

I hesitate. Should I say I am certain of it? If he had proposed marriage then and there, I would have said yes. Haven't I been emotionally engaged to him for years? Perhaps fortuitously, Marcin doesn't wait for my answer. He supplies his own. "Thirty percent. I give it a thirty percent chance."

For a few seconds I am unnerved, but I let any worry fade away. He is being practical. He is thinking like an adult, and thirty percent is not a small number.

We are back in Warsaw. Marcin drops by unannounced, as is a terrible habit, as it causes me to spend far too much time waiting, on the off chance that he might stop by.

"Let's go for a walk," he says, and he takes me by the hand, out of

Nina Lewandowska Camic

the apartment, down the steps and onto the wide boulevard that runs next to the parks.

"I want to talk to you about God," he says.

I know where this is heading. He wants to explain his religion to me. My lack of religion is a glaring imperfection, an obstacle he must overcome. And so he tells me he sees God in everything. In the leaves of trees, in a person, in all that is around us.I ask no questions. I want to seem respectful. Curious even. I listen quietly for a long time, trying to process this and imagine what it must be like to live with a God. I smile at him as if I accept his words, even as I know that this is his narrative and it has no place in my worldview, which will never shake its allegiance to scientific fact rather than Christian or any other theism.

When he is done, he plants a kiss on my forehead. We switch to talk of exams, and he walks me home.

"May I come in?" he asks.

"Of course." We enter the apartment, and we go to my bedroom. Eliza is out, and my mother is in her room, as always, behind a closed door. Marcin pulls me to the floor, and once again, I feel I am in a dream. This couldn't be happening! Is he really my lover now? Are we slated to be together from now on?

4.

The graduation dance is scheduled to take place in a lovely palace ballroom in one of the many reconstructed buildings in the Old Town. Suddenly I have a date for it. I ask my girlfriends what the appropriate dress is for the party, and they tell me it must be a long evening gown. I am dismayed. How do I get an evening gown? No store that I know of sells them. I was relieved when the school required that all girls wear navy skirts and white blouses for the most recent school dance, the *studniowka* (the hundred-day dance, celebrating the days left to graduation). Now, for the bal, I have no choice but to ask my mother for help. I can sew from a simple pattern, more or less. She, on the other hand, is an expert. In New York, she would make an evening dress in a week or less, and it would be no simple dress. She wore all her creations to the various UN functions that required formal wear.

"I don't really have time for this," she tells me now. I remain quiet. She knows that it'll be her dress or no dress. With a sigh, she agrees to do a simple shift on the condition that I find my own fabric.

I don't know what is appropriate for a formal shift. I walk past reels of material at the fabric store on Marszalkowska, somewhat bewildered by it all. Blue. Maybe it should be blue. People say I have blue eyes. The choices are limited, but there certainly are decisions to make as to fabric, pattern, and general cost.

"Mom, there's stuff at the local fabric store. But I don't know which one is appropriate for this."

The next afternoon, I am back at the fabric store with my mother. As I follow her inside, I sense her tension. And I know that this is more than just the daily disgruntlement that comes from the editing pressures that rile her so much these days. Looking at her, I can tell that she is not at ease in the store. I am somewhat surprised. Back in New York, my mother was the consummate, confident shopper. She knew where the bargains were, which stores carried the best fabrics at the lowest prices, and what accessories she could buy and use. But here, in Warsaw, she feels uneasy. She walks up one aisle and down the next.

"There, I can work with this fabric." She points finally to a blue and white brocade that seems a little stiff, not unlike fabric she used for her UN gowns, but I am so relieved that there is something acceptable that I give a light nod and say a quiet thank you.

The day of the bal, Marcin comes to my apartment, and we walk together to the taxi stand. I am nervous about the awkwardness of the dress. It has a slit, but still, I manage to trip in it and clumsily drop my purse so that it falls under the taxi cab that pulls up to where we are standing.

"What are you doing?" Marcin is looking at me quizzically as I get down on my knees and reach underneath the vehicle.

"My purse. I dropped my purse."

Marcin is doubled over with laughter. I know that this now will join the volume of anecdotes he likes to tell—life stories cataloged for any social situation that calls for someone to step forward and entertain.

In the ballroom, our group of friends sits together at a round table. I notice instantly that Grazyna is not there. In fact, I do not know this, but I will never see her again. Friends will tell me that she marries quickly, right after her first year at the university, and she has a child soon after. But none of us are thinking about such leaps into adulthood right now. For this one last evening, we are still high schoolers, partying the night away. There are a few bottles of wine at each table, and there is a band playing to the side. In so many ways, it is like any other party that we have attended at each other's homes. We dance and switch partners frequently, one after another. We banter and laugh. It's all so familiar now. I never once think about how uncomfortable I am in my long, narrow dress, but instead, I sink into a feeling of total pleasure in being with this intimate group of friends. My very best friends— Warsaw kids who will remain in Warsaw after high school, even after university studies. What I don't understand this evening is that none of it matters. Living in the same city will not be reason enough to continue our friendships. After this dance, we break up and drift apart and never come together as a group again.

The day after the bal, Marcin is again at my front door. I am surprised. He rarely stops by two days in a row.

"Nina, you know what we do ..." he's a little flustered, but he continues. "I can't go on like this. Making love—it's there for people to reproduce, to have children with the person they marry."

I swallow hard. I have just scheduled an appointment with a gynecologist. Do I not need it now? So this is it? Three weeks of intimacy, and we're done? I listen quietly as he continues.

"Let's take this more slowly. You know, I'm going to a camp in July. My family will be there and a bunch of others. Can you come too? It's a great camp. We pitch tents by a lake, and there are older people and young people, and the leader is a terrific priest we call Wujcjo (Uncle). He's really hip, and we have services in the forest every day. We take kayaks, and we cook meals on the campfire. Jerzyk is going too. Can you come?"

"I'll let you know. I'll have to ask my parents." Neither my mother nor my father knows that I am suddenly on very intimate terms with Marcin. Or am I still on intimate terms? Are we lovers still? Should I be happy with the invitation to camp?

I word my request to my parents very carefully. I am convinced that they are sleepwalking through my adolescence most of the time. But sometimes, one of them wakes up abruptly and reacts negatively to some plan that Eliza or I may hatch. I don't want this to be such a time. I say now that Marcin and his family invited me to camp with them, Jerzyk, and a few other families. My mother shrugs her shoulders.

"Go ahead," she tells me. "If Jerzyk is going, it must be alright."

5.

The entrance exams take place in early July. The math test is hard, but I feel rather confident about it. I know I need to score well, and I know that I will lack the additional points given to those who have disadvantaged backgrounds, typically those coming from rural districts. I put off thinking about the results. Those won't be posted for several weeks. In the meantime, I am preparing to go to Marcin's Catholic family camp.

If Marcin's parents are concerned about their son's current dating habits, they don't show it. His mother, a tiny woman with short blond hair and a sweet predisposition toward saying kind things about those around her, kisses me as I show up at the campsite with Jerzyk a few days later.

"Here, you'll be sleeping in this tent with Barbara. A girl your age from Gdansk. After you settle in, I want you to come to the main tent. We're having a special meeting for the women here. It's for the older women, but I want you to come too."

I set down my pack and make my way to the large tent by the cooking station. Inside, a dozen women much older than me are sitting, chatting together. I stay to the side, not sure what the meeting is about. Another woman with graying hair and a creased face comes in, and there is a hush now as she starts to talk. There is a seriousness in the air that makes me think perhaps we're about to learn something tragic. But the older woman takes out charts and pencils, and I see that the topic is ovulation and copulation. She is explaining the rhythm method of managing reproduction. It's all about thermometers and temperature taking, and now I understand that this is the preferred way for a Catholic woman to proceed with family planning. At an earlier time, I had been thinking of getting a diaphragm. Would these women reject that form of contraception? If the meeting is any indication, they would rather choose to engage in sex on days when the thermometer tells them it is safe. I am fascinated by this. I had no idea that you could manage birth by tracking your temperature in the morning.

When I return to Warsaw, even though Marcin seems to have backed away from continuing a sexual relationship, I place a thermometer near my bed and take my temperature before getting out of bed. I'm curious if I can spot a time of ovulation. But the chart I produce is confusing and irregular, and I quickly lose interest in the project. I tell myself that I'll rely on the diaphragm in the future.

At camp, mornings begin with a prayer service in the forest. The priest is indeed a boisterous man with a shaggy dark beard, bushy hair, and an affable manner. He plays the guitar too, and his services include a lot of singing with lovely songs about God and nature, and I find myself humming along even as I stand back from the rest during the actual prayers.

On Sunday, the entire group of campers, including about a dozen families and a handful of young adults without families, gets ready to hike to a nearby village church. Wujcio, the camp's priest, will be going with them. Marcin's mother asks me if I want to go too or would I mind staying behind to mind the tents. I tell her I'm happy to help by minding camp. The camp empties, and I settle in to read a book outside. An hour or two later, I look up to see the form of Wujcio down the path. He comes over to where I am sitting and smiles down at me.

"The rest are enjoying a longer hike right now. Are you liking camp?" he asks.

"Sure!" I answer, but I am not being completely honest. I like camping, but I feel like an intruder, too. Everyone knows I am not Catholic. No one mentions it, but surely they must wonder why I am here.

"Why don't you and I take a kayak out onto the lake."

I think I am about to hear more about God, and I am okay with that. It is, after all, why I am here.

I take the front seat of the kayak, and we paddle out. Wujcio is behind me, instructing me on how to work the paddle.

"That's superb!" he tells me as if I was performing some complicated task rather than merely gliding the paddle through the still waters.

"Stop for a while," he tells me. "Listen to the quiet. Watch for birds!"

I pause. Wujcio moves in the kayak, and the boat wobbles a little. He steadies it and sits down, but closer to the middle.

"Here, sit quietly here. I really want to compliment you on your paddling and your friendliness toward everyone here. You are quite special!"

He reaches for me and gently guides me so that I am sitting just by him.

"Really special," he repeats. "You deserve a kiss for that!" He grins as if he is joking, but he uses his strength to push me against him. He kisses me first on my cheek but then, quite suddenly, on my mouth. I can feel that he has an erection, and he is pressing my body against his groin. His free hand, the one not holding me close, is unbuckling his belt. He takes my hand and moves it closer to his now opened pants.

I pull away. I tell him that I would like to get back to the shore. I sit down resolutely in front and paddle with a great show of strength toward camp. Wujcio continues sitting in the middle of the boat, but he says nothing. As we approach the small sand strip, I jump out and walk away without daring to look back.

I am back in my tent, lying down, trying to understand what just happened. I listen for Wujcio's footsteps, but it is quiet outside. When I do hear a voice, it is not that of Wujcio, but Jerzyk. He comes to my tent and pokes his head inside.

"I came back to tell you that a group of us found a farmstead with a television. The owners invited us to come inside and watch the American moon landing. Come on. I'll take you to it." It strikes me then how thoughtful Jerzyk is! Had he not come to get me, would I have missed this event? We walk back to the village and chat lightly about the camp.

"Do you like Wujcio?" I ask him as we approach the farmstead.

Jerzyk lets out a short laugh. "He's okay. I don't go for all that stuff with the guitar and his big brother attitude, but I know everyone likes him. He helps a lot of the teens here. Your tent mate Barbara is one of the people he has especially helped with some of her troubles at home."

I bet he has, I think to myself. Many years pass before I tell anyone what happened in the kayak in the middle of the lake.

We find a handful of campers gathered around an old TV set at the farmhouse.

"They're about to step out of the spaceship now. We're just in time," Jerzyk whispers. Marcin gives a quick wave and continues his conversation with a fellow camper. I try to imagine that his conversations with me are more intimate and personal, but as I watch the easy laugh, the stream of uninterrupted sentences, the hand gesture that causes him to touch the elbow of the person next to him, I think that he is with others as he is with me. I turn my attention to the moment on the screen when Armstrong steps on the moon. There is a gentle round of applause in the room. It never fails to surprise me how much Poles love Americans, even as most Americans remain suspicious and largely indifferent to this European nation. On the screen, I hear American commentators with their ever-confident manner of speech and their familiar intonation. Never has the divide between the two countries seemed greater to me than now, in this small farmhouse, with the group of Catholic campers and the farmers watching intently the small screen on the kitchen table.

"Sing us a song, Nina," Marcin's mother prods me that evening as we sit around the campfire after supper. "You know the music of Joan Baez?" The American folk artist is well liked in Poland. In the next year, she will travel to this country for the Sopot Music Festival to sellout crowds. I take the guitar and sing.

How the winds are laughing
They laugh with all their might

Laugh and laugh the whole day through
And half the summer's night.
Donna donna donna donna …

6.

I am accepted into the econometrics program at the University of
Warsaw. The list of names is posted on the wall outside the university
administration building. I notice that Marcin's name is there as well.
I haven't seen him for a number of days, and I wonder if we are still
even dating. We have not been alone together since before camp. I call
him now to congratulate him, but his mother picks up the phone and
tells me that he is off with his brother and won't be back for a few days.

"Can he call you back then?"

"I'm leaving next week to go on a family vacation."

"He should be back by the weekend."

On Saturday, Marcin calls.

"Good morning! How are you?"

"We're on the university admitted students list!"

"Yes, I know. My parents told me. Listen, we're driving out to the
country tomorrow for the church service. There is this beautiful church,
and they do a wonderful mass with folk music. You might enjoy it."

"Okay. Sure, but let me check with my parents. I don't think we're
going to the village, but I'm not sure. Hold on, will you?"

I knock on the door to my mother's room. "That's Marcin. He wants
to know if I'll go with him and his family to this country church
tomorrow."

"What church?"

"It's just a regular church. They do music—"

"No, of course not." I had, unfortunately, caught her at an awake
moment.

"What? Why not?"

"Tell him you do not go to churches. Whoever heard of such a thing!
You're not Catholic! Why would you need to go to this?"

"Mom, it's just a service! I'm not joining a church!"

"I told you. No, you cannot go."

I am sobbing so hard that I can hardly get back on the phone. "I can't go," I tell Marcin and hang up. I think my mother is so completely unreasonable that I try to find support from my father. But he is indifferent to my pleading. I hear them talking now—a rare thing as they have just come off of an extended period of silence.

"They're trying to convert her. It's ridiculous," my mother says.

"She can stay home."

I close the door to the room I share with Eliza and bury my face in the pillow. What's the matter with my parents? Don't they get how important the church is to most people in Poland? If they only probed a little, they would know that I am not looking to become a Catholic. I do not believe in God. I can't even get myself to pretend that I am an agnostic. No amount of church attendance could lead me to reconsider. Nonetheless, I am living in a country full of believers. If I want to have a family someday, there is a strong likelihood that it will be alongside a Catholic spouse. In the United States, you could imagine a union of people of different faiths, but in a country like Poland, where one church has such a stronghold on an overwhelming majority of the population, I feel that a person on the outside needs to tread carefully. I can't ignore religion. It's all around me. And I have another worry. I feel that Marcin is slipping away from me. An invitation to spend time with his family is no small deal. Saying no to it hurts.

As so often happened in the past, a small matter outside their relationship cracks the wall of silence and has my parents speaking to each other again. Maybe they are surprised that they can still find themselves to be on the same side of a family dispute. Or maybe they are relieved that I have thrown them a reason to break the silence that has been in place for several months now. We are about to go on vacation, and traveling in silence would have been tough, even for a family that's used to not saying much to each other. I had been wondering if my mother would simply refuse to go. And indeed, just a few weeks ago, she had appeared quite ready to call it quits on a lot more than just the trip. She had come into the kitchen while I was getting my dinner. She was agitated, and she spoke quickly as if she wanted to say something and be done with it. "I'm thinking of leaving your father."

I put down the pot with the stewed piece of meat and looked at her.

"Really?" Now what? If she leaves, will Eliza and I stay with my father? I could never quite think of him as invested in the whole business of parenting. And where will she go?

"We'll talk more about it this evening. I'm going to see Irena right now. We're going to look at a place I may rent for a while."

When she is gone, I go back to the bedroom. Eliza is there, looking through an old magazine.

"Did you hear?"

"Yeah."

"Is it for real?"

"She seems mad. But then, she's been mad at him for several months."

My father is out for the evening with his friend Mietek Rakowski. An hour later, as Eliza and I scavenge the kitchen for more food, we hear the elevator shut and my mother's key in the front door. She comes straight to the kitchen.

"I decided to stay," she tells us, with not a small amount of drama. "Irena pointed out why it's not a good idea to leave now. For the sake of children. Well, for any number of reasons." She hangs up her coat on the hooks by the door and retreats to the bedroom.

Eliza shakes her head.

"For the sake of the children ..." she mimics my mother. "How crazy is that."

That was last month. And now we have a vacation before us that both Eliza and I are extremely eager to go on. The plan is to spend a week in Hungary and then drive further south and west for a three-day visit to Venice. It will be the first time that we'll be visiting a western country since we left the United States three years ago. My parents had cautioned us that the trip would be quick and on a shoestring budget. They do not want to spend down their western currency, and even cheap hotels out of the Frommer book I love, *Europe on 5 Dollars a Day*, cost more than they can afford.

"We'll have to stay someplace outside Venice."

"Frommer suggests camping for the rock bottom budgets," I

Nina Lewandowska Camic

comment, and after some consideration, my parents agree that we should take along camping gear. We would stay at a campground on Lido Beach, a vaporetto boat trip away from Venice proper. My parents would sleep in stable bunk beds in the permanent room-sized tents there, and Eliza and I would sleep in our sleeping bags in a small but hefty tent on loan from Jerzyk.

7.

It is now three days before our departure for Hungary and Italy. I am still feeling the humiliation of having to tell Marcin that I could not attend a church service with his family. In fact, I haven't heard from him since that phone conversation, and I worry that I will not see him before we leave. I alternate between anticipation and listlessness. And, once again, I push the limit on my assigned weekly chore of taking out the garbage. The can is almost completely full when my mother comes home from shopping. She lifts the lid to throw away scraps of paper from her trip to the market, and she slams it back down again.

"Nina!"

I drag myself to the kitchen. I am brooding, and she knows it.

"This really is the last straw. You don't do your chores. And since you don't seem willing to do your chores, I think we should call off this entire vacation plan. I don't see the point of rewarding you. Look at this! I can hardly close the lid!" She storms to my father's room. "The trip is off," she says simply.

This time, Eliza is upset as well. "What did I do?" she asks, with not a small amount of anger.

I am crying hard now, and I go to my father's room. He has put his newspaper down, but he remains in his leather chair, looking at us with a slight furrow in his brow.

"Daddy, talk to her!"

"Let's give her a few minutes," he suggests.

I leave the room and lie down on my bed. With the appropriate degree of adolescent drama spinning through my head, I think that nothing good lasts. Count on nothing. Look forward to nothing. One moment, followed by another, randomly assorted, according to a whim, a chance event.

Within a day, my mother will change her mind. There will be another penalty that she'll impose for that full can of garbage, one that will make little impression on me, but the family trip will be saved.

We set out by car, driving with as much speed as my father dares apply, given that the roads remain a shared enterprise between cars, trucks, horse-drawn wagons, and the occasional chicken. We spend a few days in Budapest touring with nameless, faceless Hungarian guides and then we proceed to Lake Balaton, where we are again guests of the Hungarian government. The accommodations are not nearly as sumptuous as they had been in Sochi, but we like the lake and the Hungarian foods that we are served for dinner.

On our final evening, we drive to a restaurant that prepares traditional meals in a colorful room with embroidered fabrics and painted roosters on the wall. Musicians play folk songs on violins and guitars, and the restaurant patrons, aided by the easy flow of a Tokaj wine of the region, join in enthusiastically. Hungary feels very different than Poland. Most of the Americans I knew had lumped all Eastern European countries into one Communist Bloc with complete oversight and control exerted by the Soviet Union. But is this accurate?

From at least one perspective, it is. As I surely learned last summer, the Soviet government did not tolerate opposition, either within its borders or in the countries of the so-called Eastern Bloc. Like in Poland, elections in the Soviet Union were a bit of a farce since the ballot offered no choice for the voter. Poland had had parliamentary elections in June 1969, and though I was too young to vote, I knew too well what parties were on the ballot. They were all under the umbrella of the PZPR (Polish United Workers' Party). In effect, you could vote either for the United Workers' Party coalition, cast a blank ballot, or not vote at all. There was no penalty for not voting, and still, many Poles did vote, if only because doing so made you not stand out. The newspaper reported that the coalition secured 99.2 percent of the vote.

Still, in my view, Poland is as far removed from the Soviet Union as Hungary is from us, its neighbor to the north. The sense of isolation and separation from the Western Bloc is most acute in the Soviet Union

Nina Lewandowska Camic

and, I would learn later, in East Germany. Hungary, like Yugoslavia, has a toe in the West. People from Budapest travel to Vienna and vice versa with a fair amount of ease. The two capitals are only two hundred kilometers apart. With a milder climate than Poland, Hungary has a greater diversity of foods in the stores. A delicatessen in Budapest has meats and sausages. A delicatessen in Poland rarely has much of either.

At the end of the week, we leave Hungary and drive without pause through Yugoslavia (currently the state of Slovenia). From there, we enter Italy. Crossing the border into Italy is a bit of a jolt. We see the billboards, the advertisements, and quite suddenly, it is as if we are in America again. We are jubilant. We put on Italian-American accents and mimic the signs using hand gestures and Italianized words. The road has taken on color, and though it is a crassly commercial color, we are made buoyant by it.

My father, as always in the driver's seat, initially says nothing. On the rare occasion when Eliza, my mother, and I have engaged in a verbal mockery of a curious facet of Polish life, he'll stay silent, but you could almost see a twinge of a chuckle wanting to escape. "Listen to that! There is going to be a Polish Fiat on the market! Do you suppose they'll use real metal parts for it?" We'd laugh, and he'd offer a half-smile. But this time, he seems bothered by our jubilation, and after a few more rounds of "Mamma mia pizzeria!" coming from the back seat, he says sharply for him, "Enough already!"

My mother challenges him. "Why? They are happy to be back in Italy. What's wrong with that?"

"It's not political, Daddy, It's just that you can't help but notice—"

"Notice what? The ads? You have missed ads?"

I consider his words, but they do not move me. He is, after all, the one who frequently travels to the West. To him, this is commonplace. Why should he be surprised that this is remarkably different to someone else? And for us, different in a familiar sort of way?

We make our way toward the Lido di Jesolo, the strip of land that juts out from the mainland toward the Venetian Islands. My mother points to the numerous small signs along the road with the word "Zimmer." They announce room rentals, clearly appealing to the budget German tourist. "We should have checked the prices in those," she comments.

But I am undaunted. The campground is sprawling and crowded, but it is right by the beach, and the water views are superb. At the campground office, we are assigned a spot right on the sand, and Eliza and I start putting together the heavy burlap tent. Still, it is hard to ignore my parents' dislike of the accommodations.

It is dark by the time we finish installing ourselves in the tent. The sky is flashing with lightning. A powerful rainstorm passes through, and as Eliza and I open our sleeping bags, we notice a leak in the tent. Water is seeping in at an alarmingly fast rate. Reluctantly, we pick up our sleeping bags and make our way to our parents' sturdier tent-like structure. It's almost like a small cabin, with a wooden floor and several bunkbeds.

"We have some water inside," Eliza says.

"You may as well stay here with your sleeping bags. There's plenty of room."

The next morning, we take the ferry boat to Venice. Three years ago, when we passed through this sumptuous and waterlogged city, I resisted warming up to it. It must have been especially warm, and I remember the stench from the canals as spoiled waste and litter bobbed right alongside the gondolas. Even after six years in New York, Venice seemed remarkably dirty. But toward the end of that visit, I had softened to it. And now, at the age of sixteen, I am fully on board. The Venetian palazzos leave me speechless. The movement of boats along the canals, some romantically serene, others hurried and loud, is mesmerizing.

"Venice is my favorite city in the world!" I say now, eating with great hunger slice after slice of the pizza that I have missed so much since New York.

Though we are traveling on the cheap, my mother tells us that she would like us to purchase a sweater and a pair of shoes each to take home for the winter. Eventually, I find a green turtleneck and a sturdy pair of brown loafers with a bronze buckle running across the front. Both are agreeable to me and the budget. It's impossible for me to forget these two items because I wear them almost every day in the fall and winter of my university years in Poland.

Nina Lewandowska Camic

Chapter 8

1.

I'm so Polish! Three years back, and it's as if I had never left. My contacts with New York have fizzled to nothing. I no longer follow the latest music, rarely get my hands on western press, and never listen to news other than what is reported on the Polish, state-controlled television. I read American novels, but this is unremarkable. Many well-educated Poles become fluent enough in a second language to pick up a book in it. True, my choices are straight from my mother's shelf of American novels, but this is merely a fleeting dabble in what I feel to be my otherwise very Polish life. And yet, every now and then, I wonder if something happened to rob me of a complete and exclusive identification with my homeland in those childhood years in New York. When I see an American movie on the Polish cinema screen, I know that I am experiencing it differently than the roomful of people watching it with me. I am flooded with Polishness, but there is that part of me that stands to the side, refusing to give in. The fit is good, but it's not a perfect match. Will it ever be a perfect match?

2.

Polish universities are like schools of higher learning in the rest of Europe. They do not open their doors to a new academic year until October. But despite this longer summer break, I do not travel to my grandparents' village home very often. I am at an age where the isolation of the house—now with electricity but still without a phone line—is palpable, and I don't like it. I do see Babcia when she comes to town each week with her usual cheeses, garden vegetables, and baked goods. Dziadek, on the other hand, remains in the south of Poland, living with his relatives near the village where he was born. He has lost all interest in Gniazdowo and stays firm in his resolve not to return. Though she does not talk about her loneliness to me, it is clear that Babcia feels abandoned. She takes the time to visit her brother in the southwest of Poland, but though he urges her to move to where he lives, I am not surprised that she resists. Her son lives in California, and her daughter is in Warsaw. If she could, she would live across the street from both. The next best thing is being a short train ride away from one.

In the middle of September, I finally take the train to visit Babcia. I walk from the station along the riverbank, and I feel a profound melancholy as I look around me. Since my spring visit here, there has been such a change in the landscape. When Marcin and Jerzyk came to see me in May, the acacia trees were covered with fragrant white blossoms, the forget-me-nots lined the shores of creeks, and poppies splashed red color between the shafts of wheat in the farmed thin strips of land. That vitality and freshness of spring is long gone. I pass stacks of hay neatly left in the fields where poppies once sprouted. The leaves on the tall birches are starting to dry out, and t. My delirious giddiness, too, has receded. Marcin had just kissed me then, and I was encapsulated in my love for him. Everything else was external and irrelevant. That was then. In the summer months following my camping trip with his family, he and I were rarely in Warsaw at the same time. Once, he wrote a letter from the southern highlands. It was chatty and, in my mind, emotionally hollow. Signing *caluje* ("I kiss you" in English, the equivalent of the ubiquitous love) never felt so empty.

I open the gate to the yard now and look up at the house. I see Babcia in the kitchen window. She hasn't noticed me yet, even as her gaze is directed toward the road. When she sees me, she quickly wipes her hands on her apron. A happy smile lights up her aging face. She seems shorter now, and when she showers me with kisses, I bend down to greet her at her own level. During this visit, I spend a good amount of time sitting with her on the bench outside the house. We don't talk much, but when I tell her a story or a piece of gossip about people she knows, she lets out soft chuckles of appreciation. I wish I had more stories to tell her. When I leave after a few days, she cries. I am not surprised. She has cried nearly every time our family car has pulled out of the yard on weekend visits. But this time, I know, and she knows it will be a while before I come again, and her sadness seems more profound. I am walking away from her as she stands bravely alone at the gate of the homestead without a phone, without a way to talk to the family that she has cared for all her adult life.

In Warsaw, I have received instructions on what I must do in the month before my studies begin. Each new university student has an obligation to do physical labor before starting classes. It is a new program to give perspective and teach respect for those employed in menial work. Some students choose to leave Warsaw, signing on for work in the struggling towns and villages of the northern regions of Poland, but I opt to stay in the city. Warsaw's city parks are taking a number of student workers, and I sign up to be one of them. On paper, it sounds good. The major parks are close to where I live, and showing up for outdoor work on warm late summer days is not unpleasant. But the parks aren't ready for the crew of young temporary workers, and the tasks assigned to us seem random and often without purpose. Occasionally we're asked to weed the edges of graveled paths. At other times, we rake and tidy remote corners of the park. Our student work crew is unenthusiastic and lethargic. Cigarette breaks are frequent, and our progress is lackluster. I am reminded of the saying that has been floating around Poland for many years: *czy sie stoi czy sie lezy, dwa tysiace sie nalezy* (whether you're standing up or lying down, you're owed two thousand zlotys—a reference to work in a socialist state, where you get paid no matter how little effort you give to the job). I do not work any more or any less than the rest, but our shared indifference to the job makes for a terribly long day.

The weeks of work in the parks offer something else that is rare for soon-to-be university students—a chance to be with a new set of people. Warsaw is a large city, but we live our days within small, loosely integrated communities. Varsovians from Srodmiescie, the city center, work in Srodmiescie, and their children attend schools in Srodmiescie. I sailed through my three years at the lycee with the same group of students. No one was added, shuffled in, or eliminated from the class of some three dozen kids. I remember America as a country of great mobility, and UNIS was in constant flux. A year did not pass without the addition of new students or someone suddenly leaving to go back to her home country.

Here, not only my school but my city too is grimly stagnant. Warsaw accepts few newcomers. If families from agrarian regions want to move to the city, they face a continuing, acute housing shortage. There is no fluid apartment rental market that I know of. Warsaw residents stay put in the places allotted to them. They'll pass on the apartment to their children as young families form. The aging grandparents will share the space and some of the household responsibilities. They'll stand in line for food and take the youngest children to the park. If a young family wants to live independently, they can buy a unit in one of the new cooperative housing blocks slowly being built at the city's periphery. Still, the wait for a unit is long, and preferences are given to those who can pay with western currencies. Ten thousand dollars may buy you a pretty little apartment (unfinished inside), but very few have access to sums that large. And so, the city sees no significant expansion after the initial burst of postwar construction. Of course, it sees no contraction either. Residents of Warsaw do not leave. Their entire lives may unfold within the same neighborhood, perhaps the same apartment, with the same stores, parks, and playgrounds, where you'll sit on the same bench that maybe your grandmother sat on when you were little. So my entrance to the university accomplishes something rare—it allows me to make new friends.

3.

Our university studies begin just as autumn comes with full force to Central Europe. The campus itself is a beautiful half-hour walk from my home along Nowy Swiat and Krakowskie Przedmiescie, the streets that form the Royal Way, probably the most picturesque set of blocks in the city. If you follow the wide avenue beyond the university, you'll be in the Old Town, a favorite destination for tourists and locals. Marcin comes up to my apartment on the first day of classes, and we head out together. But at the departmental gates, we part ways. Our econometrics group is divided into two sections. One is for students who have preferenced advanced French, and the other is for those who have chosen advanced English as their foreign language. Marcin picked French. I had hesitated in this one course choice and then decided on English—the easy route for me. It is, of course, a waste for me to select English, but I am apprehensive about being so young, and this seemed like a small compromise, considering the otherwise intense schedule of classes we had before us: Political Economy, Advanced Calculus, Introduction to Econometrics, Accounting, Economic Theory. There is no breathing room, no chance to explore or sample. From day one, our classes are completely focused on the discipline we had chosen as our major. And so, though we would share some lectures, Marcin and I have no small classes together.

I am definitely on the lookout for new friends. My lycee group has dispersed quickly, and apart from Joanna, I see almost no one else from my high school. Two girls from Zmichowska Lycee are also in the econometrics program, but they are from a different class, and I hardly know either of them. Of course, I am no different than the rest. We are all in classrooms with strangers.

The gender split in the econometrics group only slightly favors men. I have plenty of opportunities to make close friends among the young women, and I eventually find Agnieszka, a café buddy who slowly replaces Joanna as the go-to person for a quick cup of tea up the street at our favorite meeting place. But she is my only female friend. I will grow close to other university students, but they all will be men.

It is not at all surprising that the two people I notice first are Tomek and Krzys. They are both outgoing and smart. Though they are not immediately friends with each other, it is obvious to me that they are both ambitious and, in terms of academics, ahead of the pack. I develop an instant liking for both, even though these two young men seem about as different as you could imagine. Krzys is someone who has had few breaks in life. He lives in a room that he rents from an older woman in the city. His father is deceased, and his mother resides in a small provincial town south of Warsaw. He brings an inherent seriousness to all the meetups that I have with him at the coffee houses of Warsaw. There is not even a suggestion of romance between us. We are friends in the way that Polish young people play out friendship. We sip tea and we talk. I can tell Krzys is amused by my young age and my refusal to get serious about my work.

"Tell me about your weekend," he'll say as I plunge into stories of people and movies and walks in city parks.

"And you?" I ask.

"Oh, you know I do none of those things. I shopped for groceries for my landlady. She's getting old, and it's hard for her to stand in line. And then I worked." Krzys is tall, and he has the look of an older person. His hairline is receding, and his eyes show worry.

"Do you miss your hometown?"

"Miss? That's not a word I know. Besides, there's not much to my hometown."

Krzys is discreet in displaying his talents. But word spreads quickly that he shows a genius for economic analysis. Perhaps equally talented, especially in our math-related subjects, is Tomek. Unlike Krzys, Tomek is a Warsaw man through and through. His father, an economist who works for LOT Polish Airlines, has traveled extensively, and the family has contacts in Canada. Tomek attended another excellent lycee in the city. He has stayed close to Piotr and Jacek, two of his former classmates, even though they have all chosen different academic programs for their post lycee education. Tomek, Piotr, and Jacek eventually become my three best friends during my university years in Warsaw. In the decades that follow, Tomek (and later, his wife, Basia) will keep my connection to Warsaw alive.

Nina Lewandowska Camic

For now, I am a student. That, in itself, has status. Even though I am unusually young, I've moved from being a schoolgirl to being an adult. We're not called by our first names anymore. In classes, I am Pani Lewandowska. I like that. Unfortunately, I like the trimmings of student life far better than the realities of my academic discipline. The lectures in economics I find, for the most part, terribly dull. I appreciate bits and pieces. The theory of capitalism is illuminating, even if it is obvious that we are studying it from only the Marxist perspective. But as we begin to probe into supply and demand models and as the mathematical complexities grow, I wonder if I can survive the program. In the first semester, my grades are excellent. But with each subsequent semester, I find that I am slipping. Instead of working harder, I work less each month and become more and more indifferent to the enterprise. If I once had ambitions to be a journalist, writer, or professor, now I begin to see that as an econometrician, I am likely to work for a government agency, producing statistical analyses of economic data. I am not interested in aiming higher. Perhaps because at some level, I understand that, most likely, I am not good enough, and certainly, I am not dedicated enough to do the work required of, say, a professor in econometrics.

Therefore, the first year of studies is a deep disappointment from the academic side. On the emotional front, the year is tumultuous and not a little distressing. At the beginning of the first semester, Marcin and I resume our love life without prompt or discussion. He is again coming over to my home, still always with a surprise visit, and more than once, we spend a wonderful hour that closely resembles our first sexual encounter during his visit to the village house back in May. But as autumn progresses, his visits grow increasingly less frequent. He tells me he has become deeply involved with KIK (Club of Catholic Intelligentsia), and he describes in great detail the people he has met there, including a young woman named Kinga. He never suggests that his affections are now centered on her, but the more he talks about her, the more I understand that I am ignoring a blunt reality: Marcin is not in love with me. Nonetheless, I have to admit that I am an easy target. I am always available, willing to accept him when he decides to resume our wobbly love affair.

As we move into the short, dark days of winter, I know I am underwhelmed by all that is happening both in the classroom and in my social life. I'm not sure how to improve my attitude toward classes. The idea of working harder at my assignments never enters my head. If I don't like a subject, I put in minimum effort and look for distractions. I loved the years of algebra and trigonometry in high school. I do not like the greater complexity of advanced mathematical analysis at all. And still, I like my ambitious and devilishly motivated new friends. I want to spend more time with them, so I suggest a party. I tell them I'll host. I invite Tomek and his friends Piotr and Jacek and a few girls who seem to come in and out of our friendly after-class conversations. And I invite Marcin.

As I introduce Marcin to the others, I notice how picayune his stories have become in my eyes. As he throws himself into a too familiar tale, spelling out how he can handle walking on slippery icy surfaces, I find myself drifting away from the flow of the inconsequential chatter. We don't consume a lot of alcohol, yet I feel myself drifting, as if on a buoyant ocean of emptiness. Why am I not finding a niche in this group of very nice young adults now? Is it because I am suddenly feeling less connected to my own Polishness? And why do I persist in thinking that being in a relationship with Marcin would be a good thing? If I feel uneasy about any of this, I surely don't act on it. After the party ends, Marcin doesn't even have to ask. He stays in my apartment far longer than the rest, and once again, my love for this guy who is so familiar to me surges. I am again momentarily very happy.

4.

Toward spring of my first year at the university, my parents float the idea of a summer vacation. I am surprised that they should want to vacation with each other, let alone with us. Their withdrawal from family life has been solid. My mother continues to close the door to her room each day, and we assume that she is working on complicated editing projects. Or something. We rarely eat suppers together. That habit had waned and then completely disappeared. We do hear occasional passing comments from her about her stress level with respect to her editing. Some workplaces are especially affected by the rise of hostilities toward the West and by the rhetoric of anti-Semitism that remains strong in the political culture of 1970. Hers appears to be such a workplace.

These are the last months of the reign of Cyrankiewicz—my mother's Jozef. With Jaroszewicz as the new prime minister, the country will veer in a direction that will eventually lead to an economic crisis and the collapse of the current system of governance. But two more decades will pass before Poland embarks on democratic reform and the reintroduction of market capitalism. My father is passing the time at the headquarters of the Communist Party, and my mother continues to edit texts translated into English. And, as if stuck forever in a swirl of muddied waters, my parents' attitude toward each other has remained hostile. If anything, I see them even less frequently in each other's company. And yet, they cling to the family vacation ritual, perhaps fearing that if this event is scrapped, so, too, will fall any pretense of unity within our family.

My summer months now are not entirely my own. I have a month of compulsory army training, followed by a month of work as an apprentice economist at a textile factory in Warsaw. But in early September I will be free, and my parents suggest that we drive to East Germany for two weeks in the mountains there. My father tells us that quite possibly, we will be allowed to visit West Berlin for a few hours even as we surely will be staying on the eastern side of the city. I am happy to have a trip before us, but my sister politely declines to go along. If the lycee had her feeling marginalized and disconnected from her peers, she has suddenly found herself on quite good terms with many people at the university. She has a growing circle of friends, and she continues to maintain connections with some of our summer friends from the village. She has little interest in travel with my parents.

It's nearly the end of the school year. Krzys and I are sitting at a café near Polna Street, not far from where the open-air market still supports a few stalls with fresh produce in the warmer months of the year. I tell him that I am greatly looking forward to the end of the first year of studies.

"What do you think you'll do after you're done here?" I ask him now.

"I don't know. That seems a long way away, don't you think?"

He looks at me now with a half-smile, but it's a serious expression. Or maybe it's that his face always has that touch of seriousness. As I study him, I think that he seems even older now. You could easily mistake him for one of the junior faculty members at the university.

"Where are you doing your summer internship?" I ask him.

"Close to my hometown. I need to look in on my mother. She's not doing well right now."

"Do you have a brother or sister who could help her too?"

"Nope. Just me."

"Well, if you're in Warsaw, call me. We can take a walk."

———

Krzys is right, of course. After the first year, we'll have four years left to complete our master's degree in econometrics. But I am almost convinced by now that I have chosen the wrong field of studies. Even though economic theory spells out principles of behavior that have relevance to our daily life, I can't quite fish out the human elements of the discipline. Mathematical modeling bores me. It all seems terribly abstract and disconnected from everyday reality. The personal note is missing. At seventeen, I am old enough to understand what interests me in school and in scholarly work. As I stand one afternoon in front of the doors to the computing center at the Palace of Culture used by students and faculty to run programs and test our nascent computing skills, I think to myself, *I don't care enough about computer programming to spend even this little time on it. I need to do the impossible. I need to change my course of study.*

———

The summer at a textile factory in southern Warsaw confirms my fears that I have made a terrible mistake picking econometrics. As I arrive for my first day on the job, I am handed a stack of bookkeeping

Nina Lewandowska Camic

sheets, most of them in great disarray.

"You'll be tracking our production quotas," the office manager tells me. "We want to do some projections for the next five-year period, and we need to look at our numbers more closely. Let's see what you can do with these various summaries that our accountant has put together."

———

Tedious work. I know I need to produce a paper analyzing what I accomplished in the course of my internship. I doubt that the numbers I'll pull out for the head of the department will be useful. I think the job is being dumped in my lap because someone has to produce a report to comply with directives coming from outside the factory. May as well hand it to the intern.

———

If my internship leaves me feeling anxious about my future in econometrics, my second summer month puts me in a place where I don't think about my studies at all. It is the month when I am fulfilling the army requirement recently imposed on all students at the university. We are to complete basic training at a military base in Warsaw. The army campus is by the edge of the Vistula River, a pleasant forty-minute walk from my home. My unit, composed of only women, must complete both the classroom training, covering such topics as first aid and rifle assembly and the hands-on component, where we are trained in the use of firearms.

I am struck by how dated it all feels. In the classroom, we learn about trench warfare. We are taught how to stop a blood flow from a gunfire or grenade injury, clean and treat wounds, and rescue someone in the line of fire. We use books with pictures that must be at least twenty years old. Learning to use a rifle, too, seems terribly old as if we're continuing a training program held over from the Second World War or maybe even earlier. I remember the images from television that gave just a small glimpse into the war that is now taking place in Vietnam. Even to the uninformed viewer, the images portray a level of technological complexity that is missing here, at this Polish army base. Or is it that our training isn't treated as vital to any future military operation? Maybe we are placed in these instructional modules because we are students, fulfilling a requirement no one understands nor wants to fully support? In any case, I find myself enjoying the absurdity of acquiring these skills. If the artery has been severed, put your bandage in this place. When the target is moving, use your rifle in this manner. Even in this short month, I become quite adept at the shooting range. At the end of the military training, I leave the barracks feeling somewhat accomplished, even if it is an absurd and meaningless accomplishment that will fade before the summer's end.

The two-week trip with my parents to Germany, on the other hand, leaves me feeling empty. I appreciate the chance to visit Poland's neighbor to the west, but even without the burden of traveling with parents who are mostly indifferent to family life, I find it hard to really enjoy a holiday in Germany. I am far too close still to a history that has cast Germany in a light that I cannot yet stomach. It is 1970—twenty-five years since the war has ended. Twenty-five years is not a long time. And there is another layer here that I find difficult to digest. We are just nine years into the existence of the Berlin Wall. Our visit to East Germany begins in Berlin, and I am immediately looking head-on at a reality that seems downright surreal. A city split in two. A line drawn to divide. With two superpowers ensuring that travel between the East and the West would be at first merely difficult and eventually impossible.

In East Berlin, the neighborhood where our hotel is located is dreadfully somber. Without the color of an active commercial life, the city blocks are bleak, as if someone had used a sponge that wiped out any pigment other than gray and brown. Warsaw, by comparison, has a vitality despite a modest commercial infrastructure. I never felt that my city lacked color. On the other hand, East Berlin seems as if it was reconstructed in a punishing way. There is no reason to like it. It shows no warmth, no appeal to the human heart.

But what makes it infinitely worse is that if you cross the Berlin Wall—and as foreign visitors, we are permitted to enter West Berlin on a day pass—everything changes. We are dropped off in the commercial heart of the western city, and you cannot fathom how these blocks could be part of an entirety that is, at its core, one Berlin. My mother tells me that I can purchase an inexpensive souvenir in West Berlin, and I buy a cheap brown felt hat. I think it's funky and cool. I wear it that day, but it feels strange and out of place when we cross back to East Berlin. I take it off then and never wear it again.

On our way south to the hilly East German village where we are to vacation, we stop for a day in Weimar, a pretty little city that was home once to Goethe and Schiller. Both writers' residences have been preserved for visitors, and as we stroll through the rooms of the Schiller home, I fall in love with the aura of the place. It seems so perfect for a writer! Down to the beautiful desk that once belonged to the famous author. I remember that not too long ago, I had wanted to be a writer, or at the very least a journalist. The craving to write more seriously hits me again.

"Tatus," I say to my father.

"Yes?"

"Isn't that a gorgeous desk? The one Schiller used for writing?"

"It is. Why, do you want it?" His eyes are laughing at me, but his voice is perfectly serious. If he is being playful, I'm not prepared for it. Of course, my father cannot possibly guess that I want to write, in some fashion, on some surface, in some imaginary world where it would not matter that as a result of skipped grades and switched languages, I have great gaps in language usage, in literature, in other words in everything that you need to write well. Now, looking out on Schiller's desk, I say nothing about writing and opt instead for answering my father, Tatus, with the note of whimsey that surely he was injecting into his question.

"Yes, can you get it for me?" And maybe I want to believe, just for this one fleeting second, that he is just the kind of father who would do magical things to make his children happy.

"You really want it? Really?"

"I do!" I don't mean it, of course, but I do, for this one last fleeting moment, imagine that my father is capable of great deeds, magical acts that bring good things to all people, especially his family. In years to come, his might diminishes in my eyes and perhaps in the eyes of others so much that I grow to feel sorry for him. A man who my mother and his daughters once admired will have to face the indifference and perhaps hatred of one and the disappointment of the others. But in Weimar, I still allow myself to toy with an image of his cleverness and grandness, even as I know that the desk will never be mine and that I will never write in the way that I once imagined I could write.

5.

Once again, a summer passes and I have spent almost no time with Babcia. When we return from Germany, I don't go to Gniazdowo. Instead, I hop on a train and head to the south of Poland to visit my old high school friend Joanna, who is renting a room for herself in Zawoja, a village in the Beskidy Mountains. I don't know that this will be the last time I will ever see her. Unlike all my other friends, who will go on to finish their careers and eventually retire in Warsaw, Joanna will opt out of living in the city. The highlands will have lured her back, and she will abandon her career, family, and friends for a life in the mountains where I visit her now.

Very little from this trip stays with me, even though the setting, just at the foot of the summit of old Babia Gora, is magical as Joanna described it! I know that the emptiness I often felt in my high school years—a hollow ache that I attributed to my unreciprocated infatuation with Marcin—is with me now. Maybe it's that I do not like Joanna's crowd of friends. Or maybe there is a deeper unease born of the realization that I am drifting, untethered, without a credible goal, without a love or even a like for the career I have chosen. Now, in Zawoja, we climb the mountain at night to watch the sun rise at an ungodly hour. I have my guitar, and we sing endless rounds of the very plaintive Goralka Halka, and most likely, we drink plenty of cheap wine. I seem to have developed a talent for feeding my bouts of deep melancholy.

It's the end of summer. My last full summer in Poland, though I have no idea that this is the case. All I know is that I only have a handful of days left before school starts again, and I use them to finally visit Babcia.

She is not alone now. Dziadek has returned, but he is of little help to her. He is eighty-five years old and, for the most part, bedridden. I ask if I can do anything for them, but I know my offer is like a thin sliver of a benefit. Without time, I can do very little. She asks me to take some of my grandfather's urine to the nearest town. A lab can do an analysis, but she has no way to take it there herself. Babcia has never driven a car and never used a bicycle, to my knowledge. She is constrained to moving around either on foot or by horse-drawn wagon. I pedal to town, spilling some of the contents as I bump over the rutted dirt road. I stop at the clinic in town, then pedal over to the general store to pick up a few items on Babcia's shopping list. I think how impossible her chores have become. Caring for infants was tough, but at least Dziadek was available to back her up when the job became overwhelming. Now she is completely alone, with a sick old man who needs care.

I pedal back, just beating a monstrous thunderstorm. How many times have I run from storms here, in Gniazdowo? How many times have I panted on my bike, hoping that I would make it before the crashing thunder filled the quiet countryside? In the house, I enter my grandparents' bedroom and approach Dziadek's bed.

"How are you doing?" I ask, lightly, with a smile that I hope looks encouraging.

He chuckles at me. I know that chuckle. He owns it—Dziadek, with his creased forehead and smiling eyes. But I note that his eyes are wet as if he's been crying. Has he?

Just a year or two earlier, when he was still quite mobile, he and Babcia came together to Warsaw. I had never been with them to the movies, but this time Dziadek wanted to see a film about the folk group Mazowsze, so my mother, my sister, my grandparents, and I went. He sat next to me, and I could feel his deep, rhythmic breathing beside me. It was the kind of breathing I had seen when he would lean back in a canvas chair outside, in the countryside, enjoying the sunshine and the delicate chirping of birds in the garden. When I was much younger, I would pull up a canvas chair right by him, and we would both gently sway backward and forward. Once, very long ago, I noticed that a wasp had landed on his arm.

"Dziadku, swat it!"

"What for? He's not harming anyone."

"Aren't you scared that he'll bite?" "No. You see? He's happy to go away by himself." Dziadek's eyes had that distinct twinkle, and as he looked at me with a grin, I sat back in my chair and felt not a small amount of pride in the man who would not swat a wasp.

Now, at the showing of the film about Mazowsze, I glance sideways at him, and I see that he is crying. At the end of the film, I ask, "Were you crying?"

"Of course! Don't you cry when you hear something beautiful?"

As I get ready to leave the village, Babcia kisses me hard.

"I will see you in Warsaw," she tells me. "The woman from the village will come to mind him for a day next week. I will see you then."

It's a beautiful autumn in the city. Classes will start again in October, and I resolve to do better with them. One class at least offers a pleasant surprise. My uncle will deliver economic theory lectures, and I am at least a little proud that he appears to command respect among the students. I learn to like my class in logic, and I am happy enough to be learning the economics of socialism, having last year studied the economics of capitalism. But the advanced calculus class is too difficult, too abstract. Very quickly, I lose patience with it.

And I lose patience with Marcin. We never talk about being together, which is not surprising because Marcin shows little interest right now in being with me. As far as I'm concerned, we're not even friends. When I am not with Tomek and his friends, I am often alone. On my way home one afternoon, I brood about all the uncertainties piling up around me. Family life, social life, and university life all seem wobbly and without direction.

As I fret about this, I walk past the philharmonic building. I pause to read the posted notice. The International Chopin Competition, an event that takes place in Warsaw every five years, is about to begin, and as a student, I see that I can attend all the competition events free of charge. I pick up a schedule of performances and check off the ones I can go to between classes. Instead of mathematical equations, my head begins to fill with the perfect distraction—the music of Chopin. I am enraptured with the performances, and I quickly develop a love for the Americans in the competition—Emanuel Ax and Garrick Ohlsson.

I root for them at each stage and am ecstatic when Ohlsson wins. Garrick, who is a mere twenty-two years old in 1970, will return to play at the Warsaw Philharmonic in 2017, and I will be in the audience, having returned to Poland for a brief visit. After, I'll stand in a short line to meet him in the hallways. In offering my meager thanks for yet another brilliant performance, I will mention that I had been in the audience nearly fifty years earlier. Only as I walk away do I realize that nearly everyone in line has a story the same as mine.

I ask Tomek and Eliza to join me for the 1970 gala event where the finalists play for a packed house of concertgoers. I am trying very hard to move away from including Marcin in social events.

As my days hopscotch between classes and piano music, I never even notice how much I have moved away from tracking the political developments in Poland. If, before 1968, I was lost in confusion as to what direction was best for my home country, the last two years of the decade left no ambiguity there. It is obvious to most everyone who isn't part of the current power elite that the system of governance in Poland has grossly failed us. It's as if the departure of so many of the remaining Jewish people in the last decade somehow shut the door for the rest of us, locking us inside something that has no hope for a good outcome. Toward the end of 1970, Jaroszewicz steps into the post of prime minister, and Gierek replaces Gomulka as the head of the Communist Party. On the one hand, we look with approval at Gierek's credentials. Gierek spent his childhood in France, and his entrance into politics was through his joining the French Communist Party. Surely this will mean a kinder stance toward countries of Western Europe? Surely there will be changes? Greater transparency, perhaps? A redirection of governmental priorities?

We are slated to be disappointed. Very quickly we recognize that no changes will be forthcoming. The news stories flash the same propaganda about economic successes, even as consumer items are hard to come by. If I had any interest in politics early on, that interest dissipates toward the end of the decade. By the end of 1970, I not only stop watching the news on TV, but I cut myself off completely from even reading the local paper. Like so many others, I make myself deliberately blind and deaf to anything having to do with politics. At home, my father says nothing about the changes in heads of state. He continues to work for the Communist Party, and he continues with his longstanding silence on all topics related to the Polish political reality.

When winter break comes, I am surprised and delighted that Tomek has invited me and another female student at econometrics named Elka to join him and his friends, Piotr and Jacek, for ten days in the mountains.

"You should bring your skis. We all want to do some skiing," he tells me. I don't admit that I do not own skis, but I know they will not be hard to obtain. Basic Polish boards are readily available in sporting goods stores. Though there are almost no mechanical lifts or groomed ski trails in the Polish highlands, skiing still draws a dedicated following.

"Where are you thinking of going?"

"I don't exactly know. Jacek and Piotr will go a few days earlier. They'll scout out a place for all of us."

I tell my parents about the forthcoming trip. I'm only seventeen, two years younger than all my university friends, so I half expect questions, perhaps even objections. But none are forthcoming. If anything, my parents seem even more distracted and disinclined to involve themselves in decisions Eliza and I make for ourselves. By now, they are not unique in their hands-off parenting style. My university friends, too, are on their own in everything but room and board. Yes, family for all of them is important. Even as young adults, they continue to participate in events and holiday celebrations with their parents and grandparents. Except for Krzys, all of my friends live at home. Nonetheless, they maintain a high level of independence. The trip to the mountains is an example of their ability to create a life around friends, far from the inquisitive parental eye.

It is a glorious winter trip. The newly formed group has a smooth and easy dynamic, and I'm starting to feel a warmth toward all of them—a friendship that I hadn't felt since my high school years. Jacek is the funny guy you'd want to have on any trip. Slight in frame, he moves quickly and thinks creatively. Later in life, he'll be the entrepreneur of the group, extremely successful in the market economy that will take hold in Poland in the last decade of the twentieth century. Piotr is more serious and careful in his choice of words, but he, too, loves to banter with his friends. He is an engineer slated to teach at the Polytechnique. Tomek, of course, is my link to them all. In a number of ways, I think of him as my best friend in school. The one other woman in the group, Elka, is even at this early stage of econometrics, intensely focused on forging a successful future for herself. She is attentive to her appearance with a beautifully smooth face, thin, somewhat puckered lips, short and smart hair, and a slender build. She is confident and well liked by all the men in our circle of friends. Of course, we don't know yet that eventually, she will marry, then divorce Jacek. Too, she'll be the one who will set the wheels in motion for establishing the Polish Stock Market Exchange once market capitalism returns to Poland. For now, even though I think she and I are friends only at the margins, we work well together. The group will grow to include others over the years. Piotr and Tomek will bring wives into the mix. There will be kids, and they will form friendships too. But for now, we are just five second-year university students spending winter break in the mountains together.

Jacek and Piotr find a place to stay at a highlander farmstead in the hidden valley of Rynias, just at the Czech border. All along the horizon, we see the peaks of the High Tatra Mountains. On most days, the air is brilliantly crisp. The gently sloping hills here are perfect for practice ski runs. It's been a long time since I have taken to a ski slope! The farmers feed us supper and breakfast, and they let us use two of the rooms in their two-story wooden home. Elka and I take the room with the stove, and the three men take the second room, significantly colder as it is without a direct source of heat. There is no running water, and we have to make do with an outhouse for our toilet needs, but the home does have electricity. We warm buckets of water and wash ourselves over basins inside. And we laugh. Oh, do we laugh! On the slope just outside the highlander home, at lunchtime over bowls of hot soup, in the evenings spent by the warm stove, we tease, tell stories, and laugh. I am enormously happy to be with this group of friends instead of at home in Warsaw, where I would inevitably be waiting for Marcin to come and ask me out for a walk.

6.

In my second year at the university, two very important things happen. First, I get to know someone whom I grow to regard as an academic soul mate in my econometrics program—a person who appears equally disheartened by the abstract and impersonal nature of our studies. His name is Marian, and he is as smart as Tomek and Krzys, but at least at this stage of university life, he is less willing to accept without comment the tract of studies that we have before us. (Later, he will remain at the university as a professor of econometrics. He and Tomek will trade off leading the department as deans.)

"I have an idea," I say to him one afternoon as we drink tea together at my house.

Marian has a poet's gaze. He seems too easily distracted, too happy to wander off into a discussion of anything but economics.

I pick up a list of courses that sociology students are enrolled in over in the Sociology Department. Some of them look downright intriguing. I show this list to him.

"And so?"

"Well, I thought we could petition to maybe take one of these classes."

"And then what?"

"If I like it, maybe I could, over time, transfer to the Sociology Department."

"And start from scratch?"

"It wouldn't be from scratch. I'm sure there is some overlap in the areas of study."

"Okay, I'm willing to go along, only I don't think they'll agree to have us do this."

But, the university shines us a green light. In the spring semester, both Marian and I are enrolled as auditors in a seminar on social psychology. I am at least a little excited about a class for the first time.

The second important development arises in an extremely serendipitous manner, at the same time that it will, over time, completely change the course of my life.

It is early spring, and my parents are hosting a dinner. Back in New

Nina Lewandowska Camic

York, toward the end of my father's term as UN ambassador, he and my mother struck a cordial friendship with Arthur "Punch" and Carol Sulzberger. Perhaps there wasn't great substance to their friendship then. My parents were, after all, far from the intimate social orbit of the Sulzbergers. For generations, Carol and Punch were a prominent New York family at the center of a newspaper publishing empire. But there was enough of a friendliness to it that we were, as a family, invited once to their home on Fifth Avenue for a movie night with close friends and a few Sulzberger family members. And so, it was not strange that my parents would be notified that the Sulzbergers would be traveling through Warsaw, and it was obvious that my mother would want to plan a dinner party in their honor.

As was the case in previous instances when she hosted a dinner, my mother asks me now to help serve the meal and clean up afterward. And as always, I am glad to do this. When there is a dinner party at our house, life feels more normal. In preparation for it, our parents will talk to us and each other. My mother will once again care about food. And my father will open up his room and treat it more like the living room that it was once supposed to be.

Punch and Carol are agreeable guests, and the evening is moving along in a boisterous and lively fashion—something that I haven't seen for years in our home. I know my mother is pleased. She comes into the kitchen to check on the next stage of the meal, and I can see on her face the social smile that came so easily for her when we lived in New York. Toward the end of the evening, when I am just about to start preparing a tray for the final coffee, my mother is again in the kitchen. This time, she asks me to turn off the faucet at the sink. "Can you come into the living room for a minute?"

"I'm not quite ready with the coffee," I tell her. I had delayed preparing it because I wanted to soak the dinner plates first.

"No, put it down for now and come in. I think Carol wants to talk to you."

I follow my mother, thinking that this must be the time the grownups want to ask polite questions to the kids in the house.

Carol, perhaps the best-groomed person I have ever met, whose face has just the right amount of makeup, even as it can sometimes look drawn and stern, studies me carefully as I enter the room. Her whole frame softens, and she gives me a warm smile.

"Helen tells me you're in the middle of your studies?"

"That's right. I'm in my second year."

"But you have summers off?"

"I do this year. I already completed my required internships."

"I've been watching you help with the meal tonight. I'm impressed! Helen says you do this all the time?"

"Sure, I don't mind." I don't mention that there are very few dinner parties at our house these days.

"I was wondering. Our girl, Cynthia, is almost seven now, and she needs someone to look after her once school is out. How would you like to come and live with us for the summer and be her nanny?"

I look at my mother. Her eyes reveal nothing at all. But her smile is still there so that I know she has been consulted and is not opposed to the idea.

"Could I?" I ask my father with not a small amount of surprise. The idea of Polish me, daughter of a government official—not a very prominent one—but still a Communist Party official, joining the household of Carol and Punch, where Punch is now the president and publisher of *The New York Times*, seems like a script for an offbeat movie. But my father seems unperturbed.

"Of course. You would have to apply for a passport and a visitor's visa, but there's time for that."

"Can we help with getting those documents for her?" Punch asks.

"Oh, I think she is better off getting her uncle to issue an invitation. It's natural that he would. He lives in California."

My mother agrees. "Yes, Johnny can do that. He can also lend her money for the airfare."

"Then it's set. You know, Helen, we had a college girl last year, and it just didn't work out. She wasn't up for the job. I think Nina would be good for Cynthia."

And just like that, out of the blue, it appears that I have a summer job. Apart from the required internships, students don't look for temporary, seasonal employment in Poland. And yet, here I am, about to travel for work in America. Not New York exactly. The Sulzbergers have a summer house in Stamford, Connecticut, and I will spend most of my time there. Nonetheless, under these most unusual circumstances, it seems that I will be returning to my childhood haunts and to a country I had stopped thinking about for a very long while now.

7.

When classes end for the academic year, I take the train to the village to see Babcia and Dziadek. Again I do not stay long. I have the details of travel waiting for my attention in Warsaw. Dziadek is sitting up in bed in the village house, but he remains frail, and it's hard now to coax a smile to his face. I sense that he is in some amount of pain. And Babcia—the woman who has cared for family members since her youngest years—has visibly aged this winter. I can see that. She has lost weight, and her face is just a little creased. Most unusual for her. She is seventy years old, and she has had, until now, the complexion of a person half that age. I used to ask her if she secretly applied sour milk and cucumbers to her skin, and she would laugh and say that she had never used any cream or skin potion in her life! Her face is what it is. And right now, it's beginning to look old.

But it is Dziadek whom I should remember from this visit. It is the last time I will see him. He dies from what doctors assume to be stomach cancer this summer, in 1971, while I am in Connecticut taking care of Cynthia Sulzberger.

Back in Warsaw, I have already applied for a passport and a visa. My uncle in California, a genial man who refuses to let life's burdens sag his shoulders, unlike his sister—my mother—is happy to sponsor me and lend the sum needed for airfare. I purchase a ticket in the empty Warsaw office of KLM Royal Dutch Airlines, where no Polish customer ever seems to enter. If Poles travel, they fly LOT Polish Airlines, which accepts Polish currency. I purchase the KLM student special roundtrip from Warsaw to New York with my uncle's money. To make my overseas connection, I will be spending the night in Amsterdam. I'm feeling the might of this privilege. I'm about to do what few young Poles can do— hop on a plane and head west.

When I am notified that my U.S. visitor's visa application has been approved, I make my way to the American Embassy to get that coveted stamp on my passport. Inside the glass and steel building reminiscent of a short and stubby New York office skyscraper, I suddenly feel the confusion of being in a tiny slice of America in Poland. I start with an English greeting. After all, these people all speak English. Surely they are American. In the New York offices of the Polish Delegation to the UN, all the employees are from Poland. The woman at the desk answers in English but with a Polish accent. I miscalled that one. I quickly switch back to Polish. *So this is how it's going to be?* I think to myself. I'm caught between English and Polish. Which language should I claim as my own? When do I admit to which influence in my life? If I am traveling abroad and someone asks me, "Where are you from?" I should say Poland, right? But that masks a deeper truth. I am speaking as a New Yorker, too. If I speak English, must I admit to my Polishness?

Jackie, my childhood friend from UNIS, had stopped corresponding with me a few years back. I had no more contact with any of my UNIS friends. But when I write that I would be in the United States this summer, she responds immediately. Could I stay with her in New York before moving on to Connecticut? Could she pick me up at the airport? I hadn't explained to her about the Sulzbergers. Mail between the U.S. and Poland is often opened and picked through. I'm told that postal clerks search for dollars. I'm not sure if letters are read and if they are, by whom and for what purpose. My father had told me to be careful. "Don't go into great detail in your letters about where you're going and what you'll be doing."

I push back a little. "Why would I be in trouble? I'm not doing anything wrong, am I?"

"It's best not to draw attention to yourself. You know that."

Yes, I do. And yet I am puzzled by the game we play. My parents expect me to write letters from the Sulzbergers' home. Wouldn't that reveal where I am?

"People get envious if you have such contacts abroad."

People? What people? And what would that envy lead to?

My starting date with the Sulzbergers is July 1. I will be arriving in New York on June 27.

Dear Jackie,

Thanks for offering to pick me up at JFK! I'm excited about meeting your boyfriend, and I can't wait to see New York again. Love, Nina.

Chapter 9

1.

It's June 1971. I left New York five years ago as a thirteen-year-old, and now I am eighteen. A school kid in New York, a teenager in Warsaw. And here I am, on my way to America again—a place where teens have a cultural space all their own. Music, fashion style, vocabulary. Had I continued to live in New York, I would have kept up with the rock bands and worried incessantly about my physical appearance. Clothes, makeup, all of it. In Poland, a teen is simply an older kid with greater independence but without a scripted lifestyle that marks them as somehow unique, someone to be reckoned with. In my very Polish teen years, I cared about how clear my face was and how clean my hair felt. Clothes were of marginal importance. We never went clothes shopping, and I certainly didn't have a style of dressing. And now, in preparing for my summer with the Sulzbergers, I still do not fret about clothes. There isn't much to pack. A change of clothing, an extra pair of shoes. A few gifts of folk art from Cepelia, the national Polish folk art store. An overnight bag, really. My mother frowns as she looks at my packing efforts.

"You'll need to pick up some more shirts or skirts. This won't do. Johnny sent you two hundred dollars beyond the airfare. You won't need much in Amsterdam. Use the extra cash to buy a change in clothing."

"I'll try. I only have three days with Jackie before I have to show up at Punch's office."

"No, you really have to shop."

"Okay, okay. I'll buy something." Surely the Sulzbergers will understand that I do not wear the kind of clothing Americans take for granted. Still, my mother is insistent. Approximating American standards of appearance matters to her a great deal more than it matters to me at this point.

My flight to Amsterdam feels luxurious and very novel. My last airplane trip was years ago when we traveled to the Soviet Union. I barely remember what it's like to board a plane. I sit down in my assigned seat, noting that I am surrounded by foreigners. I stop hearing the Polish language. It's beginning to sink in that I am traveling on my own, away from Poland.

After two hours in the air, we land in Amsterdam. I have my old copy of *Europe on 5 Dollars a Day,* and I know that there is a public bus to town. I've circled several budget hotels that seem very nice, and the book's favorite, the Ambassade, has a cheap attic room available. At fifteen dollars for the night, it feels like a stretch for me, but I am enchanted with the look of it. The hotel opens onto the stately Herengracht Canal, and I feel I have been transported to another person's life. The clerk at the hotel desk looks at me curiously.

"One night only?"

"Yes. I'm just passing through."

"Well, now. Welcome. Breakfast tomorrow is in the second-floor room. It's included in the price," he tells me, glancing at my small American Tourister.

"Thanks. Oh, and I have a question. I want to go to the movies. I passed a movie house on the way here from the bus station. Do you know the hours of the shows? I want to see *Love Story.*" I had read the book. My father brought it back from the U.S. after one of his trips there.

"There are several showings. It's still quite popular. Here, the newspaper will tell us."

It is evening, and I am walking toward the theater. I don't stop for dinner. I have never been to a restaurant by myself, and I want to use my spare cash for the movie ticket. At the theater, I notice people are eating ice cream bars. I buy one and sink into the theater seat.

I think about love on my walk back to the hotel. Marcin knew I was traveling to the U.S. He seemed fairly indifferent to this piece of news, even though he did promise to write frequently as soon as I sent him the address. Tomek and Krzys were more curious. Krzys especially asked questions about what I intended to do once arriving in New York.

"I don't really know. Eat pizza." I laughed as I said it. I no longer even missed pizza. "I wanted to go to my UNIS graduation. My classmates are getting their high school diplomas this year. It feels strange to be thinking of them in this way. I am nearing the halfway point of my university program. But it's too late. They will have graduated several weeks before I get there. Hey, do you want me to bring you back something from America?"

"No. Nothing at all. I don't care for pop music. What else would I need?"

Although I see Krzys again in the fall semester and then once or twice in the year after, this is one of the last good conversations I have with him. A year later, I will be shocked to learn that he has died. My friends tell me he passed away in the bathtub due to a gas leak. I want to believe that my childish fear of water heaters that leaked gas was responsible for his exit from life. At the same time, I know that even good friends do not reveal themselves fully to each other. If he was looking for a way to end his life, I would not know of it. And so I return again and again to the idea that it was just a leak, just a terrible accident.

And terrible accidents, imagined and feared in childhood, do happen. A few years later, Uncle Andrzej, my economics professor and my father's brother, is fatally run down by a car trying to chase a departing bus from a Warsaw bus stop. My father, who, to my knowledge, saw him infrequently and certainly rarely in our home, will remain deeply affected by his brother's death. Long after, he'll lean forward in his chair, the same New York leather chair that made its way to the Warsaw living room, his bedroom, and his eyes will fill with tears each time.

"We shared a past, my brother and I. He understood me," my father will say. "Probably the only one who ever did."

2.

The large airplane lands at JFK Airport in New York. It should be so familiar now. I've been to this airport before. And yet, my first thoughts are how unreal it feels. I look around me and think that while I slept, America moved in a titanic shift elsewhere, to unfamiliar places. I do recognize some things. The oppressive mugginess outside is very much a New York memory. But too much has changed since I was here last. I am stepping out into a new reality.

As I come through the customs doors, I see Jackie. Or, I think this is her because she is grinning and waving at me. Five years ago, she had short, cropped hair and a few freckles on her pale face. She wore a pleated skirt and knee socks, and I'd never see her without a pair of glittery pink-framed glasses. I meet her now as a young woman with long, bushy hair pulled back in a ponytail. She is wearing jeans, but not the familiar Wranglers from five years back. These are bellbottoms, somewhat ripped at the bottom. I see no glasses. "Contacts!" She laughs as I comment on the absence of the pink frames. She gives me a great big hug, and with it, she pulls me right smack into America. In Poland, you kiss in greeting. In America, you hug. She leads me to a waiting car.

"This is Jimmy, my boyfriend." She says this casually as if they'd been together for a very long time. I smile at him. He, too, has long, dark, frizzy hair. He's standing by a big old convertible. I have never seen a car with a convertible roof in Poland.

"Get in the front seat!" Jackie tells me, and we make our way toward her home, the same home, an apartment with a sunken living room in Forest Hills, Queens.

I am too busy to keep a detailed journal now, but I jot down thoughts in short notations all summer long. My words from these first hours back: *Jackie has no bra! Cut jeans. No skirts! Radio—loud.*

Her mother greets me as if no time has passed since my absence.

"Well, look at you! I can hardly believe you're the same person!" Am I the same person? And what about Jackie? She is laughing in a stream of rapid giggles, much the same way that I have known her to laugh. But there is little of the shyness that I remember from the past. She will be eighteen this summer, but she seems to have latched onto adulthood early. If I thought myself to be independent, I had not considered that there are channels toward independence here in New York. And Jackie has definitely hopped onto one.

In the evening, she suggests we go into the city.

"Jimmy will take us. We go often to the Village. On a warm night, it can be really lively there."

The Village? I had been there maybe two or three times as a child. Always with my parents and always as a visitor in daylight hours. It was not my neighborhood, and I never went back alone. I preferred Central Park and the familiar blocks to the north of our apartment. The Village was for artists and hippies. And apparently for Jackie and Jimmy.

"Did you ever smoke marijuana?" she asks me point-blank as we crawl through the tunnel separating Queens from Manhattan.

"No, of course not. I don't know anyone who did in Poland."

"Well, you can try it! We have some. Later. But you can smell it on the streets too."

"Jackie, how did school finish for you? Did you still like UNIS?"

"No, not really. I stopped going to classes in the last year. You could do that. It was optional. If you passed certain tests, you were fine."

"How was graduation?"

"I didn't go. It's kind of considered not cool to go to a graduation."

I think I would have gone.

"But you know, we can go tomorrow to my friend's graduation out in Queens! She's not really attending the ceremony, but we can watch for a little bit! That might be fun. Want to go, Jimmy?"

"Yeah, I'll go."

I'm spinning a little. It must be the strong lights that suddenly flash at me from all sides. Or the heat. Even in the evening, the air feels damp and heavy.

I write more words in my journal: *Pot, drugs. NYC at night, traffic into town. Parking problems! Walk on Bleecker. Afros! Alive, God, how conservative I am! J's so aware and sensitive. Stuffy here, can't breathe!*

"Jackie, I have to pick up some cheap clothes. You know I have to show up at the Sulzbergers in three days."

"You can go to Alexanders. It's just across the boulevard where I live. They'll have cheap stuff there. Do you have to start work so soon?"

"Yes, I do." I say this, feeling no regret. The Sulzbergers offer shelter and predictability. My clean life, the one they wanted to hire, feels out of step with America. Jackie's not to blame, of course. I was the one who left.

Her mother asks me the predictable question. "So, what's it like back there, in Poland?"

I don't know what to say. "It's good. I'm at the university now, but it's just up the street from our home, so I haven't moved out or anything." I don't mention that most of my friends won't be moving out even after they graduate. Getting your own apartment in Warsaw when you're an adult is not a given. There are waiting lists, and you need hard currency.

"And your parents?"

"They're fine," I lie. "My sister too." Why do I insist on sticking to a storyline that's so upbeat? Is it that I think Poland will get unfairly blamed for all the issues facing my family back home?

"Well, Jackie was pretty excited that you were coming back. I hope you have some time off and come back to visit."

I quickly learn that the cheapest things are in the basement at Alexander's. I go there and look at counters of disheveled shirts. A rack to the side holds skirts. I pick out a brown pleated polyester skirt for $2.49 and an orange lace-up top for $1.49. I can't believe how inexpensive these clothes are! This outfit would be coveted and admired back in Warsaw. Here, it lies crumpled and rejected.

"No returns on that," the saleswoman tells me. "It's got a defect."

"What defect?"

"Don't know. Check it out. Oh, I see a stain and a tear. Mind you, no returns."

"I'll take it anyway."

At Jackie's friend's graduation, I feel the fissures widening between my peers and me, all the more so because I did not see this coming. I imagined we were all on parallel tracks and that living in Poland would not disrupt the familiarity that I felt with an American lifestyle. I was wrong. The school ceremony is in a park, and the risers are half empty. Everyone is casually dressed, as if for a summer picnic rather than a graduation. On the spartan stage, a student is about to speak. Jackie asks if I want to stay. I nod my head, not wanting to appear rude. I listen to the valedictorian's speech from a young man with long hair tied neatly in a ponytail. He is talking about the Vietnam War. I was deeply concerned about it as well before I was reminded in Warsaw that we weren't fully finished with the aftermath of a different war. The young man on the stage grows animated, and the audience reacts with sporadic bursts of applause. I glance at my friend chatting quietly to her boyfriend, and I realize I no longer know where her passions lie. I ask her if she is planning on going to college.

"I got accepted to the University of Washington. I thought I'd try the West Coast. But now I'm thinking of deferring. Maybe I'll go the following year."

"What will you do now?"

"Get a job! Jimmy and I want to take a car trip somewhere."

No one I know in Poland just gets a job. You enter the workforce, and when you do, you stay there. Moving in and out of part-time or full-time jobs is uncommon, indeed unheard of among young people. And not a single person our age has a car. Notes scribbled furiously in my journal: *Jackie's classes in her senior year at UNIS: The American Novel, European History, French, Psychology, Q1 Mathematical skills. Next semester: African History, Renaissance Drama, Child Development, Theater of the Absurd, Psychology.* I recall my own: Calculus, Chemistry, Physics, Biology, Polish Literature, Polish History, Geography, Workshop, languages. *UNIS teachers went by first names. Okay to skip going to class. She hardly went! Every conversation includes drugs! Talk about "the pill." Tampons! There are only two hairstyles: parted in the middle or the shag.*

Nina Lewandowska Camic

I feel so European, so out of place.

Jimmy comes back to pick us up that evening. It's late, and my head is swimming from lack of rest. I'm developing a cold. Still, we head out in his car to Jones Beach, a long strip of white sand lapped by the waters of the Atlantic Ocean. He and Jackie freely smoke pot while I look out into the darkness. I don't let on that I am a misfit now. I watch, I listen, and I eat. A lot. The food choices are incredible! Did I not see this before? Jimmy takes us to Nathan's. It's nearly midnight, and we fill ourselves with French fries. By two in the morning, we are finally back at Jackie's, and she takes out cookies and ice cream. In the next two days, we will have eaten cheeseburgers, Chinese take-out, and pizza. More French fries. Saltwater taffy. English muffins. Grapefruit and pineapple fruit cup. Minute steaks. More ice cream, this time, it's caramel walnut with warm butterscotch sauce. Not one of these items could be found in Poland. Not one.

Jackie walks me to the bus stop at the end of my stay with her. "You sure you know where you're going?"

"Yes, of course. I'm supposed to meet them at *The New York Times* building, off of Times Square."

"Call me, okay?"

"Sure, yes. Of course."

3.

"I'm here to see Mr. Sulzberger," I tell the guard at the entrance to the offices of *The New York Times*.

"Which one?"

"Mr. Author Ochs Sulzberger."

He looks at me quizzically as I put down my small American Tourister. "Is he expecting you?"

"Yes."

"Let me call his secretary." I wait while he dials the number. A minute later, he turns to me. "Okay, off you go. Take the elevator to the right. Fourteenth floor."

If the entrance to the building is busy and chaotic, as I get off the elevator on Punch's floor, I am in a quiet, carpeted world. An older woman comes to greet me and show me the way to Punch's office. "Wait here," she says. "He's just finishing a phone call."

In two minutes, Punch is out, greeting me warmly as he will always greet me when I spend time with him and his family.

"Hey! Good to see you! Carol and Cynthia are here already. They're down in the car. Let's go before the rush hour gets worse!"

I follow him down the elevator, out to the back, where, in the driveway, a station wagon is waiting. A man steps out from the driver's seat. He's wearing a gray suit and a matching gray chauffer's hat.

"Hello, Mr. Sulzberger. The keys are in the ignition. You sure you don't need us for the weekend?"

"Not at all, Lucien. See you in a few days!"

Punch tells me to get in the back seat. Cynthia, a beautiful little girl with a perky nose and long, nearly black, wavy hair that has a habit of falling over her dark eyes and pale forehead, is looking at me curiously.

"Cynthia, this is Nina."

I've thought about the moment of meeting her. Punch and Carol don't know this, but I have never babysat a young child. In fact, aside from the vacationing younger kids that trailed after us in the village during the summer, I have had no contact with little girls or boys and no experience caring for them. Still, I am young enough to remember being that age. I wait for cues from her as to how to proceed. But as I get in the car, it's Carol who turns toward me with questions and explanations.

"Our summer and weekend house is about an hour outside the city. We thought we'd have dinner together tonight, just the four of us. Tomorrow we'll show you around and introduce you to Iphigene, Arthur's mother." Carol never calls her husband Punch.

"Do you drive?"

"No, I'm sorry."

"Well, that's okay. I'll teach you to use the car on the property. Cynthia doesn't have anything planned yet for the summer. We thought we'd wait until you get here."

Cynthia is looking at me with a shy smile. She is a trusting and forgiving child, and she answers questions that I have for her politely and with a childish sincerity that is disarming. By the end of the ride, I know I am exceptionally lucky. Cynthia will be a rewarding charge— playful, affectionate, and completely loyal to her family and her new nanny.

4.

Neither the Sulzberger country house nor the East Coast affluent lifestyle that Carol and Punch so gracefully inhabit is familiar to me. Nonetheless, I feel at home in this new place, far more so than I felt when I was with Jimmy and Jackie. Carol and Punch's age, wealth, and prominence all conspire to keep them away from the symbols of the cultural rebellion taking place in America. And so, despite the immense gulf separating a Sulzberger in New York from a Lewandowski in Warsaw, I quickly begin to relax and recover my bearings.

The Sulzberger property in Connecticut is vast. A long private road curves uphill and then splits in two. A driveway to the right leads to a very modern, brown paneled building. This is where Punch and Carol stay and bring their family and friends. Had you followed the road to the left, you would have eventually come to a more traditional two-story white house where Punch's mother, Iphigene, spends most of her summer months. Punch and Carol's house looks out over a small private lake. Iphigene's home hasn't a lake view, but it has something much more coveted in the summer months—a large swimming pool. There is a poolside house too, where you can use the changing rooms and help yourself to snacks from the refreshment center. Towels and soft drinks are resupplied each day by the staff. In these summer months, I drank enormous quantities of Fresca. Of course, no one in Poland has a swimming pool. The fact that I am a strong swimmer can be traced back to my UNIS years, when we had class swimming periods weekly at the nearby community center.

Punch and Carol's house looks misleadingly simple on the outside. When you enter, you are immediately in a living area with large, floor-to-ceiling windows on opposite sides of the room, giving you the feeling that you are still one foot in the outdoor world. To the far left side of the living room, there is a game room with a small bumper pool table and comfortable chairs for movie viewing. The dining room extends to the right, and it too has large windows decorated by rows of plants and potted flowers tended by Carol. All five of the bedrooms, including mine, are upstairs. Servant quarters are down a separate corridor extending from the kitchen. By any standards, it is a large home on a large estate. But it's not the vastness here that leaves me feeling incredulous. Rather, it is how Carol and Punch, both firmly rooted in their positions of wealth and power, finesse their lives to be uniquely their own, fitting into few of the stereotypical images that I had of rich, prominent elites.

I sense right away that Punch is happiest when neither Lucien nor Juanita, the butler and maid who live with them in New York, comes to help with housekeeping chores in their country home. The estate does have Gino and Gina, groundskeepers and couple, charged with overseeing maintenance both inside and outside the two family houses. Still, for many of the days I am there, Carol and Punch are on their own, especially on the weekends when there are no houseguests. During these times, Punch takes out the grill and makes steaks or burgers for all of us, and he and I clean up after dinner.

My father often puttered in the kitchen in the evenings, but Punch's clean-up routines are significantly more impressive. Dishes are scraped and stacked in the dishwasher (a nonexistent appliance in a Polish household), and every countertop is scrubbed and wiped clean. I feel I should be cleaning the place by myself, but this is not what Punch wants. He is at the helm, even as he welcomes my help. "Bring in the glasses from the living room, will you, my dear?"

Yes, there are always glasses. Carol observes a cocktail hour, and she also likes to pour a gin and tonic for me. Punch stays with a can of beer, and Carol and I sip cocktails. Dinners are happy meals indeed.

I think of myself as an au pair, but I quickly see that I am more of a nanny. An au pair would help with any number of household chores. I listen for additional assignments besides childcare, but none are forthcoming, even though looking after Cynthia is not demanding. I make sure she is up and dressed in the only thing she will wear all summer long, a polo dress. I fix her breakfast, and then we are ready for the day. Her hours are filled with swimming, horseback riding, the occasional art class, or a play date with Gino and Gina's daughter. Perhaps the biggest surprise is that she does not like being left and clings to me wherever I may take her. I'm touched by her affection. I cannot remember ever feeling that kind of an attachment to an adult.

When Cynthia is occupied, I look for other ways to at least appear busy and helpful. I mend the occasionally ripped hemline or missing button on some of Cynthia's clothes. "You don't have to do that," Carol says. "We have a seamstress who comes in once a week back in the city." I take on other projects. I sew matching wrap-around skirts for Cynthia and myself. She sweetly wears hers, even as it keeps slipping off her little girl form. I wash windows.

"Nina, stop. You do not need to clean the house."

I have idle minutes when Cynthia is busy with a friend or family member. It's never enough time to retreat into letter writing or reading, and I do not want to call any of my long-neglected UNIS friends. I wander through the house and pick up foods for a snack, two snacks, or maybe even three. In the movie viewing room, I dig into two tall candy jars, always filled with M&Ms and peanut M&Ms. And it's not only these pieces of candy that tempt me. As a child, I paid little attention to American food, but I now find myself reeling at the enormity of choice here. And I cannot resist sampling it.

Punch and I are out picking up extra items at the small grocery store up the road.

"What do you want for breakfast?" he asks.

"I eat the English muffins with cream cheese or peanut butter that you have back at the house." Indeed I do. With honey. Or peanut butter. Or both. And late in the evening, when Cynthia is already in bed, I come down and have more peanut butter mixed with honey in a cup. In Poland, peanut butter is an unknown entity. I hadn't especially missed it, but now I can hardly stop eating it.

Punch is picking up jams off the shelf, inspecting prices. "Look at this. It's ten cents cheaper!" He puts it in the cart.

"Do you care?" I ask bluntly.

"Absolutely! I don't like to buy something for more if I can get it for less. This store is expensive anyway. You've got to be careful!"

I'm completely shocked by this. Until now, I had believed that rich people didn't care about small change. They don't have to care! I have always thought it would be wonderful to make choices based on other considerations, not money. In Poland, people seem to scrape out money from every possible source just to afford a refrigerator or a television. Here, every home has both. And Punch's homes have multiples of both. Why on earth would he care about ten cents?

I'm gaining weight. Slowly at first. One month into my stay, though, I am becoming plump. Carol, who is thin and cares deeply about appearance, calls me into the bedroom she shares with Punch. Her eyes scan my face, my form.

"Have you thought about putting blond streaks in your hair?" she asks.

"No, but I think they're really cool."

"Why don't I take you to my hairdresser. Let's see what he says."

The next day, I have streaks. Are they there to take your eyes off of my plumpness?

Carol has an older daughter, Cathy, from a previous marriage. Cathy is an adult now, living away from home, but she still keeps some of her belongings in a room at the Connecticut house. Dresses and clothes that she is likely to wear on the rare trip home but has no need for in her adult life elsewhere hang in her closet. Carol reaches into the closet and takes out a casual but long gown.

"You could wear this on Saturday. We're having friends over. A casual thing. You and Cynthia should eat with us. The dress will be perfect for you. It's quite appropriate for a summer party."

"Will Cathy mind?" The dress is full, hiding my expanding body.

"No, of course not. We'll have it dry cleaned after and put it back in her closet."

The only time I have ever worn a long dress was for my lycee graduation dance. It feels sumptuous now. Folds of white cloth with a navy blue paisley design touch the floor as I move across the room. Is it Indian? It feels exotic. A month ago, I never gave my wardrobe back home a second thought. Now I entertain the fantasy that Cathy won't like this dress anymore. "Oh, Nina, I heard you looked great in my dress. Take it with you!" I imagine her saying this even though I know I would have absolutely no use for the dress in Poland.

When New York guests come for a weekend visit, the rhythm of the household changes. Punch and Carol's maid and butler will come down from the city to help out if there is a planned dinner with many expected guests. But when it is just one or two friends, Punch will grill, and Carol will take on the job of changing the sheets on all the beds. If Punch fusses about prices in the grocery store when he doesn't have to, Carol fusses about sheets on beds even as she doesn't have to.

"I like them tight. Here, let me show you how to do a tight bed." She smiles, acknowledging her obsessive care. "I know I'm fussy. I just like beds done my way. So I do them myself."

Carol and I make countless beds in the course of the summer, even as I am only the apprentice, imitating, never setting the pace.

There are unique weekend guests, and there are repeat guests. Repeat guests are the ones who require little care or attention. One Sulzberger cousin tells me, "They are like warm slippers. Comfy and not too exciting." Unique guests are often associated with the paper. Editors Scotty Reston and Fred Hechinger, for example—men whose names I see on the masthead of *The New York Times*. They come with wives or alone. But if they talk shop, I never hear it. Carol expertly directs the social conversation, and the paper is not a topic she is likely to bring up at the dinner table.

Early into the summer, Carol tells me that she wants to get a small group of friends together for a day at the country club to which they belong.

"We don't use our membership nearly enough! I think you and Cynthia would enjoy the larger pool, and we'll end the day with dinner in the dining room there."

I've heard about country clubs. They were portrayed as elite places for those who thrive on exclusivity and privilege. I am surprised that Punch and Carol belong to one. Yes, their family wealth might suggest that they were exactly suited for such places, but from the beginning, they do not strike me as a family that likes to flaunt their status or wealth. I am curious how they would fit into a country club culture.

The club seems to me much as if you took the pool and pool house from up the hill of the Sulzberger property and expanded it tenfold, with additional trappings thrown in. Endless fresh towels. Comfortable chairs. Drinks delivered. Anywhere. Fresca for me. And at the end of a club day, there is dinner in the dining room. Carol has arranged for others to join us. I always sit with the family and their friends for the meal.

"Have you ever had lobster?" Carol asks me.

"No."

"Try it. I'll show you how to take it apart."

Like the Pygmalion that I am, I order and learn. And, quite unfortunately, I learn to like it. Not so much the club, but the lobster served there.

It is surely a summer of firsts. First lobster. First scotch and soda, gin and tonic. First smoke of marijuana.

Cynthia is a child born to Carol and Punch. Cathy, born to Carol, is adopted at an early age by Punch. Punch also has Arthur and Karen, children from a previous marriage. They're my age, and when they come for a several-day visit, their cousins also show up. Danny. Steve and his wife, June. And so on. Some stay in Punch and Carol's house, some stay up the hill, but they spend their time together, and suddenly the mood of the place changes. It becomes louder, jocular, and fast-paced. There are evening skinny dips in the pool, movie showings at the house, and lunches at the grandmother's house. Cynthia is the youngest by a good decade, but she and I are always included. When it's her bedtime, I'm typically back in my corner bedroom watching TV or writing letters, but Carol nudges me to go downstairs when the kids and cousins are there. "Go hang out with them. Cynthia will manage without you up here for the night." And I do. The kids and cousins are friendly and not unwelcoming.

"Come out on the hammock. Have you ever smoked?"

"Cigarettes, yes." In fact, I sometimes take one from Carol. It feels like a bridge to her world.

"No, not cigarettes. Grass."

"No."

The odd thing is that I have no sense of whether this is acceptable, dangerous, illegal, or commonplace. I remember when we lived in New

York, and my mother warned us repeatedly, "Don't get into trouble. If you do something wrong, it will be talked about. People are watching how you behave. Don't give them a reason to spread negative things about you." I wonder how it is that these kids, who are so much more in the limelight than we ever were, can smoke pot and drink vast amounts into the night without the worry of soiling reputations or setting bad impressions. I haven't yet grasped that if they do it and are found out, there likely will be a second chance handed to them. Still, I am a part of this group in some small way, and if they feel smoking pot is safe, perhaps it really is an acceptable behavior.

And so I try it. And it has no impact at all on me, and I am not a little relieved.

5.

Carol tells me that I need to take a day off each week.

"Go to New York! You can ride in with Arthur in the morning and come back with him after he is done with work."

I like the idea. I had gone into the city twice with Jackie, but a day on my own appeals to me even more. It gives me a chance to revisit spots that had great meaning to me as a young child. How do they present themselves now, after a five-year break?

It's very warm when I arrive with Punch in the city, though thankfully not as muggy as July days can be.

"Have a great day, Nina! And why don't you go to our apartment in the late afternoon when you're done with the city. Lucien will wait for you there."

I wave to him and turn right away toward the place of my childhood home at 46th Street East.

The building is still there, still with the awning and the washed-out lettering "The Executive House." I used to think that the name itself was so magnificent! And the building seemed beautiful too. Twelve stories and a penthouse. I never went up to that top floor, but the PH button on the elevator seemed like it might open up to something splendid and exclusive. Now the whole building looks a little less splendid or exclusive. Newer buildings have sprung up on the block, overshadowing the older ones. The yellow brick on the Executive House looks more gray than yellow. The window frames are without any color at all. I walk up the three steps to the big glass doors. A doorman holds one open for me and asks if he can help me.

"I used to live here. Can I just look around?" He smiles and nods an okay. The interior looks like it has had a modest facelift. A brass chandelier and a gold-trimmed mirror hang in the spacious hall. I pause for a minute, then head out again. The doorman waves me on with a cheerful smile. How surprised he would be if he knew that I now live in Warsaw, a city where not a single apartment building has glass entrance doors, to say nothing of chandeliers, gold-trimmed mirrors, or penthouse units on the top floor.

I continue my search for the familiar. The pizza place on Second Avenue is gone. I look around for something comparable. Toward Grand Central, there is another pizzeria, but even though the pizza fragrance is unmistakable and, in my opinion, sublime, nonetheless, I feel cheated. A reheated slice consumed standing up doesn't measure up to a whole pie, carried quickly home, eaten in front of the TV, with ginger ale on the side. Pizza nights were the only time I was allowed to reach for a soda from my father's bar during my childhood.

Despite new additions and not a small number of closures, the heart and soul of this noisy and vibrant city feel the same. There is something uniquely New Yorkian about how the sidewalks slant uphill to Fifth and how the people move determinedly, with an eye toward the changing walking light signals. The building that housed UNIS has been torn down. No shock there. But First Avenue is still First Avenue, and 42nd, 57th, the wider cross streets, have the same feeling of space that I remember when I used them in my younger years to cut through the city.

By late afternoon, I am at the Sulzberger home on 82nd and Fifth. Their apartment house belongs to an older generation of buildings. Stone arches frame the entrance hall, and an attendant operates the elevator manually. I get on half expecting a challenge, but I see that I've been cleared for passage. "Eight please," I say almost unnecessarily.

Nina Lewandowska Camic

What surprises me is that there are only two apartment units per floor. But when I enter the Sulzberger apartment, I understand why this is so. The unit is very large. It doesn't appear that way at first. The entrance hall fans out in all directions, toward the kitchen and the living room to the left and toward the den and bedroom area on the right. But these are merely portals to an even longer chain of rooms. Punch and Carol's room, Cynthia's room, and what is described as Karen and Arthur's room, though in all the time I am with the Sulzbergers, I never see them use it (their primary residence is in the city but with their mother). The living room connects to the dining room, and the kitchen connects to a series of servants' quarters. Lucien and Juanita, the general caretakers, live there. (Other service people come and go: the seamstress, the tutor, the cook for special dinners.)

Juanita offers me a soft drink, but I decline. I see that Lucien is ready to head out. I don't want to hold anyone up. We make our way downstairs again, where the station wagon is standing, double-parked, just outside the door. Lucien will be driving us to Connecticut. On weekdays, Punch uses the commuting time to review papers. I sit in the back seat and take note of the passing landscape—a stream of cars leaving the city at first, then an emptying four-lane road curving through the hills of Connecticut. The American highway. No road in Poland comes close to this.

We stay on a two-lane road on the drive out of Warsaw to the village. This is the Polish "highway." Taking your car out on these roads is never relaxing. A slow-moving vehicle like a tiny Trabant car or a horse-drawn wagon will come out of a side dirt road, and you pump the brakes furiously to avoid a collision. Then you're left to crawl behind it until the traffic coming at you provides a break long enough for you to use their lane to pass. And if the wagons and Trabants aren't enough to slow us down, there are also the cyclists and pedestrians. As the road leaves one village and passes through the next, the number of people swells, especially on Sundays, when the roads are used for an after church stroll by children and adults. An American highway knows nothing of this. Cars, an occasional truck. A ribbon of road, lovely in its simplicity. It's not boring to me. Not yet.

6.

Toward the end of August, Carol comes into the bedroom where I am attempting to compose a friendly and just a little sentimental letter to Marcin. She gets right to the point.

"Nina, how would you like to go to college in New York?"

I look up at her. Her tone is serious, but her face has traces of a genuine smile. "Well, I talked to Arthur. We would like you to live with us. You could look after Cynthia on some evenings, come with us to Connecticut on the weekends, and during the day, you could attend college. We could arrange to have your tuition taken care of. Cynthia would be thrilled."

I am dumbfounded. I have grown to be exceptionally fond of Cynthia and the whole family, but I never once thought of my stay with them as anything more than just a summer adventure. What Carol is offering would upend everything for me. Would it be a change for the better? And given my father's line of work, could I even leave Poland now?

"I don't know if I can ..."

"Punch will write to your parents. I'm sure it can be arranged. What do you think?"

"Oh, wow! Thank you! That sounds fantastic!"

But when she leaves my room, my enthusiasm immediately subsides, and I try to grasp what this would really mean. Well, no Marcin in my life, for one thing. As I finish the letter to him, explaining that I have just been invited to live with the family whose girl is my charge, I think about how he'll react. Within two weeks, I hear from both my parents and Marcin. His letter is full of details of his emerging friendship with Elka in econometrics. And he has a response to my latest news: "Take it! Take the offer! You'll have such a great experience!"

I want to say the hell with you, but instead, I let the sheet of paper fall to my lap and turn to the letter from my parents. They are cautiously encouraging.

"Your father and I realize that this is a wonderful opportunity. We haven't told you before, but your father may be returning to New York to work for the United Nations. In that case, we would both be traveling to New York next year. But regardless, we think you should return first to Poland at the end of the summer and do a formal transfer from here, applying for a student visa from Warsaw and asking for a transfer of university credits."

My mother's rather formalistic writing is typical for her, so I am not surprised by the unemotional tone. She includes no details of my father's possible future work in the letter. Later, upon my return, she explains that my father had always hoped to come back to the UN, especially now that the government in Poland has forced a direction for the country that he and countless others find unpalatable and ominously grim. Ever vigilant, used to a lifetime of sniffing out the looming threats to his country and his family, my father has been hard at work investigating avenues of possible returns to the UN even when he was still in the ambassador position. When he learned that the rotation of under-secretary-general positions would take place in the early 1970s, he made sure that his name would come up among those considered for the job. And indeed, within a year, in 1972, my parents will return to New York, and my father will be appointed Under-Secretary-General to the UN, a title that he holds onto for seven years. It is a position that offers financial security, as after his rotation ends, my parents will be able to return to Poland with a secure UN pension for the rest of their years.

They don't exactly follow that course. My parents will split up toward the end of their final New York stay. My mother will move to California, then to Madison, then to California, then Madison one last time, supporting herself with income from that pension. My father will eventually return to Poland and take over the life we had there, on Aleja Roz, only with another woman as his partner for the remaining years of his life. But surely none of this is even in my imagination right now. I have been offered a chance to live in New York, and I am weighing my decision with some consideration of the consequences.

The summer away from Poland has made me unsure about the strength of my integration into a Polish culture that had gradually accepted me back into its fold. Was I even honest in the way I presented myself to my Polish friends? So often, I limply went along with the prevailing view—not the political one, but the cultural belief system that governed daily life in Poland. When friends, especially my male friends, scoffed at that American fabrication of "women's lib," I bristled. Still, after one feeble effort to fight back their affectionately patronizing characterization of this movement, where they threw down claims that once again Americans were inventing problems because life was simply too good for too many, I learned to say nothing. I felt myself to be outnumbered.

Every day that I walk the streets of Warsaw, I notice that I live in a country populated by white Catholics who identify themselves as deeply Polish. The foods we are supposed to like, the traditions we strictly follow, the jokes and banter we like to hear, and the history we learned in school are all firmly Polish. And within that framework, women follow a very Polish, articulated path. True, under so-called communist rule, women have access to higher education. Most adult women work, many entering professions such as medicine or the hard sciences.

In the 1960s and '70s, Polish women merely had to state that their pregnancy would cause personal hardship to gain access to a free abortion. But did this pave the way toward personal freedom? Most people remained deeply rooted in their Catholic faith and were far more respectful of what a handful of church officials would say in a sermon than what a law would mandate. Still, my friends (both male and female) would argue that women these days have little reason to complain. Women have access to universities, to the arts and sciences. They don't need extra consideration. No one wants to talk about the absence of women in positions of power or that women work but also manage households, take care of babies and aging parents, prepare suppers, and scavenge stores for clothing for the family. And we scoff at the government's attempts to level the playing field. We mock the granting of additional bonus points to young people from the provinces or who can demonstrate working-class family background as they seek access to higher learning schools. It was just one of those government impositions that we disliked merely because the governmental hand in our daily lives was so heavy, so odious that we rejected nearly everything it touched.

The summer with the Sulzbergers and my days with my childhood

Nina Lewandowska Camic

friend on Long Island brought all this to the forefront for me. Again, I feel oddly out of place in Poland, with my hippie questions and women's lib ideas. Of course, Americans mischaracterized life in Poland all the time (if they even bothered to think much about it). It's not that I have jumped cultures. I am not feeling more American. I know and understand Polishness. Even after living in America for half a century, I haven't lost the ability to think like a Pole, with a mind full of that Polish history, of Polish nationhood. But as I consider my options now, I know that I am not ready to accept Polishness so completely, without question or reservation. The very plurality, the chaos, and the complexity of American life appeal to me tremendously. I am tempted to jump into that chaos, that whirligig of argument and discourse, that frenzied pace of life on the other side of the ocean.

I can think of two very strong practical reasons on the side of accepting Carol's offer. First, I want desperately to leave econometrics. A chance to study in the United States grants me academic freedom to rethink my major. And second, I want distance between myself and Marcin. An ocean between us suits me just fine. His unsentimental response to my question about what to do unnerved me. If I am incapable of telling him to stay away, then the next best thing is to move away from where he is.

Missing from my list of institutions and people I may want to leave behind is any thought to the idea that by taking up Carol's offer, I may be paving a path to an escape from Poland's current political reality. Even though I am as hostile to the current government as the next Pole, I never once thought that I should look for ways to leave Poland to create an economically stronger future for myself elsewhere. If my friends could build families and establish careers within the confines of the current Polish system of governance, so could I. It did not strike me then that the system in place could self-destruct and that there was a very real threat that, given our vigilant neighbor to the east, what would replace it could be worse. I suppose I had some small reserve of optimism. There was always the possibility that Poland could rid itself of its current authoritarian leadership and redraw its political platform to be in closer alignment with the rest of the world, specifically with the West.

In the end, I have a talent for convincing myself that change trumps stability. I don't think deeply about the consequences of leaving, and I don't worry in the slightest about moving away from my family. All four of us have drifted into our own private enclaves in the past few years, and if it was not for the shared apartment, I'm not sure we would ever track, let alone understand, each other's comings and goings. It's fine if my parents fulfill their hope of a return to New York. If they stay in Warsaw, that's equally okay by me. On the other hand, my Polish friends have woven an emotional fabric around me that remains fiercely strong. Who would play that role in New York? With the exception of Cynthia, Carol, and Punch, I feel no real connection to anyone in America. In high school, I reentered a world that is solidly Polish, and I assumed that I would now follow a Polish script in my life.

Friends indeed laughed at what they referred to as my Americanisms, but at the core, they found me to be Polish like them. And I allowed myself to slide into that mold. Because, if not Polish, then what? I've now returned to a country that has leaped into a reality that I don't fully understand. The youthful rebellions in America seem personal and very detached from the concerns facing young people living in countries like Poland. Still, I do not worry about returning to this charged environment. Carol and Punch are proposing something new, and I'm more than happy to accept their offer. I tell them now that I would like to return in February.

As my flight takes off from JFK in late September, I have none of the sadness of leaving New York. I'm eighteen years old, and I'll be returning to this city in a few months. Will it be my home now? In a year or two, will I have extricated myself from the pull of my country of birth? I can't predict any of this yet. I know only that I am happy to be reentering soon the noisy chaos of a complicated and thrilling city that had first shown its gritty yet exciting face when I got off the boat nearly a dozen years ago at the Hudson River pier where the *Queen Elizabeth* docked after her voyage across the ocean.

Acknowledgments

A book is like a fence: without solid posts, it bends, groans, and tumbles. And the author tumbles along with it. I was bending and groaning a lot when writing this memoir. Sometimes I'd stop in midsentence and not return to it for months out of exasperation or because I could not find the time to lose myself in its content. Over a dozen years, I worked on countless edits, clarifying events and themes as contemporary political changes in Poland and the United States demonstrated how easy it is for misinterpretation to occur if you don't state things clearly and honestly. My final draft is perhaps my hundredth draft.

Throughout all the time I worked on the memoir, my mate and best partner, Ed, was my most solid fence post. He knows how to encourage when the moment calls for it. He knows when to stay silent at other times. He showed me how easy it could be to transition from writing to publishing. Without his composed advice and unending support, I would have never gotten to the final stage of sending it to a press.

Absolutely stellar advice came, too, from the book's editor Shannon and from Kristin of Little Creek Press. Working with these brilliant women to move the memoir toward production was like nothing I expected. Not many authors would claim that this last stage of putting out a book is easy or fun, yet for me, it was both. I am immensely grateful to them.

Many people write memoirs so that they can leave a story behind for their children and grandchildren. I am no different. Both my daughters, Caroline and Susannah, are my closest buddies, and they, along with their husbands, Peter and Alex, have stood by me over the years with patience and understanding, allowing me to dig into family stories for my daily blog, Ocean, and never once showed anything but sweet enthusiasm for my interminable Great Writing Project. And each one of their kids, from the oldest, Serena, through Lena, Sammy, Sepi, to the youngest, Alma, is so full of gentility and love that I know they will forgive me for writing a story first about me before I can write stories for them. I could not love them all more for all they are in my life.

Others, including friends in Poland (Basia, Tomek, Piotr, Malgosia, Elzbieta, Ewa, Grzes, Karolina, Wanda, and of course Marcin, who appears heavily in this book and graciously told me to be my own guide in reflecting on the years I was so smitten with him) were an important part of the process. Friends in the U.S. (Diane, Barbara, Suzanne, Deb, Andrea, Gordie, Linda, Regan) were fence posts throughout the years of writing. I can't neglect my ex-husband either. Chas bought me a table twenty-five years ago and created a writing space for me in our home and said, "Go for it." Thank you.

My sister, Eliza, and I are almost as incongruous a match as Ed and me. She and I move in different worlds, and we're plagued by different anxieties and buoyed by different pleasures, yet I feel her right by my side, especially in our view and review of our childhood together. She and I shared a room until I left home for good. We couldn't imagine doing it any other way.

Then there are the people who made this story so much better because they invited me into their homes and lives and showed me how things worked outside my small world back in Warsaw. Three people made it possible for me to return to the United States as a young adult: my uncle Johnny (my mother's brother) and Punch and Carol Sulzberger. None of them are alive today, but I cannot neglect to mention them here. Punch and Carol especially helped me transition back to this country, even as my heart was still stuck in Poland. Too, working with their youngest daughter Cynthia made me want to aim high even though my work was not that difficult. Cynthia was a joy to me, and my au pair work was like a trip to the candy store. I do admit, though, that I ate too much candy at their house. Bowls of peanut M&Ms were irresistible.

And finally, a few words about my parents and grandparents. In retrospect, I do believe that both my mother and father, in their own way, made it a life's goal to provide for their family at a time when the horrible aftermath of the Second World War hung in the air, and you could still stumble over the rubble on the streets of a devastated Warsaw. My father's work at the Foreign Ministry and then for the United Nations opened numerous important doors for me, not the least of which was placing us in New York when I was little, which allowed me to learn English quickly and fluently. Too, he taught me to look both ways carefully, to the east and the west, before passing judgment. And I owe my American citizenship to my mother, who is ninety-eight as of this writing and lives just a few miles up the road from me. She spends her days in a room decorated with pictures of her two children, four grandchildren, and six great-grandchildren. Parenting wasn't easy for either my mom or dad, but one thing is clear—they never totally abandoned the effort. Each in their own right steadfastly clung to what must have often appeared to them to be a sinking ship with no obvious rescue in sight. From both, I quickly learned how important it is to be independent. But even they would admit that the true anchors in my young life were my mother's parents, Babcia and Dziadek. They were my source of childhood pleasures, comfort, my enduring love for all that grows and thrives in the natural environment.

In the end, though, I come back to Ed. Calm, centered, and always ready to help me figure out life so that I (and no one else) can decide what's next. I wake up to his shout. "Hi, gorgeous!" I come downstairs and hear him ask, "Are you a famous author person yet?" My heart swells, and my day is off to a great start.

Thank you all, with all my love always.

About the Author

Nina Lewandowska Camic retired from teaching at the University of Wisconsin Law School to write stories, play with her five grandchildren and grow flowers with her partner, Ed. They live in an old farmhouse just south of Madison, Wisconsin.